AF606053

A PLANETARY AVANT-GARDE

Experimental Literature Networks and the Legacy of Iberian Colonialism

A Planetary Avant-Garde

Experimental Literature Networks and the Legacy of Iberian Colonialism

IGNACIO INFANTE

UNIVERSITY OF TORONTO PRESS
Toronto Buffalo London

© University of Toronto Press 2023
Toronto Buffalo London
utorontopress.com
Printed in the USA

ISBN 978-1-4426-2974-5 (cloth)
ISBN 978-1-4426-2976-9 (EPUB)
ISBN 978-1-4426-2975-2 (PDF)

Toronto Iberic

Library and Archives Canada Cataloguing in Publication

Title: A planetary avant-garde : experimental literature networks and the legacy of Iberian colonialism / Ignacio Infante.
Names: Infante, Ignacio, author.
Series: Toronto Iberic; 81.
Description: Series statement: Toronto Iberic; 81 | Includes bibliographical references and index.
Identifiers: Canadiana (print) 20220488894 | Canadiana (ebook) 20220488932 | ISBN 9781442629745 (cloth) | ISBN 9781442629752 (PDF) | ISBN 9781442629769 (EPUB)
Subjects: LCSH: Literature, Modern – 20th century – History and criticism. | LCSH: Literature, Experimental – History and criticism. | LCSH: Comparative literature.
Classification: LCC PN771 .I54 2023 | DDC 809/.911 – dc23

We wish to acknowledge the land on which the University of Toronto Press operates. This land is the traditional territory of the Wendat, the Anishnaabeg, the Haudenosaunee, the Métis, and the Mississaugas of the Credit First Nation.

The publication of this book has been supported through research funds provided by the Dean of Arts and Sciences at Washington University in St. Louis.

University of Toronto Press acknowledges the financial support of the Government of Canada, the Canada Council for the Arts, and the Ontario Arts Council, an agency of the Government of Ontario, for its publishing activities.

Canada Council for the Arts   Conseil des Arts du Canada

Funded by the Government of Canada   Financé par le gouvernement du Canada

In memory of my mother, Teresa Infante Fernández (1955–2013)
To Jamie, Isabela, and Nicolas
because of you, as always

Contents

Illustrations

Acknowledgments

This book, like most scholarly books, I am sure, has had a complex but enriching history, and it is ultimately, and despite the ups and downs of life, the result of many wonderful conversations and collaborations throughout the last seven years with amazing colleagues, incredibly generous and energizing students, and two exceptional editors; many visits to a series of outstanding libraries and research centres across the world; and, last but not least, the support, patience, and love of my family. I am deeply grateful to everyone who has had an impact, directly or indirectly, on the completion and publication of this book, and I wouldn't have been able to complete this project without everyone acknowledged here.

At Washington University in St. Louis, I am extremely fortunate to be able to work across two fabulous departments, and, since 2018, as part of the leadership team of our Center for the Humanities. I would like to thank all my colleagues across the various sections of the Department of Romance Languages and Literatures, and particularly my various chairs (Elzbieta Sklodowska, Harriet Stone, Michael Sherberg, Andrew Brown, and Julie Singer), who have been incredibly generous and supportive of my work over the years since my arrival at Washington University in 2009, as well as all my colleagues in the Hispanic Studies Section (Billy Acree, Joe Barcroft, Andrew Brown, Nina Davis, Javier García Liendo, Stephanie Kirk, Tabea Linhard, Mabel Moraña, Eloísa Palafox, Zorimar Rivera Montes, Ignacio Sánchez Prado, Pepe Schraibman, Elzbieta Sklodowska, Akiko Tsuchiya, and Miguel Valerio) for their collegiality, commitment to the mission of our section, and collective intellectual vision – and a special thanks to Rita Kuehler for everything, as always. Since 2016, I have served as one of the book reviews editors (peninsular) of the journal *Revista de Estudios Hispánicos;* thanks go to Stephanie Kirk (general editor), Javier García

Liendo (book reviews editor, Latin America), Anna Eggemeyer (our production editor), and our editorial assistants (Francesca Dennstedt, Olivia Lott, Juan Manuel Ramírez Velázquez, Shirley Anghel, and Pili Cuairán Chavarría) for making such an outstanding editorial team, and for assembling such exciting scholarship in Latin American and Iberian studies in every single issue of the journal.

In the Program in Comparative Literature, I would like to especially thank Lynne Tatlock for her generous guidance and leadership, and her constant support of my work over the years. I would also like to thank my colleagues in the unit – Jami Ake, Kurt Beals, Nancy Berg, Letty Chen, Matt Erlin, Bob Hegel, Rob Henke, Matthias Goëritz, Caroline Kita, Joe Loewenstein, Mike Lützeler, Erin McGlothlin, Anca Parvulescu, Philip Purchase, and Gerhild Williams – for making Comp Lit such a wonderful intellectual and creative space for faculty and students alike. Finally, at the Center for the Humanities, which has become my second home and family during the last four years, I would like to thank the entire team, past and present: Wendy Love Anderson, Kathy Daniel, Alicia Dean, Shefali Chandra, Kathleen Fields, Barb Liebmann, Caitlin McCoy, Tila Neguse, Laura Perry, Trisha Sutton, and Rebecca Wanzo. I am especially grateful to Jean Allman and, more recently, Stephanie Kirk, the Center's directors during my tenure as associate director, for their groundbreaking humanities initiatives, their visionary leadership, and the welcoming, collaborative, and exciting environment that has turned the Center into such a successful hub for cutting-edge humanities research at Washington University and beyond. One of the most fulfilling aspects of working at the Center is the opportunity to regularly collaborate with numerous colleagues outside my home departments (among them J. Dillon Brown, Rachel Brown, Colin Burnett, Panill Camp, Liz Childs, Joanna Dee Das, Danielle Dutton, Gerald Early, Jonathan Fenderson, Andrea Friedman, Cathy Keane, Laurie Maffly-Kipp, Lerone Martin, Bill Maxwell, Jeffrey McCune, Paige McGingley, Anne-Marie McManus, Melanie Micir, Tim Moore, Jessica Rosenfeld, Zoe Stamatopoulou, Michelle Purdy, Samuel Shearer, Ila Sheren, Nancy Reynolds, Vince Sherry, Abram Van Engen, Anika Walke, Julia Walker, and Rafia Zafar), and to meet a remarkable array of visiting scholars, who have shaped my research and work in many ways (particularly Daphne Brooks, Caroline Levine, George Sanchez, and Walter Johnson). Being able to work with such an amazing group of colleagues at the Center has been one of the highlights of my career. This book is also the result of learning from the amazing students that I have been fortunate to work with in my graduate and undergraduate classes, and especially all the students that I have collaborated with during their doctoral studies in comparative literature and Hispanic studies, among them Baba Badji, Aaron Coleman, Rebecca Dehner-Armand, Irene Domingo, Julia Leverone, Olivia Lott, Gabriella Martin, Gonzalo Montero, and Annelise Finnegan.

Sections of this book have been presented at a variety of conferences and invited lectures. I would like to extend special thanks to Alejandro Mejías López for a most kind invitation to present my research with colleagues and students of the Department of Spanish and Portuguese at Indiana University, Bloomington, in 2015 ("'Huidobro's Hazaña': Postcolonial Translation and the Avant-Garde Poetics of *Mío Cid Campeador*, 1929"); the students and faculty organizers of the Romance Languages and Literatures Faculty Colloquium at Washington University, for their invitation to present my work in April 2016 ("Divergent Multilingual Poetry Networks: On the Politics of Postcolonial Poetics in the Philippines"); and the Rutgers University Comparative Literature and Film Studies communities for their warm invitation to visit New Brunswick again after so long and present my work in 2018 ("The Specter of Translation") – especially Susan Martin-Márquez and Andrew Parker for organizing the event, and my former mentors at Rutgers, Elin Diamond, William Galperin, Nicholas Rennie, Tom Stephens, Ben Sifuentes Jáuregui, and Janet Walker. I would also like to thank the Modernist Studies Association, and their Executive Board, on which I proudly served as international relations chair between 2016 and 2018, for providing such a welcoming, encouraging, and inspiring scholarly community (special thanks to MSA presidents Rebecca Walkowitz, Jessica Berman, Stephen Ross, and Laura Winkiel). The MSA also organizes one of the best annual scholarly conferences out there, and I was able to share sections of this book in different MSA roundtables, seminars, and sessions, including: "José Garcia Villa, and the Anxious Forms of (Post)colonial Poetry in the Philippines," part of the "Tracking Modern Anxieties Seminar," led by Leah Flack and Sarah Keller (Modernist Studies Association Conference, November 2016, Pasadena); "Iberian and Latin American Modernismos, Planetarity, and the Challenges of Periodization," a seminar I co-organized with María Del Pilar Blanco (Modernist Studies Association Conference, August 2017, Amsterdam); and, finally, "Feuilles de Route, 1924: Cendrars's Journey to Brazil, and the Divergent Temporalities of the Planetary Avant-Garde," part of the "Photography and Print Culture" seminar, led by Jordana Mendelson, Andrés Zervigón, and Antonella Pelizzari (Modernist Studies Association Conference, November 2018, Columbus, Ohio).

The research leading up to this book has been generously supported by a Maxwell C. Weiner Research Fellowship and a Summer Faculty

Research Grant from the Center for the Humanities at Washington University, as well as the research support provided by the Office of the Dean of the Faculty of Arts and Sciences, led by Barbara Schaal, and more recently by Feng Sheng Hu, for which I am extremely grateful. I am particularly indebted to the amazing library staff and grateful for the archival resources at the following libraries and research centres: Biblioteca de Andalucía, Biblioteca Nacional de España, Library of the Getty Research Institute, Los Angeles Public Library, UCLA Libraries. In addition, of course, I am grateful to everyone at Washington University Libraries, and for materials provided by the MOBIUS consortium.

This project wouldn't exist in this form without the support of the University of Toronto Press, particularly the editorial vision of Siobhan McMenemy in its earlier stages and the patience and generosity of Mark Thompson throughout the entire process leading up to the completion of the manuscript – I am indebted and forever grateful to both of them, and to the entire team at UTP, especially Simon Coll, Mary Lui, and Stephanie Mazza. The anonymous readers who read the manuscript for the Press provided extremely generous and considered feedback that improved key aspects of my argument, for which I am deeply appreciative. I am thrilled for this book to have found such an ideal scholarly home, and such esteemed company, as it has in the Toronto Iberic series.

This book is dedicated to my late mother, Teresa Infante Fernández. Those who were able to know Teresa – her true joy and sophisticated zest for life, her amazing warmth and generosity, her deep love for her family and many friends, her laughter and beautiful smile that just solved everything – know how lucky I was to have her as my mother, teacher, and friend ... *Teresa, siempre impresionante y magnífica, te echamos tantísimo de menos ...*

Finally, there is no way I would have been able to write this book, be here now, or really do anything that I do, without my true team, my incredible family: my love and partner in life, Jamie Zorigian Infante, and our children, Isabela Adele Infante and Nicolas John Infante. The three of you are everything that I could have ever dreamed of, and having each of you in my life makes everything as satisfying, real, magical, thrilling, and joyful as life can be, all the time. Jamie – every day the beautiful dream continues ... forever changes, always; and Bela and Nico – I am so proud of who you are, and always know that your true awesomeness and amazingness are totally unique and invaluable: *Os quiero con todo mi corazón, siempre.*

A PLANETARY AVANT-GARDE

Planetary Engagement, the Historical Avant-Garde, and Iberian Colonialism (1909–1929)

A Planetary Avant-Garde develops a critical history of experimental poetics emerging within key transnational literature networks during the historical avant-garde, considered both as a historical period (here specifically circumscribed by the years 1909 and 1929), and as a pivotal category within modern literary and art history. As a period closely intertwined with and determined by two interrelated events in world history – namely, the modern expansion of Western colonialism, capitalism, and industrialization across the globe during the first decade of the twentieth century on the one hand, and the global political realignment after World War I on the other – the historical avant-garde represents a rich and complex process when a multiplicity of transnational artistic movements are newly articulated, imagined, and experienced. Within this larger historical context, the avant-garde artwork represents an "embattled" condition, that, as Marjorie Perloff has importantly argued in relation to the historical avant-garde and the Great War, is located at the political space between "revolution and liberation": "The avant-garde is by definition embattled, and for the European avant-garde of the early century, war signified, at least at the outset of the conflict, both revolution and liberation."[1] It is precisely due to the "embattled" nature of avant-garde poetics as a radical experimental challenge to and rupture from previous aesthetic forms that the avant-garde can traverse diverse literary, linguistic, and media boundaries, challenging assumptions of particular institutions, national identities, and aesthetic traditions.

As explored in this book, between the years 1909 and 1929, a series of experimental literature networks developed via paths that were often geographically fragmented and temporally unstable, suggesting the underpinnings of an avant-garde phenomenon directly affecting artistic expression that transcends a purely European geopolitical centre.

Through a sociohistorical and critical mapping of key transnational networks of experimental poetics, I expose a political dimension of experimental literary production and cultural circulation during the historical avant-garde. This critical mapping moves beyond European and Anglo-American geopolitical frameworks traditionally used to understand this movement within the academic fields of modern art and literary history. In the particular experimental networks studied in this book, the experience of temporality and history appears to be inseparable from the pervasive sense of alterity at the core of various forms of avant-garde poetics, unveiling conflicting experiences of modernity that are related to the hegemonic impact of Western definitions of history and progress as they are encountered in different parts of the world as dominant epistemological forces.

In the pages that follow, I examine how experimental form – as embodied in the avant-garde artwork in various geographic contexts and manifestations – is not only endowed with a new aesthetic and political value, in terms previously acknowledged by critics, but also constitutes an aesthetic and historical realm in which different identities, languages, traditions, and histories coalesce in radically new and conflicting responses to differing manifestations of modernity. Caroline Levine has recently argued in her groundbreaking *Forms* that there appears to be a growing scholarly interest in tracing the ways in which forms in general, and literary forms more concretely, "do political work in particular historical contexts."[2] Levine's own work successfully highlights the political value of form itself, persuasively demonstrating the ways in which "literary forms emerge out of political situations dominated by specific contests or debates."[3] Following Levine's recent re-evaluation of formalism, *A Planetary Avant-Garde* undertakes the critical re-examination of experimental form at the core of the historical avant-garde as emerging from a series of transnational "political situations," in Levine's words, that within the scope and framework of this book are specifically related to the impact of Iberian colonialism across the world.

A Planetary Avant-Garde explores this particular political dimension of the historical avant-garde – and the related collaborations established between writers, as well as connections across literary texts, forms of poetics, and conceptualizations of history – through what I define as *planetary engagement*. This notion constitutes a direct response to Peter Bürger's formulation of the "political engagement" that he locates at the core of the historical avant-garde. In his influential *Theory of the Avant-Garde*, a study that remains, more than thirty years after its publication in English, one of the most influential approaches to the period, Bürger defines his conceptualization of "engagement" within the historical avant-garde in the following terms:

> In a theory of the avant-garde, a section on engagement is justified only if it can be shown that the avant-garde has radically changed the place value of political engagement in art, the concept of engagement prior and subsequent to the avant-garde movements is not the same. It is our intent, in what follows, to show that this is the case ... It is this: through the historical avant-garde movements the place of political engagement in art was fundamentally changed.[4]

According to Bürger, the ability of the avant-garde to change what he terms as "the place of political engagement in art" is directly connected to his "two-fold definition of the avant-garde," namely "the attack of art as institution and the coming into existence of a nonorganic work of art."[5] By emphasizing the "social effect" of a work of art within its institutional framework as a response to socio-economic conditions, Bürger underscores a new form of political engagement as a "function" of the avant-garde artwork. As Bürger further argues, during the historical avant-garde, "it became apparent that the social effect of a work of art cannot simply be gauged by considering the work itself but that its effect is decisively determined by the institutions within which the work 'functions.'"[6] Consistent with Bürger's recognition of this new form of political engagement of the work of art at the institutional and social level, I posit that the avant-garde artwork articulates a specific geopolitical engagement with the world that goes beyond national categories and institutionalized traditions. During the first three decades of the twentieth century there emerge various networks of avant-garde poetics (or what Bürger has described as "nonorganic form") that articulate and imagine various forms of alterity that explicitly respond to specific historical, cultural, and socio-economic forces.

A Planetary Avant-Garde moves beyond the aesthetic and institutional dimensions highlighted by Bürger to trace further historical evidence and poetic manifestations of planetary engagement across different languages and various geographical areas around the world during the historical avant-garde. In order to expand the notion of engagement presented by Bürger, my project reconceptualizes Gayatri Chakravorty Spivak's influential conceptualization of "planetarity" – a term Spivak originally coined in 1997 – as an extremely helpful linguistic figuration of the world that emerges as an alternative to the notion of the "global." Spivak's original formulation of "planetarity" emerged as a concept intrinsically differing from the transnational framework provided by globalization, a paradigm understood as a global and totalizing system both in its scope and socio-economic articulation. As argued by Arjun Appadurai, globalization as a system is "inextricably linked to the current workings of capital on a global basis."[7] As opposed to the "global," and the totalizing logic of globalization in the terms highlighted by Appadurai, Spivak's influential conceptualization of "planetarity" serves as a key notion through which we can linguistically figure and conceptually imagine a particular realm of "alterity" in which "we inhabit" beyond the self, the local, or the nation. In what is perhaps the most concise definition of this key critical term, Spivak conceptualizes the invocation of "the planet" at the core of her notion of "planetarity" as follows:

> The planet is in the species of alterity, belonging to another system, and yet we inhabit in it, on loan. It is not amenable to a neat contrast with the globe. I cannot say "the planet, on the other hand." When I invoke the planet, I think of the effort required to figure the (im)possibility of this underived intuition. Since to be human may be to be intended toward the other, we provide for ourselves transcendental figurations (translations?) of what we think is the origin of the animating gift of life: Mother, Nation, God, Nature. These are names (nicknames, putative synonyms) of alterity, some more radical than others ... If we imagine ourselves as planetary subjects rather than global agents, planetary creatures rather than global entities, alterity remains underived from us.[8]

Spivak's notion of planetarity highlights a sense of alterity and an intendedness towards the other which is intimately related to our own experience and sense of being in the world. However, while Spivak's notion highlights a contemporary imagining of alterity in relation to late twentieth-century globalization as an alternative framing and understanding of subject formation (i.e., "planetary subjects" vs. "global agents"), my study of planetary engagement within the historical avant-garde departs from Spivak's conceptualization in two main ways. First, I historicize the notion of planetary engagement as a form of transnational relationality and experience of alterity primarily articulated through experimental form, as part of a larger geopolitical process that is traceable across a diverse range of literature networks emerging during the historical avant-garde. Thus, each of the following chapters traces the political dimension of the avant-garde artwork as articulating divergent transnational forms of planetary engagement that operate outside the strictly European geopolitical centre at the core of Bürger's critical framework in his *Theory of the Avant-Garde*. Adopting a much broader comparative critical perspective than Bürger's approach, this book considerably expands the forms of political engagement at the core of the historical avant-garde beyond the institutional framework considered by Bürger, which operates mostly at a local and national level within its specific focus on the European avant-garde.[9]

This necessary expansion of both the archive and geopolitical dimensions of the historical avant-garde leads to the second way in which the conceptualization of planetary engagement developed in this book differs from Spivak's notion of planetarity: the various manifestations of planetary engagement I examine reflect an experience of temporality and history in which a local or national event or condition is conceptualized in relation to wider and, at times, conflicting forms of history and historiography. As a sense of alterity that appears within these experimental literature networks, planetary engagement is specifically grounded on divergent experiences of modernity, both as a sense of temporality and a historical process, deeply connected to, and generally in tension with, various forms of Western colonialism and imperialism as hegemonic forces across the world.

At the same time, the methodology in the critical approach in this book goes beyond the Eurocentric understanding of the social context of the avant-garde provided by Bürger's historicizing method, into broader transnational and transcultural geopolitical contexts. *A Planetary Avant-Garde* thus considerably expands the understanding of the avant-garde as a historical category and critical paradigm that, for Bürger, is essentially understood in purely European-centred critical terms, and mostly based on French and German avant-garde authors and archives. In contrast to Bürger's model, the specific avant-garde artworks themselves examined in this book constitute key actors within a larger network of social assemblages and historical conditions to which they are inextricably connected in complex ways that are hard to universalize into a single theoretical, geo-political, or historical model. For Bürger, on the other hand, the avant-garde artwork is valued in its historical dimension that results from the relationship between the institution of art and the actual context of each work, which Bürger affirms as historically defined in a radical new way during the avant-garde, as he argues here:

> If the history of the subsystem "art" is to be constructed, I feel it is necessary to distinguish between art as an institution (which functions according to the principle of autonomy) and the context of individual works. For it is only this distinction that permits one to understand the history of art in bourgeois society as a history in whose course the divergence between institution and content is eliminated. In bourgeois society (and

> already before the bourgeoisie seized political powered in the French Revolution), art occupies a special status that is mostly succinctly referred to as autonomy.[10]

The sense of the historicity of the avant-garde unveiled in this book transcends the historical premises that Bürger ascribes to it in two main ways: first, it understands the role of the avant-garde artwork in a much more fluid and less dialectical understanding of its social dimensions, and thus of the key connection between the work of art within its historical and political context, as well as its dimension as an institution that Bürger considers as a key historical condition. One of the central aspects of traditional theoretical or historiographic models for the analysis of the avant-garde such as Bürger's is how the avant-garde's own historicity – not only as emerging in a particular moment in history, but also as constituting a new historical rupture with the past – is theorized in part through an understanding of its historical dimension in a way that reinforces a European-centred archive as central to its very theorization.[11]

Bürger's particular historicizing strategy is also shared by other influential theoreticians of the avant-garde, particularly Theodor Adorno, as well as José Ortega y Gasset. While Adorno's emphasis on the autonomy of the avant-garde work of art is highly influential for Bürger's theory, Ortega y Gasset's critique of the social value of art within bourgeois society has historically determined a particular reading of the avant-garde for various generations of readers of the work of the influential Spanish philosopher. Similar to Bürger's approach, a key aspect of Adorno's and Ortega's respective understandings of the avant-garde is that they both see its historicity as related to a "particular geography" that, as Martin Puchner has highlighted, depends on the "temporal orientation of modernity" at the core of Hegel's understanding of history:

> Modernity has often been seen as depending on temporal constructions such as progress as opposed to the spatial orientation of postmodernity. This temporal orientation of modernity found a particularly influential formulation in Hegel, for whom geography was but the passive recipient of history, an array of transient places occupied by the progress of the spirit in time. While the temporal axis is marked by steady progress, the geographic plane is marked by gaps, white areas, and the graveyards of past cultures.[12]

In understandings of the avant-garde as a project of European modernity, the geographic implications of "temporal orientation of modernity" just highlighted by Puchner thus entail a form of historicizing that essentially posits, on the one hand, European avant-garde cultural forms as "historical," in the strict sense highlighted by Bürger, and on the other hand, non-European experimental literature networks as essentially not sufficiently modern or original to the avant-garde as such. In my approach, I argue instead for a new conception of the avant-garde artwork and of experimental form itself within a transnational and planetary context, while contributing to recent scholarship on avant-garde and modernist studies from a multilingual and comparative perspective.[13] Within this framework, planetary engagement constitutes a political dimension of the historical avant-garde that is central to the experimental condition of the avant-garde artwork as such, and thus to the series of experimental literature networks established beyond a European centre during this period.

Planetary Engagement and the Avant-Garde Artwork as Network

A key aspect of my approach in this book is the consideration of the avant-garde artwork as constituting an active actor within the larger literary and cultural networks in which it circulates. My critical methodology is in this sense related to Bruno Latour's distinction between a conceptualization of the network as a "result," versus an understanding of the network as "process." Latour develops this fundamental distinction in *An Inquiry into Modes of Existence* through what he describes as the "double movement" of networks.[14] As Latour argues, for his hypothetical inquirer, the experience of a network as "result" is very different from an experience of the same network as "process," and it is the latter understanding of the network that Latour highlights as the one that calls for and requires a more complex critical consideration:

> The "network" in the usual sense of technological network is thus the belated result of the "network" in the sense that interests our investigator. The latter, were she to follow it, would oblige her not to verify the quality of a signal but rather to visit in turn the multitude of institutions, supervisory agencies, laboratories, mathematical models …: these have all *ultimately* contributed to the signal she gets on her phone. The distinction between the two senses of the word network would be the same if she were interested in railroads: following the tracks is not the same as investigating the French national railroad company. And it would still be the same if, taking the word more metaphorically, she wanted to investigate "networks of influence": here, too, what circulates when everything is in place cannot be confused with the setups that make circulation possible.[15]

Through a critical exploration of the network as process that articulates its own configuration, *A Planetary Avant-Garde* opens a related series of historical and theoretical implications that are intimately connected to the experience of alterity at the core of various networks of avant-garde poetics across the world. It is by newly reading this historical encounter and event as a complex spatio-temporal network that we can open the door for the emergence of a sense of alterity, and a related sense of planetary engagement within these particular networks as a political dimension central to our understanding of the historical avant-garde.

A growing number of contemporary scholars have recently used the notion of the planetary as an alternative framework to the concept of the "global" or "globalization" for the study of transnational literature and culture, leading to an emerging interdisciplinary scholarly field within the humanities and social sciences that Amy Elias and Christian Moraru have referred to as "the planetary turn." Elias and Moraru conceptualize the planetary as a key feature and radical sense of the contemporary moment in relation to a series of "spatial-cultural reconfigurations" that have emerged across the world:

> Planetarity: our moment. A way of being and a way of measuring time, space and culture in the human sciences and on the planet at large. Whether a break with modernity, as some argue, or its extension into the twenty-first century, as other contend, the new moment involves, more than other geosocial shifts of the modern era, spectacular spatial-cultural reconfigurations on a global scale.[16]

Consistent with the recent "planetary turn" described by Elias and Moraru, scholars in several humanities disciplines have used the notion of the "planetary" and "planetarity" as a way to frame and explore new configurations of transnational and transcontinental cultural forms.[17]

Out of this growing body of scholarship, Susan Stanford Friedman's "planetary" approach to modernism is perhaps the most closely related to *A Planetary Avant-Garde*. In *Planetary Modernisms*, Friedman further develops her critical examination of a "planetary" form of modernity originally articulated in her influential 2010 essay "Planetarity: Musing Modernist Studies" (first published in the journal *Modernism/modernity*). Friedman uses the idea of the planetary to disrupt a purely anglophone and Euro-American paradigm for the study of modernism – both in a more traditional approach and in Rebecca Walkowitz and Douglas Mao's so-called "New Modernist Studies." In particular, Friedman's take on the planetary considerably extends the historical range traditionally associated with modernism as an aesthetic category and the related notion of modernity as a historical event, applying the concept to cultural objects and events spanning a wide range of world history – from Tang dynasty tomb figures and thirteenth-century Persian representations of war images related to the Mongol Empire, to Oswald de Andrade's 1928 *Manifesto Antropófago* medieval Basra pottery, or Aimé Césaire's *Cahier d'un retour au pays natal*, among many others.[18]

While I share Friedman's deep commitment to moving modernist studies beyond a purely Eurocentric and Anglo-American framework, the main objective of *A Planetary Avant-Garde* is not to expand the scale, range, and applicability of the anglophone conceptualization of "modernism" itself as a critical category. My approach to planetarity in this book builds upon Friedman's challenge to monolingual and nationally based approaches to modernist and avant-garde cultural forms, while considerably differing in both scope and focus from Friedman's project. As Friedman argues, her use of the "planetary" in *Planetary Modernisms* mainly functions "to invoke this greater expanse of time and space, to signal my attempt to break with periodization altogether."[19] Moreover, Friedman's planetary approach attempts to replace the notions of "alternative" or "global" in relation to the study of modernism, as has been relevantly pointed out by Rebecca Walkowitz in relation to Friedman's critical understanding of the "postcolonial turn in modernist studies."[20]

While the notion of planetary engagement developed here aims to contribute to what Walkowitz has described in terms of the kind of "larger aesthetic geography" as one the key contributions of Friedman's "planetary modernism" to modernist studies,[21] my methodology in *A Planetary Avant-Garde* remains strictly focused on the much more concise scale and defined temporal specificity of the period generally understood as the historical avant-garde. Thus, the notion of planetary engagement in my book constitutes a political dimension of the avant-garde that I trace historically as well as materially within a series of experimental and multilingual poetry networks that explicitly emerge between the years 1909 and 1929. As I argue in this book, the forms of geopolitical alterity that I trace through the notion of planetary engagement have, for the most part, been buried in traditional historiographic attempts to conceptualize the historical avant-garde as a period and artistic movement originating and taking place in Western Europe, and subsequently, and only in its aftermath, emerging in other parts of the world, as the story has been traditionally told. *A Planetary Avant-Garde* thus aims to challenge this normative narrative of the historical avant-garde, opening and unveiling new lines of enquiry related to the various experimental literature networks I study.

When considered collectively, the different manifestations of planetary engagement explored in this book reflect the complex history of imperialism and colonialism across the world and its impact on the development of the historical avant-garde. From this perspective, one of the main premises of this book is that it is precisely through the exploration of various forms of planetary engagement during the historical avant-garde that one can potentially respond to recent important challenges to European and Anglo-American paradigms as the hegemonic critical model for the study of modernism and the avant-garde. One such important question is voiced by Elleke Boehmer and Steven Matthews: "Might we detach ourselves from the assumption that creative production elsewhere, across the world, was merely reflective and derivative of Euro-American Modernism?"[22] My study responds to this query in the most positive terms through an alternative comparative understanding of the historical avant-garde and the modernist period. I submit, however, that in order to sustain a critical answer to Boehmer and Matthews's crucial questioning of the normative model of Euro-American modernist studies as the main scholarly referent for the study of modernism, it is imperative to expand the historical, geographic, and linguistic parameters used for scholarly analysis within this context.

The Historical Avant-Garde and the Legacy of Iberian Colonialism

Working within the larger scholarly framework of transnational literary and cultural studies, and particularly related to Laura Doyle's notion of inter-imperiality, my use of the concept of planetary engagement for the study of the historical avant-garde also highlights what can perhaps be best described as the inter-imperial density – in geopolitical, linguistic, and historical terms – of various poetic responses to the legacy of colonialism during this period.[23] Within this inter-imperial framework, I examine how particular experimental literature networks developed during the historical avant-garde politically and aesthetically respond to a series of "dispersed" or "scattered hegemonies," as Ella Shohat and Robert Stam have aptly employed this concept, while particularly adapting this focus to the legacy of Iberian colonialism across the world.[24] Rooted in this wider re-examination of the "scattered hegemonies" of colonialism proposed by postcolonial scholars such as Grewal, Kaplan, Shohat, and Stam, among others, my study considerably expands what Boehmer and Matthews have described as the "colonial landscape of Modernism" beyond the case of the British Empire. In particular, I focus on how the "dispersed" and inter-imperial hegemony of both Portugal and Spain's colonial regimes across the world can be traced in particular avant-garde networks established in different parts of the world, and how these networks respond specifically to Iberian colonialism during the first three decades of the twentieth century.

A Planetary Avant-Garde builds upon the groundbreaking work of key Latin American and Iberian studies scholars who have examined particular aspects of the legacy of the Spanish Empire in late nineteenth- and early twentieth-century cultural production across the Atlantic.[25] Partly expanding this scholarly context through a wider comparative and multilingual methodology, I examine the transhistorical and inter-imperial connections of both Spanish and Portuguese colonialism and imperial ideologies in the first three decades of the twentieth century, as well as their overlap with other forms of imperial hegemony – particularly represented by nineteenth-century British colonialism, as well as early twentieth-century United States imperialism. This book thus examines avant-garde responses to the inter-imperial "scattered hegemonies" of Spanish and Portuguese colonialism across Europe, Latin America, West Africa, and Asia, and how they affect the development of experimental literature networks during the historical avant-garde. Hence, one of the primary objectives of *A Planetary Avant-Garde* is to expand our understanding of the relation between Western colonial and imperial ideologies of the early twentieth century – and their related political and institutional manifestations – and the development of experimental poetics across the world during the historical avant-garde. As Richard Begam and Michael Valdez-Moses observe in their introduction to their collection *Modernism and Colonialism* (2007), scholarly studies in this particular area of research from a comparative perspective are lacking: "Few studies have provided a sustained and comprehensive account of the relation between modernism to colonialism. The comparative absence of such scholarship is puzzling, given the political and historical imperatives of the modernist period."[26] Since the publication of *Modernism and Colonialism*, only a relatively small number of monographs and edited collections have researched the relationship between colonialism and either modernism or the avant-garde. At the same time, most of the works published in this area since Begam and Valdez-Moses's work have generally focused on the particular influence and impact of the British Empire in the formation of modernism, as well as its relation to anglophone literary responses to British coloniality and its postcolonial aftermaths.[27]

Two relevant examples of recent scholarship in the field are *Unseasonable Youth: Modernism, Colonialism, and the Fiction of Development* by

Jed Esty (2011) and Rajeev Patke's *Modernist Literature and Postcolonial Studies* (2013). Through a study of the *Bildungsroman* form during British modernism in writers such as Kipling, Conrad, Wells, Joyce, and Woolf, Esty explores a "shift in scale, where the thematics of uneven development attached increasingly to metropole-colony relations within the global frame rather than to urban-rural relations within the national frame."[28] Esty's formulation in *Unseasonable Youth* relies on Eric Hobsbawm's conceptualization of the "age of empire," particularly in relation to the "quickening and formalizing of European colonialism in the 1870s and 1880s – a global process for which the Berlin Conference of 1884–1885 stands as a concrete marker."[29] Esty's analysis of this "shift in scale" within a "global frame" proves essential for a deeper understanding of modernism in its relation to colonialism, as well as the related category of "uneven development" in our understanding of modernity. I argue, however, that we must expand the analytic framework beyond a purely anglophone geopolitical context – a context that also determines Hobsbawm's theorization of empire, as invoked by Esty – in order to arrive at a more nuanced, multilingual, and diverse understanding of modernism and the avant-garde in relation to colonialism. This is something that Rajeev Patke tries to articulate in *Modernist Literature and Postcolonial Studies*; however the forms of modernism and postcolonialism invoked by Patke focus mostly on the legacy of the British colonial regime, from a literary perspective that relies on an archive consisting mainly of canonical anglophone modernist figures – William Butler Yeats, Ezra Pound, T.S. Eliot, Jean Rhys, Virginia Woolf – to which Patke adds studies of more contemporary figures, such as Nick Joaquin from the Philippines and Arun Kolatkar from India.[30]

I contend, therefore, that while a "shift in scale" occurs at the core of modernism as described by Esty, a richer and more complex understanding of this same "shift," and its various political, aesthetic, and historical implications, requires that we look beyond the British Empire as the primary paradigm. It is of paramount importance that, in order to articulate a more complex and nuanced understanding of modernism and the historical avant-garde in relation to colonialism, the scope of enquiry must also include a set of different "metropole-colony relations within the global frame," as well as a wider geopolitical framework. Specifically, consideration of both Spanish and Portuguese colonial regimes not only remain central to the same "age of empire" proposed by Hobsbawm – particularly based on Portugal's active role in the Berlin Conference and its aftermath – but also in terms of the historical importance of the Spanish-American War that culminated in the 1898 loss of Spain's colonial American and East Asian territories; the United States intervention in Cuba; and the US annexation of both Puerto Rico and the Philippines. Thus, by not only including London, Paris, and New York, as Esty does, but also adding other cities of parallel and overlapping colonial and imperial regimes, as proposed in this book, such as Madrid, Barcelona, and Lisbon, as well as Manila, São Paulo, Buenos Aires, and Santiago, we can posit and explore a wider conceptualization of the history of experimental poetics across the world and its relation to colonialism. These are in fact urban centres that have a considerable impact both on what we understand as modernity across the world and on the development of the historical avant-garde from a comparative and multilingual critical paradigm.

Moreover, the consideration of the colonial legacies of both Spain and Portugal in this book is based on two interconnected methodological premises intrinsically related to the critical approach to the historical avant-garde adopted here. The first is related to the field of Iberian studies, which, as Joan Ramon Resina has argued, particularly in his own recent reformulation of the field, "can be considered a subfield of comparative studies."[31] In this sense, Resina notes that the "intrinsic relationality" of Iberian studies reorganizes "monolingual fields based on nation-states and their postcolonial extensions into a peninsular plurality of cultures and languages pre-existing and coexisting with the official cultures of the state."[32] Methodologically, therefore, *A Planetary Avant-Garde* expands upon Resina's important comparative approach to Iberian relationality by applying this comparative method beyond the geographic, cultural, and linguistic confines of the Iberian Peninsula, as well as by examining a larger conflation of different borders, languages, and artistic modes that are an integral part of the larger history of Iberian colonialism and empire across the world.

Therefore, by assessing the political and historical impact of the colonial and neo-colonial institutions of the modern Spanish and Portuguese nation-states on the development of the historical avant-garde, my study broadens the comparative approach to Iberian relationality both temporally and spatially in two main ways. First, I look beyond what is traditionally assumed to be the historical "end" of the Spanish and the Portuguese colonial projects and empires during the nineteenth century in general, and the year 1898 in particular. At the same time, I trace the impact of Iberian colonialism beyond an Atlantic context, or what Jeremy Adelman has referred to as the "Iberian Atlantic," examining the reach of Spanish and Portuguese colonial institutions and traditions within a larger geopolitical framework. As I show in this book, this particular spatio-temporal expansion of Resina's model of

"Iberian relationality" in this context – as manifested, for example, in the legacies of the Iberian colonial regimes across Southeast Asia – provides a valuable critical framework in order to trace the impact of these empires on various forms of cultural production during the historical avant-garde, as well as other contemporary and overlapping forms of imperiality, such as those of Britain and the United States in the early twentieth century.[33]

The second and related comparative methodological premise of this book with regard to Iberian studies is connected to historian Tamar Herzog's important observation that Iberia "coexisted on both sides of the Ocean for hundreds of years," rather than presume "that one shore ceased to matter after the other came into being."[34] In this context, I use the term *mutual self-constitution* to describe the sustained influence of each state and its institutions on the other. Herzog relevantly conceptualizes "Iberia" not only as the political and legal interaction of the Spanish and Portuguese nation-states, but also, and more importantly, as "an accumulation of actors, interests, activities and jurisdictions [that] resulted in a highly dynamic, open-ended process that involved individuals and groups that did not necessarily represent a state but that nevertheless ended up constructing and defining one."[35] As argued in similar terms by Adelman, the colonial interdependency of both empires extended across material, legal, and symbolic realms, constituting in fact a complex inter-imperial network of relations: "The metropoles of Lisbon and Madrid and the colonies in the Americas were locked in an integrated struggle over the sovereignty of the empires. Each side constituted the other mutually, if not always amicably ... Empires were not about 'Spain,' 'Portugal,' or their colonies, but about the transactions and relationships between the various peoples of their domains."[36]

By considering networks of self-constituting relations within what Herzog defines as a "unified space that existed contemporaneously,"[37] Herzog's and Adelman's respective approaches to Iberian history facilitate the kind of comparative analysis that I undertake here to expand our understanding of modernism and the avant-garde in relation to colonialism. One of the benefits of an Iberian comparative framework that transcends the geographic limits of the Iberian Peninsula for the analysis of what Esty refers to as the "metropole-colony relations within the global frame" is that it allows for a consideration of a more complex series of political, linguistic, and ideological relations that emerge after Spain and Portugal lose effective control of most of their overseas empires during the nineteenth century. As Adelman also argues, this gradual imperial collapse happens to magnify some of the key ideological and legal implications at the core of the Iberian colonial project as a whole:

> In the Americas, colonial societies made of pluri-social peoples of the Atlantic world and mapped out since the Treaty of Tordesillas (1494), the simultaneity of the struggles for sovereignty magnified the meanings and complexities of freedom. It also made the relations between them very explosive once the legal structures that shaped centuries of exploitation, domination and transatlantic exchange began to collapse.[38]

It is precisely in the sense of mutual self-constitution connected to Iberian colonialism and empire across the world highlighted by Adelman, a concept consistent with the transhistorical and complex inter-imperial process described by Doyle, that my examination of the notion of planetary engagement unveils a new dimension to the study of the historical avant-garde: an alternative (and at times utopian) way of conceptualizing a series of transnational connections and understandings of history emerging as direct political responses to Iberian colonialism in particular, and which can be traced through different manifestations of experimental form across particular avant-garde networks during this period.

A Planetary Avant-Garde adopts this larger critical framework to examine instances of experimental literature networks that divergently connect Western Europe, Southeast Asia, West Africa, and the Americas. By tracing key manifestations of planetary engagement within experimental literature networks, this book explores different forms of transnational connectedness (multilingual, transhistorical, translational, and transcultural) that have only recently begun to appear within studies of the historical avant-garde, as well as of modernist art and literature. Overall, *A Planetary Avant-Garde* aims to partially fill what still remains an important gap in comparative modernist and avant-garde studies by establishing a critical framework able to expand the canonical paradigms of both anglophone modernism and the European avant-garde in the standard terms that have traditionally determined the transnational study of this historical period.

As a critical history, *A Planetary Avant-Garde* is specifically bookended by two historical moments marked by the years 1909 and 1929, which frame my comparative understanding of planetary engagement within the historical avant-garde developed here. As explored in more detail in chapter 1, 1909 marks the publication of the "Futurist Manifesto" by F.T. Marinetti. Marinetti's manifesto is foundational within the larger history that my book presents: an early and extremely influential attempt to engage the world politically through experimental poetic form that relies, at the same time, on transnational circulation and transmission as part of its very form and geopolitical project. The second date, 1929, on the other hand, closes my study with two historical events not generally considered together: the first, and perhaps the most obvious, is the Wall Street Crash, which created the first global economic crisis after World War I. Due to the socio-economic significance of the Crash, 1929 has been deemed a year central to the critical establishment of the traditional categories of "high" and "late" modernism within the field of modernist studies, as noted by Paul Saint-Amour: "For more than five decades, modernist studies has affirmed this splitting of the interwar period, disposing 'high' and 'late' modernism on either side of the 1929 crisis."[39]

Within the context of *A Planetary Avant-Garde*, the Crash of 1929 represents the early stages of a global economic and geopolitical realignment after World War I that would cause a radical shift on the political dimension of the historical avant-garde, and in its gradual commodification by particular cultural institutions and nation-states. I therefore highlight the state-driven institutionalization of key avant-garde practices and networks of experimental poetics across the world as related to two other notable events of 1929, namely a pair of world's fairs occurring in Spain: the Barcelona International Exposition and the Ibero-American Exposition held in Seville. These two international expositions had major repercussions for both Iberian nation-states, and as I argue in the coda to this book, in terms of the location and relevance of experimental form within both institutional projects of government propaganda, as well as for the subsequent social life and political impact of the historical avant-garde.

Both 1929 events in Spain were organized by the government of the military dictator Miguel Primo de Rivera, during the final years of the reign of King Alfonso XIII, before the establishment of the Second Republic in 1931. These two world's fairs aimed to display and promote expressions of modern totalitarian ideology, aligned with the historical development of fascism in Europe, and represented political and economic efforts by the Spanish state to articulate a sense of Iberian neo-colonialism. Both expositions assimilated the work of well-established experimental and avant-garde artists, as well as previously established modernizing and technologic efforts, ultimately promoting an imperial and traditionalist version of modernity and history. From this perspective, 1929 signals the eventual collapse of both the centrifugal and utopian transnational impulse related in my book to the notion of planetary engagement, as well as the geopolitical breakdown of most of the literature networks that articulated this impulse in different parts of the world since 1909.

The first chapter of this book, "The Geographies and Temporalities of Futurism: Almada Negreiros, Portuguese *Modernismo*, and European Colonialism in Africa," rethinks the standard geopolitical dimension of Futurism as one of the earliest avant-garde movements and experimental literary networks belonging to the historical avant-garde, by focusing on the work of the Portuguese writer and visual artist José de Almada Negreiros (1893–1970) and his Futurist network in Portugal. Through an analysis of some of the key theoretical premises of Futurism as originally conceived by F.T. Marinetti, as well as of the Futurist works of Portuguese writer Fernando Pessoa and visual artist Guilherme Santa-Rita, this chapter traces the cultural and historical impact of Futurism as an avant-garde aesthetic on Almada Negreiros's oeuvre in particular, and on the Portuguese modernist movement in general. Almada Negreiros was a key member of the collective that created the Portuguese modernist journal *Orpheu*, and, together with Pessoa and Mário de Sá-Carneiro, played a major role in the circulation of Futurist poetics within other avant-garde groups. The chapter considers Almada Negreiros's early embrace of Futurism as an experimental poetics through which he was able to engage both his own West African origins and the impact and legacies of Portuguese imperialism and colonialism in the region during this same period. In this context, one of the generally unacknowledged aspects of Almada Negreiros's Futurist work is how it can highlight both the geopolitical expansion of Futurism as an avant-garde aesthetic in general, and in relation to the impact of European and Portuguese colonialism in Africa during the late nineteenth and the early twentieth centuries. Through a close reading of the Futurist pieces included in the two published issues of the journal *Orpheu* (especially the work of Pessoa's heteronym Álvaro de Campos, and Santa-Rita's Futurist collages), as well as Almada Negreiros's main publications of the period – such as *Manifesto anti-Dantas* (1915), *A cena do ódio* (1915), and *Ultimatum Futurista às gerações portuguesas do século XX* (1917), among others – I approach the impact of Almada Negreiros's work within the larger framework of Portuguese *modernismo* and the larger circulation of Futurist poetics across the world during the historical avant-garde. Ultimately, I show how Almada Negreiros's personal experience in West Africa and his own critical engagement with the colonial legacy of Portugal in the African continent constitutes a complex historical force that fully shapes his own approach to experimental form, and that consequently shapes the larger literary and artistic networks constructed around it.

Chapter 2, "Placing Vicente Huidobro within the Historical Avant-Garde: Experimental Poetics and the Planetary Critique of European Historicism," re-examines the planetary dimension of the work of Vicente Huidobro (1893–1948), an avant-garde poet whose oeuvre was produced across Santiago de Chile, Paris, and Madrid. The complex and diverse work of the Chilean writer is constituted through a transnational network of experimental literature and art that included different languages (Spanish and French), various literary genres and visual forms (lyric poems, prose poems, novels, screenplays, and visual artworks), divergent political ideologies, and an extensive group of collaborators that included Juan Gris, Pierre Reverdy, Douglas Fairbanks, Gerardo Diego, Sonia Delaunay Terk, and Robert Delaunay, among others.

While most of the scholarship on Huidobro over the past few decades has analysed his avant-garde poetics, referred to as *creacionismo*, from a formal perspective in relation to changes in the representational system related to Cubism, I analyse how the forms of planetary engagement displayed by Huidobro's experimental work offer a geopolitical response to European-centred forms of historicism related to the historical avant-garde, which I read in relation to the work of historian Dipesh Chakrabarty. In the case of Huidobro, these forms of historicism gravitate around the legacy of Spanish colonialism and imperialism in Latin America, and the related forms of literary history that he encountered on both sides of the Atlantic. Through my analysis and close reading of some of Huidobro's key works of this period – particularly *Ecuatorial* (1918) and *Mío Cid Campeador* (1929) – I show the ways in which his avant-garde project, as fruitful as it was controversial, constitutes a complex creative response to the various forms of European historicism that emerge around the historical avant-garde.

Chapter 3, "Away from Montmartre: Blaise Cendrars, Tarsila do Amaral, and the Travel Notes of the Historical Avant-Garde," explores the forms of planetary engagement emerging across the network of experimental poetics that link during this period Europe with Brazil, primarily through the work of Swiss-born writer Blaise Cendrars, born Frédéric-Louis Sauser (1887–1961), and major figures in the Brazilian modernist movement, particularly Tarsila do Amaral (1886–1973) and Oswald de Andrade (1890–1954). Cendrars's oeuvre is critical to the early development of the historical avant-garde, and together with Apollinaire, he is generally considered one of the earliest and most influential avant-garde poets and artists in Europe. Moreover, Cendrars's work develops a wider transnational experience of modernity from a geo-political perspective; his avant-garde project literally moves from his origins in Western Europe, to Eastern Europe, North America, and, later in his career, Central and South America. Moreover, the experience of travel and the transnational dimension evident in Cendrars's early works – such as *Prose of the Trans-Siberian* (1913), *Les Pâques à New York* (1913), and *Le Panama* (1918) – dramatically expands after World War I, when he embarks on a series of transatlantic journeys.

Cendrars records one of his journeys to the Americas in *Feuilles de route* (1924), a poetry collection that documents his first journey to Brazil in 1924. In this chapter, I explore how *Feuilles de route* forms part of a much larger transnational literary and artistic network that relates different histories and conceptualizations of experimental poetics, and that powerfully connects Cendrars's work with the key group of Brazilian writers and artists actively involved in the development of a modernist poetic revolution in Brazil, particularly Tarsila do Amaral, arguably one of the most influential Brazilian artists of the twentieth century. Analysing Cendrars's avant-garde project in *Feuilles de route* in relation to Tarsila's role in the development of Brazilian *modernismo*, I map the exploratory dimension of his avant-garde poetics in relation to different colonial (and postcolonial) paradigms of discovery and route-making. As examined in this chapter, Cendrars's incorporation of Brazil as part of his avant-garde project happens to occur while the Brazilian *modernista* collective articulates a new cultural rediscovery of Brazilian culture and traditions as central to their own avant-garde poetic movement outside of European canons. As I show in this chapter, the critical analysis of Cendrars's *Feuilles de route* in correlation with the visual work of Tarsila do Amaral, and the development of the *Pau Brasil* poetic movement by Oswald de Andrade during this period unveils a crucial instance of experimental poetics that appears to be paradigmatic, while not unique in itself, for a more complex exploration of planetary engagement as a key political dimension of avant-garde "non-organic" forms – to use Bürger's terminology. Ultimately, this is a network of experimental poetics connecting Brazil with Europe that, due to its planetary dimension, emerges as central to a wider comparative understanding of the historical avant-garde.

The fourth chapter, "The Spectre of Translation: Angela Manalang Gloria, José Garcia Villa, Claro Recto, and the Comparative Poetics of Modernism in the Philippines," explores the complex multilingual context of Filipinx culture during the first three decades of the twentieth century, and various experimental poetry networks emerging within this context.[40] In particular, I focus on the work of Filipino American writer José Garcia Villa (1908–97), Filipina poet Angela Manalang Gloria (1907–95), and their respective embrace of experimental

English-language poetics, and how their work contrasts with the poetics embraced by Spanish-language poets in the Philippines, especially embodied in the work of Claro Recto (1890–1960), one of the most influential writers of the so-called "Golden Age" of Spanish-language literature in the Philippines during the twentieth century.

In "The Spectre of Translation," I compare how during the same period these three poets articulated opposing poetics, responding in divergent ways – from the perspective of language, sex, gender, and politics – to the postcolonial condition of Filipinx literature as influenced by both Spanish colonialism and the early twentieth-century imperialism of the United States. Within this larger historical context, Garcia Villa – particularly in his experimental collection of poetry "Man-Songs" (published in 1929) and his related early poetry of this period – and Manalang Gloria's early poems contemporaneous to Villa's – which would be later collected and published in the volume *Poems* (1940) – both seek to unsettle a series of normative principles connected to the "dispersed" hegemony of Spanish colonialism that characterized society in the Philippines prior to the United States occupation that began after 1898. The sociohistorical implications of the divergent careers and poetics embraced by the three postcolonial Filipinx poets whose work is examined in this chapter highlight the various forms of planetary engagement at the core of their different approaches to modernist and experimental poetics. At the same time, their divergent careers as young poets in the Philippines eventually led to different personal paths: while Garcia Villa's move to the United States in 1929 led him to become an award-winning poet (including a Guggenheim, Bollingen, and American Academy of Arts and Letters awards), a creative writer instructor in various New York City colleges, and associate editor with the publisher New Directions, and Claro Recto became a major political figure in the Philippines, (including Majority leader of the Senate of the Philippines in the 1930s and minister of foreign affairs in the 1940s), Manalang Gloria lived most of her life after the 1940s in rather difficult financial and personal circumstances that forced her to stop her literary career in order to support her family. By comparing the conflicting conceptualizations of modernist and avant-garde forms in the early work of Garcia Villa, Manalang Gloria, and Recto, as well as their divergent and at times opposed political positions, I illustrate the multilingual and geopolitical dimensions of (post)colonial Filipinx poetry within a planetary framework to demonstrate further the ways in which the avant-garde developed outside of Europe, while still being historically impacted by the legacy of Iberian colonialism, as well as US imperialism.

Finally, in the coda, "Ludwig Mies van der Rohe, Lilly Reich, and the Barcelona World's Fair of 1929: Experimental Form as Network and the Traditionalist Politics of Empire," I highlight how the international exposition taking place in Barcelona during 1929 displays a traditionalist sense of history and ideology that marks the institutional rise of fascism in Europe, as showcased by the military dictatorship of Primo de Rivera in Spain, as well as the regime of António de Oliveira Salazar in Portugal. I argue that these two parallel Iberian political processes represent the gradual development of totalitarian politics, complete with the assimilation of avant-garde expression as an ideological tool of nationalist propaganda. In particular, the Barcelona World's Fair reveals an institutional project designed to control the political, economic, and cultural institutions of Spain as a nation-state, in a process that eventually leads to the military *coup d'état* against the Spanish Second Republic in 1936 by Francisco Franco, and the fascist realignment of Europe related to both the end of the Spanish Civil War, and the start of World War II in 1939. I expose, in particular, how the Spanish state under the Primo de Rivera military dictatorship exploited in 1929 the "modern" appeal of the avant-garde in this process, celebrating a national sense of modernity and progress as State instruments, thereby collapsing and eliminating any sense of formal experimentation as resistance to totalitarian and hegemonic forces. I argue that the use and commodification of certain avant-garde forms in this context – such as Mies van der Rohe's and Reich's influential Barcelona Pavilion designed for the International Exhibition – as well as the parallel exposition taking place in Seville that same year, both sponsored by the government of Spain, correlate with the eventual collapse of the critical networks that had sustained the historical avant-garde across several continents during the previous three decades.

By co-opting the sense of "revolution and liberation" at the core of the historical avant-garde,[41] or what Gregory Betts has referred to as the "historical avant-garde's endeavor to replace existing language with new language,"[42] this commodification of experimental form by increasingly totalitarian political regimes, in this case in the form of Iberian fascism in both Spain and Portugal, underscores a dramatic shift of focus within the experimental literature networks explored in this book. It constitutes a move away from the revolutionary dimension of experimental form itself, and a reinforcement of a traditionalist understanding of history and experience towards the locally focused exertion of radical politics and ideologies for specific institutional purposes.

Chapter One

The Geographies and Temporalities of Futurism: Almada Negreiros, Portuguese *Modernismo*, and European Colonialism in Africa

The publication of Filippo Tommaso Marinetti's "Fundazione e Manifesto del Futurismo" in 1909 is generally regarded as one of the key works marking the onset of the historical avant-garde, both through Marinetti's influential use of the manifesto form, as well as through Futurism's embrace of modernity as a radical rupture with tradition. Despite the unquestionable influence of Futurism as a movement within the avant-garde, its overall status has been considered less central to critical understandings of this period when compared to other avant-garde movements, such as Dada, Cubism, or Surrealism. As Marjorie Perloff, arguably the most important US literary critic in the comparative evaluation of this avant-garde movement, has argued, the fact is that "a hundred years after its inception, Futurism remains a curiously misunderstood movement."[1] Perloff partly ascribes this "misunderstood" condition of Futurism – which Perloff brilliantly defines through the question "Dead end of modernism or enduring inspiration?"[2] – to the avant-garde movement's dispersed manifestations across a range of peripheral geographic origins:

> Here geography is central. Futurism was born, not in the "advanced" capitals of Europe – Paris, London, Berlin – where bourgeois culture was firmly established, but in what were only recently industrialized and still markedly backward nation-states on the periphery. Italy, after all, became a unified nation only in 1861, the same year serfdom was abolished in Russia. The citizens of both nations were regarded by the French and Germans, and especially by the British, as not quite civilized.[3]

Perloff's understanding of the origins of Futurism here provides a crucial comparative framework for conceptualizing both the complex geopolitics and historical conditions of the Futurist movement, while highlighting in contrast the hegemonic centrality of French, German, and British culture within the literary and cultural history of the avant-garde. By highlighting a peripheral geopolitical dimension of Futurism within the historical avant-garde, Perloff's assessment provides two key critical foundations that are central to this chapter in particular, and to *A Planetary Avant-Garde* as a critical project as a whole: on the one hand, the inclusion of geopolitical considerations as central to our understanding of the historical avant-garde; and on the other, an analysis of the historicity of key manifestations of experimental form during this period as traditionally determined by an avant-garde archive essentially centred around British, French, and German traditions and cultural capitals. From this critical perspective, Futurism constitutes an avant-garde poetics that does not take root as such within the hegemonic framework instituted by the European cultural centres generally associated with this period, or, for that matter, that is not related to the specific manifestations of modernity that these national cultures represent – during this period itself, but also as critically understood since then. As Perloff's overall argument highlights, the Futurist movement challenges, from its inception, the centrality of these three hegemonic national cultures in the definition of the avant-garde from a historical and theoretical perspective.[4] One such instance of Futurism's peripheral dimension suggested by Perloff can be seen in Peter Bürger's foundational *Theory of the Avant-Garde*. Bürger's heavy reliance on exclusively French and German avant-garde art in order to ground his influential study precisely illustrates the geopolitical dynamic outlined by Perloff. Even though Futurism as a movement arguably produces the earliest radical critique of art as a bourgeois institution, Bürger includes only a few brief references to Futurist montage in his study, and none to the work of Marinetti.

A parallel claim to Perloff's understanding of the geographical origins of Futurism as central to the development of the movement is provided by Harsha Ram, who sees Futurism not only as originating in divergent ways in Italy and Russia, but, more importantly, as being determined by each national culture's complex and "tenuous" relation to modernity:

> Militantly Italian yet lucidly addressing Paris as the center of cultural modernity and aesthetic modernism, the manifesto's chosen site and language of publication, no less than its contents, betray some of the essential tensions of futurism as a whole. Promoting itself as the supreme expression of aesthetic modernity, futurism came into being in two regions – a belatedly unified Italy and the sprawling if tsarist *ancien régime* – whose

> relationship to the modern was tenuous at best. Italy's heyday was widely lamented as long past, even as it heavily encumbered the present, while Russia's greatness was often proclaimed to be imminent.[5]

This paradoxical aspect of Futurism highlighted by Ram – that is, Futurism as a "supreme expression of aesthetic modernity" developed in nations where the experience of modernity (as a "relation to the modern") appeared to be distant, both geographically and temporally, from the sense of modernity that pervaded European capitals of the period, such as Paris – underscores one of the problems in relation to the scholarly study of Futurism in particular, apart from its deep ideological connections with the rise of fascism in Italy.

Moreover, and parallel to its peripheral dimension within the historical avant-garde, Futurism has traditionally been analysed as a relatively short-lived movement following the original publication of Marinetti's Futurist manifesto in *Le Figaro* in 1909. While this understanding of Futurism has been expanded by scholars into a larger and more complex sense of its own temporality and historical range, there has been a tendency to describe Futurism as a comparatively brief "moment" within the larger history of the avant-garde.[6] However, as Perloff's and Ram's arguments highlight, despite its peripheral geopolitics and its alleged brevity, the fact remains that Futurism has had a lasting and impactful legacy. Thus, while it did not expand to any great extent across France, Germany, or England, as Claudia Salaris has argued, Futurism, particularly as conceived and promoted by Marinetti, did circulate widely across the world, having an impact across various disciplines and artistic forms.[7]

Much like its Italian and Russian counterparts, the particular case of Futurism in Portugal examined in this chapter emerges as an instance of an experimental literature network that fits within Perloff's critical paradigm: Portuguese Futurism represents a form of avant-garde poetics belonging to a nation with a smaller bourgeois population and one considerably less industrialized when compared to France, Germany, and England at the time. However, unlike the Futurist movements of Italy and Russia highlighted by Perloff and Ram, this unique period of Portuguese modernism has, until very recently, rarely entered the critical study of Futurism within a wider transnational and comparative critical framework outside of its original national and Iberian context.[8] Moreover, as an avant-garde movement, Futurism in Portugal has also generally been studied as a relatively brief moment within the larger development of Portuguese modernism.

As argued in this chapter, the status of Portuguese Futurism presents an invaluable opportunity to critically reassemble some of the traditional categories that have defined Futurism as a poetics, as well as its place within the historical avant-garde within a transnational framework. As I will examine here, the Portuguese Futurist movement is determined by various transnational literary and artistic networks that morph, transform and ultimately coalesce into other larger, and perhaps more visible, avant-garde movements and manifestations of experimental poetics during the period. In what follows, I focus in particular on the key role within the Portuguese Futurist network of one of the founding and most influential figures of Portuguese modernism, José de Almada Negreiros (1893–1970), widely considered one of the most important figures and prolific artists of Portuguese literature, culture, and the visual arts of the twentieth century. While Almada started his artistic career, at the young age of nineteen, as a caricature artist and illustrator in 1911, producing his first graphic designs by 1913 with his first recorded exhibit at the Escola Internacional de Lisboa, he had a long and highly influential *oeuvre* that span more than seven decades. Almada is generally regarded as one of the most influential artists of Portuguese *modernismo* and of his generation, and worked as a writer in a variety of literary genres – including poetry, fiction, and drama – as well as a dancer, painter, muralist, stage designer, and visual artist.[9]

As I will show in this chapter, Almada played a central role in the circulation of Futurist poetics across Southern Europe (and primarily connecting key literary and artistic networks in Portugal, France, Italy, and Spain).[10] I will particularly focus in the pages that follow on Almada's early embrace of Futurism as an aesthetic project, as well as the close conceptual and historical relation of the Futurist movement in Portugal to Marinetti's early formulation of Futurism during the second decade of the twentieth century, culminating in the Conferência Futurista held in Lisbon in 1917. One key aspect of Almada's Futurist work during this period is how it engages different political and aesthetic interpretations of Portuguese and European colonialism, particularly across Africa, in ways that considerably expand the geopolitical implications of our understanding of Futurism as an avant-garde poetics and its various articulations of planetary engagement. By tracing Almada's collaborations, as well as his various works and manifestos, as part of a larger Futurist network, I demonstrate how Futurism as a movement has a complex ideological and historical relation to the process of European colonialism across Africa during this period, in ways that expand both the geographic and historical parameters previously used to study the Futurist movement from a comparative perspective. In other words, my analysis sheds light on the highly relevant dimension of planetary engagement emerging at the core of Almada's own Futurist "moment," highlighting a paradoxical dimension of his work, and consequently of the Portuguese modernist movement more generally, in relation to and tension with the colonial legacy and imperial dimension of Portugal as a nation-state since the early modern period.

The "Futurist Effect": Marinetti's Foundational Manifestos and the Emergence of Portuguese Futurism in *Orpheu*

As Renato Poggioli argues, Futurism originally emerged as an aesthetic and poetic movement that epitomizes an avant-garde "task" to radically reject the past, which Poggioli defines as "the down-with-the-past movement": "Futurism chose as its own task the creation of a taste favorable to the actual contents of modern culture and in fact formulated the *aesthetic of the machine*."[11] It is precisely this dimension of the Futurist project as being tasked with embodying a radically new sense of modernity – through its emphasis on technological and industrial advancements – as a sign of its future-driven critique of bourgeois culture, that appears prominently in the following passage from Marinetti's foundational Futurist manifesto, (originally published in French as "Manifeste du Futurisme" in *Le Figaro* on 20 February 1909):

> 11. We shall sing the great masses shaken with work, pleasure, or rebellion: we shall sing the multicolored and polyphonic tidal waves of revolution in the modern metropolis; shall sing the vibrating nocturnal fervor of factories and shipyards burning under violent electric moon; bloated railway stations that devour smoking serpents; factories hanging from the sky by the twisting heads of spiraling smoke; bridges like gigantic gymnasts who spans rivers ...; adventurous steamships that scent the horizon, locomotives with their swollen chest, pawing the tracks like massive steel horses bridled with pipes, and the oscillating flight of airplanes.[12]

It is through Marinetti's original re-articulation of the manifesto as an avant-garde form, as shown here, that he can "sing the great masses," while claiming through the same action a new aesthetic relation to an incipient experience of modernity. This dual performative use of the manifesto as an experimental form not only provides Marinetti with a new lyrical voice that is powerfully projected to his audience in an innovative avant-garde tour de force, but also allows for this voice to provide a new "singing," and thus a vision, of a new technological era.

Thus, a key aspect of Marinetti's performative conceptualization of Futurism, both throughout his first manifesto of 1909 and in subsequent ones, is how it manages to disassociate the manifesto form itself from the influential model provided roughly sixty years earlier by Karl Marx and Friedrich Engels in their *Communist Manifesto* (1848). As Martin Puchner has already suggested, part of the original relevance within the history of the avant-garde of both Futurism as a movement in general and Marinetti's work in particular lies precisely in how Marinetti's critique of Marx is articulated through an original use of the manifesto as an aesthetic form, constituting an extremely influential artistic innovation that is defined by Puchner as the "futurist effect":

> A crucial moment in the emancipation of the art manifesto from the socialist manifesto is Filippo Tommaso Marinetti's Fascist critique of Marxism. This critique, drawing on the French syndicalist Georges Sorel, allowed him to forge a new manifesto, one that continued to function as a political document but whose primary focus was now artistic. The impact of futurist manifestos, what I call the "futurist effect," can be fathomed from the strong reactions they caused in the European semiperiphery of industrialization such as Italy and Russia, but also in England and Latin America … Whether the manifesto was greeted with enthusiasm or suspicion, everyone, including its detractors, was now relying on it.[13]

As argued by Puchner, this specific "futurist effect" marked by the appearance and circulation of Marinetti's 1909 manifesto – an event through which, in fact, "the manifesto enters the sphere of art in the early twentieth century" – constitutes a truly foundational moment within a larger understanding of the historical avant-garde.[14] The avant-garde impulse of this "futurist effect" is also evident in Marinetti's other manifestos of the period, for example his "Proclama futurista a los españoles" (Futurist Proclamation to the People of Spain) of 1910. In this short manifesto, translated into Spanish by a young Ramón Gómez de la Serna (1888–1963) and published in the Madrid-based literary magazine *Prometeo* – edited by Gómez de la Serna's father – Marinetti carries out a parallel "proclamation" to the earlier "Manifeste du Futurisme." In "Proclama futurista," Marinetti not only reasserts his own avant-garde voice as a singer of a new experience of modernity, but also provides a poetic vision of a new era that, within Marinetti's Futurist project, aims to expand across the globe, as the following passage shows:

> ¡Futurismo! ¡Insurrección! ¡Algarada!… ¡Voz juvenil á la que basta oír sin tener en cuenta la palabra!:—¡ese pueril grafito de la voz!—¡Voz, fuerza, *volt*, más que verbo! … ¡Intersección, chispa, exhalación, texto como de marconigrama ó de algo más sutil volante sobre los mares y sobre los montes! ¡Ala hacia el Norte, ala hacia el Sur, ala hacia el Este, y ala hacia el Oeste!

> (Futurism! Insurrection! Upheaval!… Youthful voice that can just be heard without considering any words!: – that childish trace of a voice! – Voice, force, *volt*, more than the word! … Intersection, spark, exhalation, text as a Marconigram or something more subtle flying over the seas and over the mountains! Wing toward the North, wing toward the South, wing toward the East, and wing toward the West!)[15]

As these sections from Marinetti's "Manifesto of Futurism" of 1909 and the 1910 "Proclama futurista" show, one of the foundational dimensions of Marinetti's early articulation of Futurism is how he is able to proclaim the new sense of modernity at the core of Futurism, as well as provide a model for the avant-garde to assert its historicity while simultaneously expanding its geopolitical reach. This dual dimension of Futurism as a foundational movement for the historical avant-garde has been underscored by Harsha Ram in relation to the larger "competitive spatial organization of the global literary system" and its tension with the more fragmentary and concrete local practices that characterize Futurism. Ram defines this tension as dependent on the distance, and thus inequalities, between to two different spatial logics "that separate and distinguish the world's centers from their peripheries," namely that of the world market on the one hand, and that of the system of competing nation-states on the other: "These distances, and the inequalities they generate, are perceived as the necessary by-products of two spatial logics, that of the expanding world market and that of the modern Westphalian system of sovereign and competing nation-states."[16] Furthermore, within this dialectic and tension between the centre and the periphery, Italian Futurism provides for Ram a model for how to connect the temporal dimension of modernity with the spatial logic of a global literary system:

> Italian futurism can be said to have established the parameters by which subsequent avant-garde movements could relate the temporal logic of modernity to the verbal properties of language, the cultural efficacy of negation, provocation and scandal, and the competitive spatial organization of the global literary system. For this very reason no unified or cohesive international movement could have accompanied futurism's emergence as a transnational movement.[17]

Overall, the three key foundational dimensions of Marinetti's Futurism examined here – namely the "aesthetic of the machine" that for Poggioli characterizes Futurism, the "futurist effect" theorized by Puchner around the re-articulation of the manifesto as an avant-garde form, and

Ram's interpretation of Futurism's fragmentary and "discrepant visions of modernity"[18] – were aspects also rearticulated by Almada through his early adoption of Futurism during the second decade of the twentieth century. As will be shown in the rest of this chapter, Almada's role in the development of Futurism in Portugal explicitly engages and establishes through a series of manifestos and literary works a particular geopolitical relation between Portugal, Europe, and the rest of the world, thus articulating an original sense of planetary engagement that considerably expands previous critical paradigms used to understand this "futurist moment," to use Perloff's term, within the historical avant-garde.

The standard interpretation of the development of Portuguese Futurism has been provided by João Alves das Neves's canonical history of the movement in *O movimento futurista em Portugal* (1966).[19] For Alves das Neves, the Portuguese Futurist movement as such lasts eight months ("cronológica e oficialmente, o movimento futurista português teve apenas a curta duração de oito meses" [chronologically and officially, the futurist movement only lasts the short period of eight months]).[20] This "official" period of Portuguese Futurism gravitates, according to Alves das Neves, around the first Futurist Conference of 14 April 1917, as well as the publication of the journal *Portugal Futurista* that same year. However, the work of the two main Portuguese Futurist figures – Almada and Guilherme de Santa-Rita (1889–1918) – together with that of Fernando Pessoa's Futurist heteronym, Álvaro de Campos, already appears in the two issues of the influential modernist journal *Orpheu* published two years earlier in 1915. In this sense, the publication of Almada's and Santa-Rita's work, as well as Campos's, in arguably the most important and influential literary journal of Portuguese modernism of this period, considerably expands the canonical chronology that Alves das Neves ascribes to Portuguese Futurism.[21]

Together with Pessoa (1888–1935) and Mário de Sá-Carneiro (1890–1916), Almada was one of the key members of the foundational Portuguese modernist group created around the journal *Orpheu* (Lisbon, 1915–16). While Fernando Pessoa had arrived to Lisbon in 1905 after spending most of his childhood in Durban, South Africa, Mário de Sá-Carneiro had spent his formative years between Coimbra, where he and Pessoa met as law students, and Paris, where he continued his studies at the Sorbonne.[22] This Lisbon-based collective of then extremely young poets, which also included Santa-Rita – whose work will be examined in more detail below – and the painter Amadeo de Souza Cardoso (1887–1918), set itself against the more established literary figures of Portuguese literature at the time. As argued by Maria Aliete Galhoz, the *Orpheu* writers quickly positioned themselves as an avant-garde group in contrast to the main literary figures of the period, in an attempt to rearticulate Portuguese literature:

> A literatura oficial, quer dizer, os autores que tinham a consagração do momento, ostentou uma superior ignorância a seu respeito. Atitude perfeitamente justificada pela condição do seu prestígio e pelo impetuoso à-vontade com que essa geração nova, a de *Orpheu*, lhe voltava as costas e lhe apregoava a sua medular oposição.
>
> (The official literature, that is, the group of established authors of the moment, boasted a superior ignorance about the *Orpheu* collective. This appears to have been an attitude perfectly justified by the status of their prestige and by the impetuous will with which this new generation turned their back on official literature and proclaimed their frontal opposition to the literary establishment.)[23]

It was precisely during the time of their collaboration in *Orpheu*, and as part of a collective avant-garde challenge to the literary establishment in Portugal, that Almada encountered and soon embraced Futurism as an avant-garde aesthetic. The first issue of *Orpheu*, edited by António Ferro, included, among other works, Almada's "Frizos," a series of prose poems, as well as Álvaro de Campos's influential "Opiário" and "Ode Triunfal." These two prose poems by Campos highlight the new sense of poetic modernity associated to Futurism that would become central to the modernist revolution in Portugal. Described by Irene Ramalho Santos as "the obvious Whitmanian heteronym of Pessoa" and the "sensationist Álvaro de Campos, futurist and decadent at the same time,"[24] Campos emerges within Pessoa's own "drama em gente" as Pessoa's central singer of a new sense of modernity emerging during the 1910s. Moreover, Campos also appears as the closer heteronym to Pessoa himself "ele-mesmo," as suggested by K. David Jackson in the following passage:

> Naval engineer and poet of modernity, both Portuguese and English, who from 1915 to 1917 captured the shock and novelty of a new age at its onset by publishing four of his most significant works – "Opium Voyage," "Triumphal Ode," "Maritime Ode" and the manifesto "ULTIMATUM" – Álvaro de Campos is the most versatile of the heteronyms and the "person" most associated with Fernando Pessoa as a companion in the literary life he led under his own name.[25]

As works by arguably the "closest" heteronym to Pessoa himself, according to Jackson, the two influential poems by Campos published in the first issue of *Orpheu* deserve a closer look within the examination of the development of Futurism in Portugal developed in this chapter. While "Opiário" – dedicated to Sá-Carneiro – is pervaded overall by a melancholic and decadent tone, and takes place over a ship across the Suez Canal (the poem is dated "1914, Março, no Canal de Suez, a bordo" [1914, March, at the Suez Canal, aboard]), "Ode Triunfal" has a more evident Futurist tone and takes place in a European metropolitan setting (the poem is dated "Londres, 1914, Junho" [London, 1914, June). Both "Opiário" and "Ode Triunfal" can thus be considered as a poetic sequence, not only in terms of the temporal sequence constituted by the months of March 1914 and June 1914 that Pessoa adds to each poem, but also as a thematic sequence that highlights the development and progression of the experimental poetics represented by the work of Pessoa's "Futurist" heteronym.

Campos's "Opiário" – a long first-person lyric following a quatrain stanza – is pervaded by a sense of loss, longing, and melancholia that is embodied in the consumption of opium experienced by the poetic voice in the poem. Thus, a key thematic feature of the poem is the way in which the image of opium itself is endowed with a relevant geopolitical dimension through which the poetic voice appears to be reflecting on a sense of longing for an experience that is no longer available: "E eu vou buscar ao ópio que consola / Um Oriente ao oriente do Oriente" (And I search for the opium that consoles / an Orient to the East of the Orient).[26] As a substance that can console the condition of the poetic voice, this geopolitical figuration of the experience of opium consumption in "Opiário" is of extreme importance in order to trace and recuperate various forms of planetary engagement at the core of Portuguese Futurism and their relation to the legacy of Iberian colonialism.

While Campos's poem describes a journey back to the West from the East through its setting in the Suez Canal, it makes explicit reference to the colonial history of Portugal in relation to the emotional decadence that overwhelms the historical and sensory experience of the poetic voice. As the poem progresses, Campos correlates a sense of melancholia as an affect that is experienced by the poetic voice with the complex legacy of Portuguese colonialism as a defining feature of the experience of modernity in the early twentieth century, which is so central to this poem, and to Campos's work as a whole:

> Escrevo estas linhas. Parece impossivel
> Que mesmo ao ter talento eu mal o sinta!
> O facto é que esta vida é uma quinta
> Onde se aborrece uma alma sensível …

Pertenço a um género de portuguêses
Que depois de estar a India descoberta
Ficaram sem trabalho. A morte é certa.
Tenho pensado nisto muitas vézes.

(I write these verses. It seems impossible
For me to have talent, when I barely feel it!
The fact is that life is an estate
In which a sensitive soul gets bored …

I belong to Portuguese kin
Who after having discovered India
Were left without a job. Death is certain.
I have thought about this many times.)[27]

Thus, the physical passage across the Suez Canal described in the poem also constitutes a temporal journey away from Portugal's colonial past, to a more uncertain present moment in which this imperial dimension and legacy appears to be essentially gone. From this perspective, the arrival in London, as a modern European metropolis, represented in "Ode Triunfal" constitutes a radical revolution for the poetics of Campos in the two poems included in the first issue of *Orpheu*. In contrast to "Opiário," "Ode Triunfal" presents a form of writing that is "electrified," as it were, by the pulsations of modernity embodied by the modern cityscape, and through which Campos's poetics move closer to the tone and imagery characterizing Marinetti's original formulation of Futurism, as highlighted in the first opening lines of the poem:

Á dolorosa luz das grandes lâmpadas eléctricas da fábrica
Tenho febre e escrevo.
Escrevo rangendo os dentes, féra para a beleza disto,
Para a beleza disto totalmente desconhecida dos antigos.

Ó rodas, ó engrenagens, r-r-r-r-r-r-r eterno!
Forte espasmo retido dos maquinismos em fúria!

(The painful light of the big electric lamps in the factory
I am feverish and I write.
I write grinding my teeth, raging by the beauty of it,
By this beauty totally unknown to the ancients.

Oh wheels, oh gears, eternal r-r-r-r-r-r-r!
The strong spasms of this furious machinery!)[28]

These opening lines of "Ode Triunfal" demonstrate the radical embrace of technological modernity through which Campos's poetry connects with the key features of Futurism. Throughout the ode, the poetic voice carries out a fervent singing of new senses and sensations of modernity in which the vibrancy and dynamism of various developments – ranging from the technological (electricity, mechanical forces, transportation, newspapers, etc.) to the social (local and transnational commerce, social gatherings, sports, opera shows, travel, etc.) and the urban (avenues, factories, hotels, etc.) – connect in the poem with the affective and temporal experience of the present. From this perspective, Campos's "Ode Triunfal" is thus characterized by a radical embrace of the "aesthetic of the machine" as defined by Poggioli, as well as the manifesto-like tone that Puchner identifies as the "futurist effect," as two of the key dimensions that characterize the experimental poetics of Futurism, as examined earlier in this chapter.

In contrast to the revolutionary dimension of Campos's poetry already present in the "Ode Triunfal," Almada's work published in the first issue of *Orpheu* has a nostalgic tone and symbolist imagery that is closer to Campos's "Opiário." Almada's *Frizos* (Friezes), which would also be reprinted as *Frisos*, constitutes a series of eleven short prose poems that through dense imagery present various interrelated pastoral settings. From a thematic perspective, each of the eleven pieces follow a series of different figures – mainly the figures Pierrot and Colombina, stock characters of the European *commedia dell'arte*, as well as the figure of a Black Amazon shepherdess ("A amazona negra") and the biblical figures of Adam and Eve, among others. As a result, the eleven pieces that configure *Frizos* are structured as poetic versions of bas-relief units in an architectonic or decorative frieze, and are pervaded by a decadent tone and classically inspired imagery, as shown, for example, in the fragment titled "Ruínas" (Ruins):

Pandeiros rotos e coxas taças de cristal aos pés da muralha.
Heras como Romeus, Julietas as ameias. E o vento toca, em bandolins distantes, surdinas finas de princesas mortas.
Poeiras adormecidas, notas fidalgas de minuetes de mãos esguias e de cabeleiras embranquecidas.
Aquelas ameias cingiram uma noite pecados sem fim; e ainda guardam os segredos dos mudos beijos de muitas noites.

(Broken tambourines and shattered glass vases at the foot of the wall.
Strings of ivy like Romeos, and battlements like Juliets. And with distant mandolins, the wind plays delicate, silent sounds of dead princesses.
Sleepy dust, noble notes of minuets with slender hands and whitened hair.
Those battlements encircled an endless night of sin; and they still keep the secrets of silent kisses of many nights.)[29]

As this fragment shows, the poetic vision provided by Almada in "Frizos" is articulated through a rich display of sensuous images able to articulate complex emotional and sensorial aesthetic objects evoked in the poem through lyrically dense descriptions of the settings and various figures related through the series. Thus, Almada's pre-Futurist poetry is imbued with the orphic and erotic poetics of "sensationist" (*sensacionista*) aesthetic that was being theorized by Pessoa at the time, and put into practice by Álvaro de Campos, as previously explored in relation to "Opiário."

The second issue of *Orpheu*, also published in 1915, makes an explicit reference to Futurism through the inclusion of four collages by Santa-Rita, who is introduced on the cover of the issue as a Futurist artist: "Colaboração especial do futurista Santa-Rita Pintor" (Special collaboration by the Futurist Santa-Rita Pintor [Painter]). The publication of Santa-Rita's and Almada's works in *Orpheu* highlights a key aspect in the early stage of Futurism in Portugal, namely, that both shared an interest and background in the visual and graphic arts. While Almada continued to work as both a writer and a visual artist throughout his artistic career, Santa-Rita focused exclusively on the visual arts following his training in Paris, where he had direct contact with Marinetti's work during the early 1910s and up to his sudden death in 1918. Immediately preceding his passing, Santa-Rita apparently requested all of his works be destroyed, with only a few of his series of avant-garde artworks remaining, in part thanks to their reproduction in the second issue of *Orpheu*.

While he is considerably less known than either Pessoa or Almada, the role of Santa-Rita is crucial in the earlier stage of the development of Futurism in Portugal: apart from bringing from Paris his own version of Futurist art after World War I began, Santa-Rita was passionately committed to the circulation of Marinetti's manifestos in his native country. As Mário de Sá-Carneiro announced to Fernando Pessoa in a letter sent from Paris in July 1914, Santa-Rita was planning to return to Lisbon that September, and had already asked Sá-Carneiro to find an editor for the translation of Marinetti's manifestos: "Veio-me pedir para eu arranjar um editor para a traducção portuguesa dos manifestos de Marinetti (livro 'Le futurism' e os outros trabalhos)" (He asked if

I could find a publisher for the Portuguese translation of Marinetti's manifestos [the book "Le futurisme" and other works]).[30] Santa-Rita's own commitment to spread the "Futurist effect" at the core of Marinetti's project throughout Portugal appears to be clear from the testimony provided by this letter mentioned by Sá-Carneiro.

Santa-Rita's collages included in the second issue of *Orpheu* explicitly display the kind of "aesthetics of the machine" that characterize Marinetti's Futurism. One such instance of his work is the piece *Sensibilidade mechanica* (Mechanical Sensitivity), an artwork produced in Paris in 1914 that relevantly connects Santa-Rita's articulation of Futurist poetics with some of the key theoretical tenets of Marinetti's "Technical Manifesto of Futurist Literature" (1912), particularly Marinetti's "lyrical obsession with matter."[31] Santa-Rita's *Sensibilidade mechanica* is configured by a series of material elements (metal, paper, ink) and simple geometrical figures (circles, squares, rectangles, lines) as they mechanically constitute, as a "scientific study," the form of a human head. Santa-Rita's piece thus features a highly dynamic visual experience that is articulated by the spatial interaction between the different materials and shapes that converge to configure a human head. As seen in figure 1.1, the material configuration of the piece is summarized through the formula at the footer of the image: "Estojo scientifico de uma cabeça + aparelho ocular + sobreposição dynamica visual + reflexos de ambiente x luz" (Scientific sketch of a head + ocular device + visual dynamic overlay + ambient reflections x light).

As a collage that rather literally articulates the semblance of a human figure with the spatial and sensorial interaction of a range of materials, *Sensibilidade mechanica* constitutes a work of art that closely follows the tenets of Marinetti's Futurist precept to "destroy the I in literature," particularly as developed in the eleventh point of his 1912 "Technical Manifesto of Futurist Literature." In this manifesto, Marinetti argues for a form of art that reduces any trace of subjectivity or psychological element – which the Italian poet figures as a "masculine" form or substance – from the realm of artistic representation. Moreover, Marinetti proposes the substitution of the traditional mimetic model of representation, based on the subject's perspective, with a more intuitive and affective, almost somatic, artistic experience of matter:

> So abolish him in literature. Replace him with matter, whose essence must be grasped by flashes of intuition, something physicists and chemists can never do. Auscultate, through things in freedom and capricious engines, the breath, the sensibility, and the instinct of metal, stone, wood, etc. Replace the psychology of man, now spent, with a *lyrical obsession with matter*.[32]

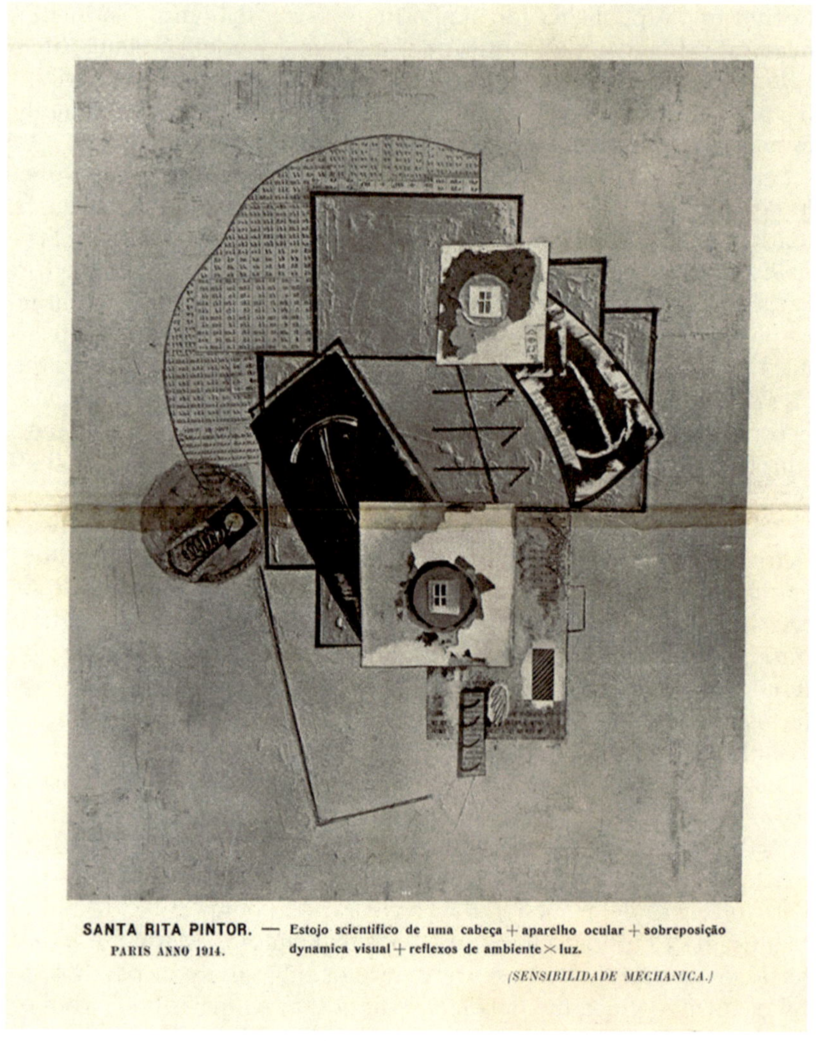

Figure 1.1. Guilherme de Santa-Rita, *Sensibilidade mechanica* (1915). Source: *Orpheu*, no. 2 (2015).

From this perspective, in Santa-Rita's *Sensibilidade mechanica* the figurative dimension of the image is both composed and recomposed, figured and reconfigured, through a series of material objects and traces that, while constructing the visual figure of a human head, simultaneously disrupt an organic perception of human semblance. Santa-Rita's compositional strategy is thus characteristic of Futurist collage, representing a creative and poetic transformation that, as noted by Perloff in relation to Umberto Boccioni's futurist sculpture, ultimately establishes a creative "process of graft or citation, a process by means of which we make the public world our own":

> As the mode of detachment and readherence, of graft and citation, collage inevitably undermines the authority of the individual self, the "signature" of the poet or painter. "Our renovated consciousness," declares Boccioni, "does not permit us to look upon man as the center of universal life. The suffering of a man is of the same interest to us as the suffering of an electric lamp" (FM 29) … Indeed, to collage elements from impersonal, external sources – the newspaper, magazines, television, billboards – is to understand, as it were, that in a technological age, consciousness itself becomes a process of graft or citation, a process by means of which we make the public world our own.[33]

It is precisely through a parallel process of "grafting" in the Futurist sense highlighted by Perloff, that Santa-Rita's *Sensibilidade mechanica* achieves a parallel effect to Boccioni's critique of human authorship and subjectivity. Through a deeply material process of configuration, Santa-Rita attempts to visually articulate a "scientific" study of a male human head through the experimental juxtaposition of a series of different geometric shapes and material elements – indeed, as a mechanical attempt to articulate a sensory experience into a new Futurist aesthetic totality. The logic of aesthetically disrupting the inner stability of the "I" through a mechanical grafting of a "public world" mentioned by Perloff, and which was examined previously as put into practice by Santa-Rita, soon acquires a crucial political valence in Almada's Futurist work, particularly in relation to the Portuguese nation, and the complex legacy of its colonial empire. As I show in the rest of this chapter, by explicitly connecting the experimental form of avant-garde poetics with the process of European colonialism in Africa during the last decade of the nineteenth century, the planetary implications of Almada's work considerably expand the traditional scholarly approach to Futurism from a temporal and geopolitical perspective.

Portuguese Colonialism and Almada Negreiros's Futurist Nationalism: *A cena do ódio* and *Manifesto anti-Dantas* (1916)

The emergence within the pages of *Orpheu* of the avant-garde poetics of Futurism through the network configured by Pessoa, Santa-Rita, and Almada coincided with a complex moment in Portuguese history right in the middle of World War I, both socially and politically. This historical period was marked by the aftermath of the overthrow of the old monarchical system, with the exile of King Manuel II to England and the declaration of the First Portuguese Republic in 1910. As historian António Costa Pinto observes, this was a moment of great political flux and uncertainty for Portugal, as one of the first republics declared in Europe during the twentieth century, and at a time in which key aspects of the Portuguese nation-state and national identity were being redefined by the new republican elites:

> The republican elites did carry out a timid but radical "mass nationalization," always being conscious of the social and political "siege" of the rural areas still dominating Portuguese society. These elites were the principal movers behind the creation of the national symbols and school socialization apparati that would characterize 20th century Portugal. They would also be the "sanctifiers" of the colonial empire as a central element of the Portuguese "nation's" viable identity. A new national Flag and Anthem, a new civil liturgy with its own holidays, a model of "citizen building," a populist-type political mobilization, and an accentuated "nationalization" of teaching programs accompanying the expansion of school system, characterized the 1910 rupture.[34]

Within this larger historical context, both marked by the growing logic of nationalization highlighted by Costa Pinto at a local level developing since 1910, and the start of World War I at the international level in 1914, Almada's Futurist work, as well as the work of some of the key members of the *Orpheu* collective, gradually gained an important political dimension. By 1915, the year in which Almada composed the poem *A cena do ódio* (The Scene of Hatred), his poetic style had suffered a major transformation that can be ascribed to his contact with Futurist poetics via Santa-Rita's work and his various efforts to spread Futurist poetics in the literary and artistic scene in Lisbon at the time.

While *A cena do ódio* (with the title *A scena do ódio*, dated 14 May 1915) was expected to appear in the third unpublished issue of *Orpheu*, it was published in its entirety only in 1958, more than forty years later. *A cena do ódio*, a poem that Almada dedicates to Álvaro de Campos, displays a newfound sense of political urgency not previously present in Almada-Negreiros's work, a feature that appears to be closely connected with Marinetti's notion of "destruction of the I" as central to Futurist poetics. The "scene of hatred" taking place within Almada's poem essentially constitutes a complex dialectical struggle between a first voice and an absent second voice (repeatedly invoked by the second person pronoun "tu") that aims to disrupt a sense of a determined personal identity, as briefly shown in this passage:

> Sou Narciso de Meu Ódio!
> …
> O Meu Ódio é Dilúvio Universal sem Arcas de Noé: só Dilúvio Universal! …
> Ah! que eu sinto, claramente, que nasci
> De uma Praga de ciúmes!
> Eu sou as sete pragas sobre o Nilo
> E a Alma dos Bórgias a penar! …
> Tu, que te dizes Homem! …
> Tu, que aperfeiçoas sabiamente a arte de matar.
> Tu, que descobriste o cabo da Boa-Esperança
> E o Caminho Marítimo da Índia
> E que levaste a chatice a estas terras.
>
> (I am Narcissus of My Hate!
> …
> My Hatred is Noah's Universal Deluge without the Ark: just a Universal
> flood! …
> Oh! I feel, clearly, that I was born
> From a plague of jealousy!
> I'm the seven plagues of the Nile
> And the soul of the languishing Borgias! …
> You, who has said you are Man! …
> You, who has wisely perfected the art of killing.
> You, who has discovered the Cape of Good-Hope
> And the Indian Sea Route
> And who has brought trouble to these lands.)[35]

The powerful tension expressed by the poetic voice in this fragment is aimed at some other self (embodied by both "tu" [you] and in the notion of "Homem" ["Man"]), whom the "I" of the poem keeps confronting as a reflection of its own self. This dialectical tension, which functions as the manifestation of both an inner and external conflict articulated across a range of poetic images in *A cena do ódio*, eventually disrupts the stability of the poetic voice within the poem: "E eu vivo aqui sepultado vivo / Na Verdade de nunca ser Eu" (And I live here buried alive / in the Truth of never being myself).[36] What is particularly relevant here about Almada's experimental formulation of his own attempt to "destroy the I in literature," in Marinetti's terms explored in this chapter, is precisely how Almada frames this conflict in *A cena do ódio* through explicit geopolitical terms specifically connected to the legacy of Portuguese colonization in Africa and Southeast Asia: "You, who has discovered the Cape of Good-Hope / And the Indian Sea Route / And who has brought trouble to these lands." Thus, an essential aspect of *A cena do ódio* is how the figure of the "Man" as the "you" in the poem embodies the force of the colonizer "who has brought trouble to these lands" as the "discoverer" of the "the Cape of Good Hope." This dialectical tension between the first and the second person – the colonized and the colonizer, the I ("eu") and the you ("tu") – is ultimately left unresolved in the poem within its own logic of indeterminate self-reflection, envisioning a form of poetic creation that disrupts the emergence of a determinate subject: "Eu invejo-te a tí, ó coisa que não tens olhos de ver" (I invent you today, thing which does not have eyes to see).[37]

Therefore, from this geopolitical critical perspective, if the poetic voice of *A cena do ódio* constitutes a "Narcissus of Its Hate" as a reflection of the loathing at the very core of its own subjectivity, it is a hatred that in the poem is intrinsically connected to the act of conquest and subjection at the core of the colonial encounter determining the modern history of both Portugal and its empire. Thus, a central aspect of Almada's incorporation of Futurist poetics into his work in this period is the particular way in which he ascribes a planetary dimension to the negation of the "I" (as a sense of human stability) in terms similar to the work of Marinetti and Santa-Rita. In the hands of Almada, this act of aesthetically making the "public world our own" that Perloff ascribes to Futurist collage is endowed with a deep geopolitical dimension that connects the fields of both Portuguese modernism, and Futurist poetics in particular, with the larger socio-political project of European colonialism in Africa, both in terms of its longer history and during this period. In this sense, this key geopolitical feature of *A cena do ódio* closely connects with the colonial implication of the experience of melancholia also explored by Pessoa through Campos's "Opiário," as examined above, and to which Campos's Futurist "Ode Triunfal" is specifically responding.

The next stage in the development of Almada's Futurist project was provided by his first "official" Futurist piece, the *Manifesto anti-Dantas e por extenso* of 1916. This Futurist manifesto, which he signs as "José de Almada-Negreiros poeta d'Orpheu futurista e tudo" (Futurist Poet of *Orpheu* and Everything), adopts an even more pointedly geopolitical dimension than *A cena do ódio*. In *Manifesto anti-Dantas*, Almada carries out a radical critique of contemporary bourgeois art and culture in Portugal, embodied in the work of Júlio Dantas (1876–1962), writer, politician, and member of the Academia das Ciências de Lisboa. The opening lines of Almada's *Manifesto anti-Dantas* thus continues the Futurist critique of the literary establishment central to the collective avant-garde ethos of the *Orpheu* group, but emerging here with a new, more radical, avant-garde tone:

> +BASTA PUM BASTA+
> UMA GERAÇÃO, QUE CONSENTE DEIXAR-SE REPRESENTAR POR UM DANTAS É UMA GERAÇÃO QUE NUNCA O FOI! É UM COIO D'INDIGENTES, D'INDIGNOS E DE CEGOS! É UMA RESMA DE CHARLATÃES E DE VENDIDOS, E SÓ PODE PARIR ABAIXO DE ZERO!
> ABAIXO A GERAÇÃO!
>
> (+ENOUGH BLAST ENOUGH+
> A GENERATION THAT ALLOWS TO BE REPRESENTED BY DANTAS IS A GENERATION THAT NEVER WAS! IT IS A HIDE-OUT OF THE BANKRUPT, UNDIGNIFIED AND BLIND! IT'S A PACK OF CHARLATANS AND SOLD OUTS, AND IT CAN ONLY PRODUCE NEGATIVE ZERO!
> DOWN WITH THE GENERATION!)[38]

As Almada develops in *Manifesto anti-Dantas*, the bourgeois condition represented by the figure of Dantas constitutes a cultural state to be transcended for Portugal to gain a new sense of national identity within its current historical moment. Following a Futurist logic, the figure of Dantas embodies for Almada an older reactionary condition that needs to be overcome in order to unveil a new future for the Portuguese people, one enabling them to surmount what Almada considers their cultural degradation at the time. The manifesto concludes with a critique of the current cultural conditions, which are described in terms that considerably expand the complex geopolitics that we also saw emerging in Almada's *A cena do ódio* connected to Portuguese colonialism and imperialism:

> PORTUGAL QUE COM TODOS ESTES SENHORES, CONSEGUIU A CLASSIFICAÇÃO DO PAIZ MAIS ATRASADO DA EUROPA E DE TODO O MUNDO! O PAIZ MAIS SELVAGEM DE TODAS AS ÁFRICAS! O EXILIO DOS DEGREDADOS E DOS INDIFERENTES! A AFRICA RECLUSA DOS EUROPEUS! O ENTULHO DAS DESVENTAGENS E DOS SOBEJOS! PORTUGAL INTEIRO HA-DE ABRIR OS OLHOS UM DIA
>
> (PORTUGAL THAT WITH ALL THESE GENTLEMEN HAS BEEN AWARDED THE TITLE OF MOST BACKWARD COUNTRY IN EUROPE

> AND THE WORLD! THE WILDEST IN ALL OF AFRICA! THE EXILE OF CONVICTS AND THE INDIFFERENT! THE CAPTIVE AFRICA OF EUROPEANS! THE REFUSE AND LEFTOVERS OF THE DISAVANTAGED! PORTUGAL IN ITS ENTERITY HAS TO OPEN ITS EYES ONE DAY)[39]

By describing Portugal as the "CAPTIVE AFRICA OF EUROPEANS," Almada is not only critiquing the intellectual condition of the Portuguese bourgeoisie at the time, but is doing so by problematically and paradoxically juxtaposing – through the compositional strategy of Futurist collage – the African and European continents as signifiers in relation to each other, and more specifically through the colonization of Africa by Europe. It is evident in this passage that the signifier "Africa" represents for Almada a subaltern identity colonized and imprisoned by Europe within the historical context of the 1910s, as well as the longer history of European imperialism in Africa. On the one hand, this key moment of the *Manifesto anti-Dantas* denotes a form of Futurist signification that is deeply problematic from an ideological and historical perspective as it conceptualizes Africa as an abject Other commodified by Europe; on the other hand, it formally constitutes a strict Futurist compositional logic in the way that Almada's figuration of this key moment of the manifesto articulates an aesthetic and geopolitical image collaging and juxtaposing three different signifiers (Portugal, Europe, and Africa) in explicit historical tension with each other.

It is very important here to highlight that this Futurist rhetorical strategy in *Manifesto anti-Dantas*, through which Almada uses Africa as signifier to refer to Portugal's cultural and socio-economic marginalization within Europe in 1916, has a wider personal dimension, and forms part of a larger geopolitical strategy that lies at the very core of his own avant-garde project. Moreover, this is a crucial connection with the African continent at the core of Almada's Futurist project that was also shared by Fernando Pessoa, as mentioned above. Almada was born in what was then the Portuguese colony of São Tomé and Príncipe, two small islands located in the Gulf of Guinea and the equatorial Atlantic roughly 150 miles from mainland Africa.[40] His parents were the Portuguese council administrator of the West African islands between 1892 and 1893, António Lobo de Almada Negreiros, and Elvira Freire Sobral, also born in São Tomé and Príncipe, who was the daughter of an important Portuguese colonial merchant, José Freire Sobral, and of Leopoldina Amélia de Azevedo, who was born in Angola and whose mother, Luzia, was of African descent.

Soon after the death of Almada's mother, three years after his birth in 1896, he moved with his father back to Portugal. During the time in which Almada's father was involved in the colonial government of these islands, São Tomé became a very important source of economic revenue for the Portuguese colonial project, as Tony Hodges and Malyn Newitt note:

> Between 1890 and 1914, São Tomé played a major role in the Portuguese economy and in sustaining the interest of the Portuguese commercial classes of the empire. Portugal and its empire suffered from chronic budgetary deficits, depressed industrial and agricultural markets, and permanent problems with the balance of payments. The diminutive island of São Tomé, by itself, went a long way toward enabling Portugal to balance its books.[41]

Moreover, Almada's father was not only the Council Administrator of São Tomé and Príncipe, but was in fact a key figure of European colonialism during this period, as well as a member of important scientific European societies involved in the colonization of Africa after the Berlin Conference, such as the Geographic Society in London, the Société de Géographie de Paris, the Union Coloniale Française, and the International Colonial Institute.[42]

While the scope and range of António de Almada Negreiros's colonial works are beyond the specific focus of this chapter, I will briefly describe here how his ethnographic writings, and the conception of Portuguese colonialism and nationalism that pervades them, relate to the Futurist writings of his son within the context of this chapter. In particular, António de Almada's geographic and socio-economic study of São Tomé, *Colonies portugaises. Île de San-Thomé; avec cartes*, covers a wide series of topics ranging from the history and climate of the islands, to traditional musical instruments used on the islands and quality of its mineral water. Focusing at the end of his book on the effects of Portuguese colonization on its native population, however, António de Almada highlights what for him constitutes the imperial success of Portugal in these equatorial islands as a manifestation of what he describes as the colonial prowess and ingenuity of the Portuguese "audacious race":

> San-Thome est, essentiellement, une colonie portugaise ; et cependant on entend dire souvent, que ce peuple portugais a toujours colonisé lentement ; que le génie de cette race aventurière est contraire à une grande expansion méthodique et productive des forces collectives de la nation, etc. C'est une erreur de la part de ces juges. L'état de quelques-unes des colonies du Portugal est là pour prouver le contraire, pour ne citer que : l'Angola, où il domine vraiment sur un très vaste territoire; et particulièrement,

> San-Thomé qui, il y a trente ans, végétait encore dans la misère … Il est alors intéressant de voir sortir victorieux de la lutte, le génie travailleur … d'une race qui a eu sa période de gloire en découvrant le monde, et qui reconnait, aujourd'hui, le besoin d'opposer au sentiment de conquête la raison et l'étude, pour parachever, à travers les âges, son œuvre si grandiose. Ce petit peuple, qui n'occupe qu'un petit coin de l'Europe Occidentale, étend toujours son pouvoir souverain, impose encore sa langue, ses mœurs et sa religion, á plusieurs millions de sujets, sur une étendue territoriale vingt fois plus grande que la mère-patrie. N'est-ce pas le meilleur éloge qu'on eu puisse faire ?
>
> (São Tomé is, essentially, a Portuguese colony; and yet we hear often that Portuguese people colonized slowly; and that the genius of this audacious race goes against a large methodical and productive expansion of the collective forces of the nation, etc. This is an error on the part of the judges. The situation of some of the colonies of Portugal is here to prove otherwise, to name a few: Angola, where Portugal in fact dominates a vast territory; especially, São Tomé, which thirty years ago was still vegetating in misery … It is interesting to see emerge victorious in the struggle … a race that had in its heyday discovered the world and that today recognizes the need to oppose the feeling of conquest with reason and study to complete, through the ages, such a grand work. This small nation, which occupies only a small corner of Western Europe, still extends its sovereign power, still imposes its own language, customs, and religion, to millions of subjects over a territorial area twenty times larger than the mother country. Isn't that the best praise that one can offer?)[43]

The colonial logic of António de Almada at work in this passage of *Colonies portugaises* explicitly posits the relative marginality of Portugal within the contemporary geopolitics of Western Europe at the time. For the elder Almada Negreiros, what may seem the more moderate and less systematic Portuguese mode of colonial occupation constitutes a sign of their impressive success in the colonial exploitation of São Tomé since the late nineteenth century. As he argues, this is a form of colonization that has revived a region that "thirty years ago was still vegetating in misery." It seems, therefore, that the "praise" that the Portuguese colonization of São Tomé can give to the Portuguese nation in 1901 ultimately fails to corroborate the potential revival of the Portuguese Empire's colonial revival in the twentieth century, as António de Almada argues. On the contrary, his hyperbolic and enthusiastic description of the colonial extension of a Portuguese "sovereign power still impos[ing] its own language, customs and religion, to millions" highlights what was then the dire situation of the Portuguese economy and its historical and cultural crisis, illustrating, overall, its marginal condition within Western Europe at the time. Thus, while his argument supports the notion that São Tomé did play a fundamental role in sustaining the Portuguese national project at the time, it also highlights the socio-economic degradation of the Portuguese Empire by the end of the nineteenth century, precisely in the terms suggested by Hodges and Newitt in their historical analysis of the period, a condition of crisis to which the Portuguese Futurist movement were explicitly responding in their own terms through their literary works and manifestos.

More important, and in contrast to the ethnographic work of António de Almada Negreiros and his conception of the Portuguese Empire that ultimately looks back on an earlier colonial period as a moment of national pride, the Futurist project of José de Almada Negreiros is clearly pointing towards a potential future moment of renewal in which Portuguese culture will be able to confront its socio-economic crisis and overcome its geopolitical marginalization within Europe. Even though Almada's Futurist poems and manifestos were written less than fifteen years after the publication of the ethnographic works of his father, it is evident that he is gradually distancing himself from his predecessor's hyperbolic and idealistic assessment of the past and the images of the "force" and "vitality" of the Portuguese nation and colonial empire at the time. However, while they are based on deeply contrasting premises, both intellectual projects do share two fundamental features: the first is the importance of Africa as geographic realm, a historical reality, and ultimately as a signifier central to the Portuguese imaginary for a national reconceptualization of itself at two key different moments of the early twentieth century; the second is how this geopolitical and historical connection between Portugal and Africa is seen and imagined in relation to the peripheral relevance and relative marginalization of Portugal as a nation within Western Europe during the same period.

Futurism, and its new sense of modernity and temporality, therefore provides the young Almada Negreiros with an aesthetic and political logic capable of questioning the stability of the Portuguese national project itself, in relation to both Europe and Africa. As José argues in his Futurist "Manifesto da Exposicão de Amadeo de Sousa Cardozo" of 1916, the age of colonial discoveries is something that the Portuguese nation can no longer experience as part of its present historical condition:

> A Raça Portugueza não precisa de reabilitar-se, como pretendem pensar os tradicionalistas desprevenidos; precisa é de nascer pró século em que vive

> a Terra. A Descoberta do Caminho Marítimo prà Índia já não nos pertence porque não participamos d'este feito fisicamente e mais do que a Portugal este feito pertence ao século XV.
>
> (The Portuguese Race does not need to rehabilitate itself, as the unready traditionalists wish to think; what it needs is to be born in the century in which it is living on Earth. The Discovery of the Sea Route to India no longer belongs to us since we do not participate physically in this event, even more since for Portugal this event belongs to the fifteenth century.)[44]

Through the "the down-with-the-past" logic of Futurism, Almada is able to establish a dual aesthetic and geopolitical relation to his own national culture in a way that allows him to distance his Futurist vision from the colonialist legacy of his father, and thus from a traditionalist understanding of Portugal's history and its place in the world. This explicitly anti-traditionalist feature of his version of Futurist poetics as manifested in his writings is therefore more than just an aesthetic strategy connected to the "aesthetic of the machine" generally ascribed to the Futurist movement – in an attempt to articulate through art a new sensorial or perceptual re-composition of the human condition, as we saw in the case of Santa-Rita.

For Almada, therefore, this geopolitical dimension at the core of his approach to Futurism, which connects both Europe and Portugal with Africa, configures a form of planetary engagement that clearly shapes and determines his Futurist works, as shown here, and which highlights the larger planetary implications of Portuguese Futurism as a poetics during this period. While the traditionalist understanding of Portugal's past embodied in his father's writings would gradually become a central dimension of the political project of the dictatorial regime established in Portugal after the military coup of 1926 and the eventual development of António de Oliveira Salazar's *Estado Novo*, as will be explored later in this book, Almada is positing here an attempt to reconceptualize the colonial legacy of Portugal for a new sense of national identity and political future through the experimental poetics of Futurism.[45]

The forms of planetary engagement, and the particular geopolitical dimension as it pertains to Africa, at the core of Almada's Futurist project constitute a dimension of Portuguese Futurism that connects directly not only to the early work of Fernando Pessoa (as I have examined elsewhere in detail), but also to the work of Marinetti. Like Almada, Marinetti was born in Africa, in his case in Alexandria, Egypt, in 1876, and lived there for about seventeen years until 1893, when his family moved back to Milan. While the impact of his experience living in Egypt during his childhood has not traditionally been analysed in relation to Marinetti's development of Futurism, it appears to constitute a fundamental aspect of his life and work that determines a number of the key ideological and nationalistic features of his oeuvre. This geopolitical connection with the African continent constitutes a relevant aspect of Marinetti's Futurist project that has been analysed by Cinzia Sartini-Blum as follows:

> Marinetti's own writing turns out to be caught in the paradoxical dynamics of the exoticist project. The futurist leader may seem an obvious paragon for colonial writers: the son of an Italian lawyer who made his fortune in Egypt, he covered the Italian campaign in Libya as a reporter, participated as an officer in the Ethiopia war, and throughout his career wrote several books staged in Africa.
>
> …
>
> The most conspicuous aspect of Marinetti's "incorporation" of Africa is, of course, his celebration of Italian colonialism inspired by the Libyan and Ethiopian campaigns: *La Batagglia di Tripoli*, (The Battle of Tripoli, 1912), *Il poema Africano della Divisione "28 Ottobre"* (The African poem of the "October 28th" Division, 1937), where the poet-turn-colonizer transfigures war into a source of aesthetic pleasure providing artistic justification for imperialistic violence.[46]

As Sartini-Blum suggests, Italian colonialism in Africa – as a process preceding the emergence of Futurism in Italy as a movement, as well as that of fascism – provides a geopolitical arena in which a Futurist artist like Marinetti is able to extend and exert an "imperialistic form of violence" at the core of his aesthetic project into a particular historical situation and political project. However, Marinetti's own personal experiences as a child in Egypt, and the related "exoticist nostalgia" that Sartini-Blum traces in Marinetti's work, problematize that canonical reading of the relationship between Italian Futurism and colonialism after World War I, at a historical moment, as she describes it, "well into the age of New Imperialism, but early from the standpoint of Italy's colonial ambitions."[47]

Similarly to this dimension of Marinetti's Futurist project highlighted by Sartini-Blum, the case of Almada within the larger development of Futurism in Portugal, specifically in terms of his personal relationship with the African continent, considerably expands and complements the importance of Africa for the Futurist movement as a whole, from a geographic, political, personal, and symbolic perspective. This transnational connection between the figures of Marinetti and Almada examined here, and consequently between the Futurist movements developed in Italy and Portugal, thus opens a new line of enquiry – transnational as well as inter-imperial – in which the Futurist "moment," to use Perloff's term, is expanded into a larger network of various artistic and cultural connections not just critiquing the realm of art as an institution – using Bürger's model for the theorization of the avant-garde – but also intimately responding in much wider and complex ways to the legacies of European colonialism as a whole, and consequently to its geopolitical relation to the historical avant-garde more widely.

European Colonialism, the Great War, and the Culmination of Portuguese Futurism: Almada's *Ultimatum Futurista*

Portuguese Futurism culminated as a project in 1917 with the first and only Futurist Conference in Portugal, Conferência Futurista, and the parallel publication of the only issue of the journal *Portugal Futurista.* The Conferência Futurista took place on 17 April 1917 at the Teatro República in Lisbon, and included a presentation and performance of Almada's own *Ultimatum Futurista às gerações portuguesas do século XX* (Futurist Ultimatum to the Portuguese Generations of the Twentieth Century), as well as the "Manifesto Futurista da Luxuria" (Futurist Manifesto of Lust) by the French writer Valentine de Saint-Point (1875–1953) and "Music-Hall et Tuons le clair de lune" by Marinetti.[48] Overall, Almada's Conferência Futurista was aimed at officially presenting Futurism to Portugal, with the political intent to provide a new vision of the Portuguese nation as a direct response to the various challenges facing the country at the time. As a result, the course of World War I becomes the key historical framework for determining this important Futurist conference in Lisbon in April 1917, and in particular Almada's central role within it.

While Portugal was initially neutral in World War I, by 1916 it had officially joined the conflict in order to respond to the German campaign in Angola of 1914–15. As Miriam Halpern Pereira shows in her historiographic analysis of this complex period in Portugal, at the time of the conference, in fact a few months before the military coup of Sidónio Pais in December 1917, Portugal was actively involved in the war:

> On 9 March, 1916, the German government declared war on Portugal, in direct response to the seizure, two weeks earlier, of the seventy German

ships and two Austrian ships that had taken refuge in Portuguese ports (mainland Portugal, islands and colonies). Portugal had been requested to take this action by Great Britain, under the scope of the Interallied Maritime Transport Council and the traditional alliance between the two countries. At that time, Afonso Costa's second government was already in office (29 November 1915–15 March 1916), but the entry into the war required the formation of a government of national unity … This government would be overthrown by the coup led by Major Sidónio Pais on 10 December 1917, which immediately called into question Portugal's participation at the war's European front.[49]

Within this particular context of war and upheaval, the 1917 Conferência Futurista, as a social and historical event, powerfully embodies the final, more revolutionary phase of Portuguese Futurism.[50] It was at this moment that Almada adopted what Poggioli refers to as a "prophetic and utopian phase" in relation to the Futurist movement: "This means that in the psychology and ideology of avant-garde art, historically considered (from the viewpoint of what Hegelian and Marxists would call the historical dialectic), the futurist manifestation represents, so to speak, a prophetic and utopian phase, the area of preparation for the announced revolution, if not the revolution itself."[51]

Almada's *Ultimatum Futurista às gerações portuguesas do século XX* is one of the most explicit political expressions from the realm of Portuguese avant-garde art to establish a social and cultural revolution, as well as to present a poetic vision for a new historical future for Portugal articulated during this period. Moreover, the fact that the manifesto was originally conceptualized as an event performed in public lends Almada's "Ultimatum" a quintessentially Futurist dimension of theatricality, in the terms suggested by Martin Puchner regarding the futurist manifesto as experimental form: "The futurist manifesto is infused with a particular form of theatricality. The manifesto had always been a genre singularly intent on theatrical posing, on claiming an authority it did not yet possess, but the art of the manifesto takes this theatricality to an extreme."[52] The specific impact of the work of Marinetti in Almada's "Ultimatum" and its performance is thus an essential feature of this piece as a Futurist work; as Almada himself describes in the brief introduction of the published version of the manifesto, Marinetti's influence is central to both the tone and form of *Ultimatum Futurista*:

Consegui, inspirado na revelação de Marinetti e apoiado no genial optimismo da minha juventude, transpor essa bitola de insipidez em que

> se gasta Lisboa inteira, e atingir ante a curiosidade da plateia a expressão da intensidade da vida moderna, sem duvida de todas as revelações a que é mais distante de Portugal.
>
> (I managed, inspired by the revelation of Marinetti, and encouraged by the enthusiastic optimism of my youth, to overcome the aura of insipidity in which Lisbon was subsumed, and to reach, in front of the curiosity of the audience, the expression of the intensity of modern life, without a doubt the furthest revelation available to Portugal.)[53]

The opening of Almada's *Ultimatum* highlights how the performative and aesthetic dimension that we saw as central to his incorporation of Futurism in the earlier *A cena do ódio* now appears to be overshadowed by the inherent political intention of this later Futurist piece. Presenting his project as a "constructive" rearticulation of Portuguese identity, and imbued with Futurist performativity, Almada's *Ultimatum* opens with the following lines:

> Eu não pertenço a nenhuma das gerações revolucionarias. Eu pertenço a uma geração constructiva.
>
> Eu sou um poeta portuguez que ama a sua patria. Eu tenho a idolatria da minha profissão e peso-a. Eu resolvo com a minha existência o significado actual da palavra poeta com toda intensidade do previlegio.
>
> Eu tenho 22 anos fortes de saude e de inteligência.
>
> (I do not belong to a revolutionary generation. I belong to a constructive generation.
>
> I am a Portuguese poet who loves his country. I have idolatry for my profession and I take it to heart. And I answer with my existence the current meaning of the word poet with all the intensity of this privilege.
>
> I am a 22 year-old full of strength and intelligence.)[54]

This opening statement in the first person embodies the process of collaging in Almada's Futurist project explored throughout this chapter in its most political dimension in two main ways: on the one hand, the manifesto is constituted through a constructive poetics aiming to juxtapose different forms, signifiers, and materials in order to recreate the historical experience of the present moment; on the other hand, the manifesto functions as an aesthetic project that, as we saw in *Manifesto anti-Dantas*, attempts to articulate in that same constructive process a new experience for the poetic voice – and its intended audience – and thus a new geopolitical position for the Portuguese nation in relation to both Europe and Africa, beyond the colonial legacies of Portugal's imperial past. The opening lines therefore present us with a poetic and political voice that, by asserting its own present "existence" as both a youth and a Portuguese patriot, provides self-evident proof that the Portuguese people can not only break with their past, but ultimately become a nation able to accommodate the newness, vitality, and strength embodied in the Futurist aesthetic experience presented by Almada to his audience:

> Hoje é a geração portugueza do seculo XX quem dispõe de toda a força criadora e construtiva para o nascimento de uma *nova patria inteiramente portugueza e inteiramente actual* prescindindo em absoluto de todas as epochas precedentes.
>
> (Today it is the Portuguese generation of the twentieth century who has all the creative and constructive power for the birth of a new country entirely Portuguese and entirely current, dispensing in absolute terms of all the preceding epochs.)[55]

Almada's *Ultimatum* thus aims to unveil a new Futurist beginning for a new Portuguese generation. By connecting the political and performative dimensions of the manifesto, particularly within the context of war, Almada is rearticulating within a different geopolitical context the merging of theatrical performance and politics at the core of Marinetti's conceptualization of the "arte-azione," which, as Walter Adamson has shown, explicitly emerges during Italy's intervention in World War I: "The interventionist campaign, which lasted roughly nine months, afforded the Futurist numerous opportunities for engaging in what Marinetti called *arte-azione* (art-action) – the introduction of the "fist into the battle for art."… Indeed, it is not too much to say that, at least in 1914 and 1915, Futurist theatrical performance and Futurist politics were wholly merged and inseparable."[56] Ultimately, while the previous formulations of Portuguese Futurism examined in this chapter remained mostly within an explicitly aesthetic realm, Almada now embraces in *Ultimatum* the act of "war" as the only way to effectively create a new Portugal within Almada's Futurist vision:

> FINALMENTE: é preciso criar a patria portugueza do seculo XX.
> DIGO SEGUNDA VEZ: é preciso criar a patria portugueza do seculo XX.
> …
> Gritae nas razões das vossas existencias que tendes direito a uma patria civilizada.

Aproveitae sobre tudo este momento unico em que a guerra da Europa vos convida a entrardes prá Civilização.

O povo completo será aquele que tiver reunido no seu maximo todas as qualidades e todos os defeitos. Coragem, portuguezes, só vos faltam as qualidades.

(FINALLY: it is necessary to create the Portuguese homeland of the twentieth century.

I SAY IT AGAIN: it is necessary to create the Portuguese homeland of the twentieth century.

...

Shout out the reasons for your existence to have the right to a civilized homeland.

Use specifically this unique moment in which the European War invites you to enter Civilization.

The complete people will be that which has gathered to its maximum force all qualities and all defects. Courage, my fellow Portuguese, you only lack the qualities.)[57]

As in the case of Marinetti in Italy, Almada collapses at the culmination of his Futurist period the power of art to transform reality by fusing civilization with war in the context of his manifesto – ultimately aligning with the experience of war and political violence as a way to effect radical change in society. As shown in *Ultimatum*, for the young Almada, war constituted the ultimate manifestation of the experience of modern life and a utopic Futurist vision of political renewal.

Ultimatum therefore articulates a characteristic "aestheticiza[tion] of the political," in Marjorie Perloff's formulation, that pervades the entire 1917 Futurist manifesto, as well as the Conferência Futurista.[58] As Perloff suggests, this productive tension between the aesthetic and the political is a feature of the critical categories of Futurism in particular, and the historical avant-garde in general, that can be fully determined only by a close analysis of the "actual historical realities" ultimately shaping that tension through a close analysis of specific instances: "Indeed, 'aestheticizing the political' and 'politicizing the aesthetic' may turn out to be two sides of the same coin. Perhaps the difficulty with all such definitive assessments of terms like Modernism or Avant-Garde or Futurism is that the actual historical realities continue to elude their totalizing power."[59]

As demonstrated in this chapter, Portuguese Futurism, while constituting a marginal and brief manifestation of experimental poetics within the wider transnational history of Futurism, and thus within the historical avant-garde, provides key insight into the historical relation of the larger Futurist movement with European colonialism in Africa. In this sense, as I have examined here, Almada's Futurist work presents us with a series of geopolitical connections between the transnational development of Futurism as an avant-garde movement and the impact of European colonialism in Africa during this same period, particularly in relation to Portuguese colonialism. In my analysis, the historical relevance of the legacies of Portuguese colonialism for the understanding of the different geopolitical implications of the networks articulated around Almada's *oeuvre* – as a central component of both Portuguese *modernismo* and European Futurism – opens a planetary dimension to his work that challenges exclusively local, national, and continental approaches to the historical avant-garde, while at the same time, challenging a reading of the historical avant-garde as somehow detached from the complex legacies of European colonialism.

As shown in this chapter, Almada's poetic and political attempt to reconceptualize the relation and connection of Portugal to the rest of the world as a central dimension of his Futurist project is a direct reflection of the complex colonial experience that shaped not only his life and his poetics, but ultimately that of the place of Futurism as an experimental poetic response to politically engage the world. From this perspective, the forms of planetary engagement within Portuguese Futurism traced in this chapter provide an alternative reading to the historical avant-garde as a response to a series of geopolitical questions that are central to the manifestations of experimental form during this period. As shown here, these Futurist forms of planetary engagement transcend the traditional interpretation of the question of "scale" in this context as determined by the tension between the unifying global literary system and the fragmentary manifestations previously highlighted by Ram. Almada's own complex legacy as the historical product of a series of unresolved racial and cultural questions at the core of the relationship between Portugal and Africa, on the one hand, and between Portugal and the rest of Europe, on the other, finds in Futurism a poetics through which he can reimagine and reconstruct not only himself, but ultimately the modern world in which he lives.

Chapter Two

Placing Vicente Huidobro within the Historical Avant-Garde: Experimental Poetics and the Planetary Critique of European Historicism

The poetic project of Chilean avant-garde writer Vicente Huidobro (1893–1948) provides a unique body of work through which to trace and historicize the notion of planetary engagement as a relation to a world beyond the local or national, articulated through a series of experimental literature networks developed during the historical avant-garde. The work of a Latin American writer who lived on both sides of the Atlantic most of his life, Huidobro's avant-garde poetic project, which he called *creacionismo*, bridges and connects, while also challenging, the particularities of different languages and national cultures. As a result, Huidobro's work allows us to analyse the historical avant-garde from a planetary perspective able to confront the forms of historicism, briefly described in the introduction, that have traditionally defined it as a movement and period. By tracing the transnational development of Huidobro's avant-garde project and its series of assemblages and connections within various networks as it circulated across the Atlantic, I examine here how Huidobro's work encourages us to undertake a geopolitical critique of the various forms of European historicism – particularly as related to Spanish national culture and its colonial legacies – that his work, and its reception, encountered throughout Europe and the Americas.

As I show in this chapter, what is at stake in re-examining from a comparative perspective the question of Huidobro's place within the historical avant-garde is a larger enquiry concerning the role of experimental poetics as part of a world literary system that transverses national histories, languages, and geographic boundaries during the period examined in this book. As Martin Puchner has already pointed out, Huidobro's project importantly opens up a series of "patterns of encounter," which elucidate a "hemispheric consciousness" that incorporates a series of "nodal points" of avant-garde cultural production across a transnational network connecting different cities and artists across the world:

> Paris is not so much a center as one of the nodal points where avant-garde activity is concentrated. Other points, for Huidobro, are New York, Milan, Madrid, Barcelona, Zurich, Berlin, and Buenos Aires. The crossing paths of figures such as Tzara, Picabia, Huidobro – one could add Huelsenbeck, Duchamp, and Breton – do not respect origins (although they may try to create and project them), but patterns of encounters and cross-fertilization.[1]

As highlighted by Puchner here, Huidobro's syncretic and idiosyncratic experimental literature project invites a new transnational critical approach to the study of the historical avant-garde beyond the limitations of a traditional European framework, which tends to marginalize the impact and relevance of non-European writers. While Huidobro's avant-garde project constantly crossed borders – both geopolitical and artistic – the question of origins is also central to the theorization of the avant-garde, and thus of its own historicity, as Puchner also mentions. At the same time, Huidobro's project poses a challenge to the centre-periphery logic of models of scholarship that claim non-European writers as a central for literary histories of the avant-garde according to locally based critical paradigms – models that struggle to overcome the historicist and ideological centrality of Europe as the "origin" of the avant-garde from a historical and critical perspective.

Creacionismo's Critique of Historicism: Locating Huidobro beyond National and Monolingual Paradigms

Overall, the instance of planetary engagement provided by Huidobro's avant-garde project entails a larger questioning of the practice of literary history, and, in particular, of conflicting versions and forms of the literary history of the historical avant-garde, as conceptualized and theorized in different geopolitical contexts. On a primary level, my analysis of Huidobro's place within the historical avant-garde emphasizes the ways in which his work disrupts the production of a traditional literary history as measured against two main paradigms that have grounded scholarly and historiographic efforts to study this period: the monolingual paradigm, on the one hand, and the national (and continental) paradigm, on the other. From the time of his arrival in France in 1916, Huidobro used both French and Spanish to write most of his key works, constituting one of the essential features of his avant-garde poetics. Huidobro's *creacionismo* was therefore a bilingual literary project. Some of his poetry collections were fully composed and originally published in French: *Horizón Carré* (1917), *Hallali. Poème de guerre* (1918), *Tour Eiffel* (1918), *Automne régulier* (1925), and *Tout à coup* (1925). Others were composed and published in both French and Spanish: *Ecuatorial/Equatoriale* (1918) and *Temblor de cielo* (1931) / *Tremblement de ciel* (1932). Still others were composed and published in Spanish: *Ver y palpar* and *El ciudadano del olvido* (both published in Chile in 1941). The bilingual nature of Huidobro's avant-garde project is further evident in the fact that some of Huidobro's poetry collections originally published in French were also contemporaneously published in book form in Spanish, as composed by Huidobro, while some were translated into Spanish by other writers, such as *Halali. Poema de guerra* (1919) and *Torre Eiffel* (1919). Moreover, some of Huidobro's poems or fragments published in Spanish were also originally written in French: *Poemas árticos* (1918) and *Altazor* (1931). Thus, the interplay of Spanish and French in Huidobro's work constitutes a complex bilingual and translational creative practice that has generally been lost in scholarly approaches to his work due to the monolingual dimension of traditional national literary histories. As Spanish poet Gerardo Diego has already suggested, apart from being somewhat of an offence to his "native" or literary tradition in Spanish, Huidobro's use of the French language crucially marks his overall attempt to arrive not so much at a bilingual poetics, but rather at a "universal" form of creative expression not necessarily determined by a single national or local origin, or specific literary form of genre.[2]

At the same time, Huidobro's bilingualism makes the insertion of his work within a traditional literary history – which tends to be monolingual, with a local or national geopolitical focus – a particularly complex proposition. A relevant instance of this problem is the difficult relation that Huidobro's work has with the field of French literary history. Due to his personal connections with key members of the Parisian artistic scene, Huidobro played a foundational role in the development of avant-garde poetry in France. His well-known controversy with Pierre Reverdy regarding the origins of *creacionismo* has led to a fascinating series of scholarly discussions and articles.[3] Indeed, based on both his use of French as a key linguistic medium for his poetic project and his residing in Paris during his most productive two decades, Huidobro could be legitimately studied as an author belonging to the fields of French and Francophone literature, save for the fact that he was a Latin American writer from Chile. The fact is that, unlike writers such as Apollinaire, Max Jacob, and Reverdy, with whom Huidobro collaborated closely for years, Huidobro has rarely been studied within the field of French literary history, or as a key writer belonging to the avant-garde in France.[4]

On the other hand, some scholars of modern Latin American poetry have pointed to Huidobro's new life in Paris starting in 1916, as well as his embrace of French as a medium for his poetics from that moment on, as an explicit rejection of his Chilean and Latin American origins. For example, Greg Dawes, in *Poetas ante la modernidad*, an important study of aesthetics and politics in the work of César Vallejo, Huidobro, Pablo Neruda, and Octavio Paz, underscores Huidobro's separation and detachment from his Chilean origins as a feature of his avant-garde project:

> Producto de la oligarquía desprestigiada en Chile, como es el caso de todos los vanguardistas latinoamericanos; se quiere "desprovincializar" y fomentar un proyecto de modernización cultural. Busca elaborar este proyecto en *terra incognita* para despojarse de toda huella de su Chile subdesarollado: su producto universal carece casi completamente de referencias a su patria y a América Latina en general … En resumidas cuentas, el mundo artístico que crea Huidobro para 1925, se empareja con el vanguardismo europeo para que así no quepa duda que es un "moderno" bautizado francés.

> (Product of a discredited oligarchy in Chile, as is the case of all Latin American avant-garde artists; he wants to "deprovincialize" himself and to promote a project of cultural modernization. He seeks to develop this project in a terra incognita in order to shed all traces of his underdeveloped Chile: its universal product makes barely no reference to his own country or Latin America in general … In short, the artistic world created by Huidobro about 1925 joins the European Avant-Garde so that there is no doubt that he is a "modern" baptized French.)[5]

Dawes's interpretation of the geopolitics at the core of Huidobro's avant-garde project presents a crucial aspect of the complex transnational dimension of Huidobro's work. For Dawes, Huidobro's move to France in the second decade of the twentieth century, and the aesthetic project he subsequently developed while mainly based in Europe, constitutes a "deprovincializing" and "modernizing" strategy in order to move beyond his "underdeveloped" Chilean and Latin American origins. By contrasting Huidobro's movement away from a "provincialized" Chile to a "modernized" Europe, Dawes unveils a postcolonial trajectory in Huidobro's work that reads the aesthetic dimension of his avant-garde project as part of a geopolitical dynamic productively connecting the modern European metropolis of Paris to Chile as the former Spanish colony, and thus Latin America with Europe. However,

Dawes's description of Huidobro's "French baptism" into European modernity does not completely address the complex tensions and dynamics of the process of cultural translation inherent in Huidobro's work in relation to European culture, which, in my analysis, goes beyond an effort to "become" French, or for that matter, to adopt a "European" sense of modernity as a central tenet of his own avant-garde poetic project when considered in its own terms.

As I will show in what follows, Huidobro never left his Latin American origins behind in his overall articulation of *creacionismo* as an avant-garde poetics in itself (whether these origins are defined in national, cultural, linguistic, or political terms). There is no doubt that from the moment he arrived in Paris, Huidobro explicitly tried to enter a genealogy of experimental literature production occurring in Europe during the historical avant-garde movement, and to explicitly insert himself into the logic of European modernity to which he was originally a foreigner, as Dawes suggests. However, as Juan Larrea has stated, Huidobro's dual status as both foreign and Latin American – "condición de extranjero y sudamericano" (condition as a foreigner and South American)[6] – was an aspect of his identity that clearly marked the reception of his work in Europe by contemporary avant-garde artists, editors, and publishers in France and Spain, as well as eventually by critics and scholars. From his perspective as a Latin American author, this same insertion into the logic of European modernity constitutes for Huidobro a geopolitical engagement that radically problematizes European culture as the exclusive putative origin of the forms of modernity that the avant-garde articulated poetically and historically. Based on Dipesh Chakrabarty's postcolonial critique of historiography, I argue that Huidobro's avant-garde project aims to unsettle and decentre the European avant-garde from its own historicist centre, if not "provincializing" the European avant-garde as such, to use Chakrabarty's concept, at least considerably expanding the planetary reach of the avant-garde in scope and focus from within. Huidobro's work thus opens up a series of crucial historical connections and theoretical questions for a comparative and planetary understanding of this moment and its historiographic and critical analysis that are central to the larger argument of *A Planetary Avant-Garde*.

In this context, a crucial aspect of Huidobro's avant-garde poetics of *creacionismo* that has not been sufficiently acknowledged to date – and is the main focus of this chapter – is how it as a project entails a radical critique of European historicism, and of its different manifestations that Huidobro encountered throughout his career. As I show in what follows, Huidobro's *creacionismo* disrupts the forms of historicism that lie at the core of the avant-garde as an event and critical category. From this critical perspective, Huidobro's avant-garde project confronts and challenges a positing of Europe as the "origin" of the avant-garde – from both a temporal and a geographic perspective – from his own Latin American positionality. This Eurocentric positing is determined and articulated mainly through a historicist narrative of a European-centred modernity, as is manifested, for example, in Bürger's influential definition of the avant-garde as "historical," one of the central tenets of his *Theory of the Avant-Garde*. In his effort to "historicize a theory" of and for the avant-garde, Bürger ends up reasserting a historicist understanding of the avant-garde that reinforces the positing of a European centre as its historical origin.[7] As Chakrabarty has influentially described, European historicism precisely posits modernity as a historical event "spreading outside it":

> Historicism is what made modernity or capitalism look not simply global but rather as something that became global *over time*, by originating in one place (Europe) and then spreading outside it. This "first in Europe, then elsewhere" structure of global historical time was historicist; different non-Western nationalisms would rather produce local versions of the same narrative, replacing "Europe" by some locally constructed center … Historicism thus posited historical time as a measure of the cultural distance (at least in institutional development) that was assumed to exist between the West and the non-West.[8]

Chakrabarty's understanding of historicism as happening "first in Europe, then elsewhere" is immensely important for understanding Huidobro's place within the historical avant-garde, especially as a way of conceptualizing the avant-garde project of the Chilean writer as a planetary critique of the European-centred temporality of historicism. From this perspective, Huidobro's overt insertion of *creacionismo* into the logic of European modernity during the historical avant-garde does not necessarily mean that he ignores or repudiates his Latin American origins, or that his Chilean national identity plays no significant role within the geopolitical dimension of his poetic project. In fact, for Huidobro, these are historical events originating outside of Europe and thus are understood as a historical time that is determined by the distance that historicism places between the West and the non-West, as Chakrabarty highlights:

> Historicism thus posited historical time as a measure of the cultural distance (at least in institutional development) that was assumed to exist

> between the West and the non-West. In the colonies, it legitimated the idea of civilization. In Europe itself, it made possible completely internalist histories of Europe in which Europe was described as the site of the first occurrence of capitalism, modernity, or Enlightenment. These "events" in turn are all explained mainly with respect to "events" within the geographical confines of Europe (however fuzzy its exact boundaries may have been).[9]

In a way, through his avant-garde project, Huidobro essentially tries to occupy with his own poetic project the very "cultural distance" that Chakrabarty locates at the core of historicism: through his development of *creacionismo*, Huidobro aims to inhabit the space between the West and the non-West, the centre and the periphery, the native and the foreign, the past and the present, as a series of categories that are reimagined as poetic "events" to be integrated into a larger and more complex planetary project able to overcome these dichotomies, at least as a utopic future horizon of possibility.

Indeed, Huidobro's critique of historicism at the core of his poetic project, and its aim at a poetic future disconnected from a previously known history, explicitly appears in Huidobro's work as early as 1914: "Amo a los que sueñan con el futuro, y solo tienen fe en el porvenir sin pensar en el pasado" (I love those who dream of the future, and only have faith in what is to come without thinking about the past).[10] As I have explored elsewhere in detail, the radical newness of the sense of *poiesis* at the core of Huidobro's *creacionismo* completely pervades the creative potential of his avant-garde poetic project as a whole.[11] Perhaps the best-known and most influential manifestation of this new creative impulse appears embodied in the figure of the "golondrina" (swallow) – "Ya viene la golondrina" (here comes the swallow)[12] – and the various forms of spatial and temporal change that configure the dynamics of Huidobro's poetic vision in his masterpiece *Altazor*:

> No hay tiempo que perder
> Y si viene el instante prosaico
> Siga al barco que es acaso el mejor
> Ahora que me siento y me pongo a escribir
> ¿Qué hace la golondrina que vi esta mañana
> Firmando cartas en el vacío? …
> Eco de gesto en gesto
> Cadena electrizada o sin correspondencias
> Interrumpiendo el ritmo solitario.
> ¿Quiénes están muriendo y quienes nacen

Mientras mi pluma corre en el papel?
No hay tiempo que perder …

(There is no time to lose
And if the prosaic moment comes
Please follow perhaps the best ship
Now that I am sitting down and start writing
What is the swallow that I saw this morning doing
Signing letters in the emptiness? …
Echo from gesture to gesture
Electricized chain or without correspondences
The lonely rhythm interrupted
Who is now dying, and who is born
While my pen scribbles on paper?
There is no time to lose …)[13]

In this sense, Huidobro's creative critique of historicism opens up a new experience of history – for which "there is no time to lose" – which correlates to what Luis Correa-Díaz and Scott Weintraub have identified as the "futurity of Huidobro's modernity." As Correa-Díaz and Weintraub argue, Huidobro's understanding of modernity conceives "the 'new' as an interruption that is the condition of possibility of the metaphorical narration that constitutes history," one that connects the newness of *creacionismo* to a larger impulse, as a historical "interruption" that points forward towards "humankind's cosmic fate."[14] Therefore, from its inception, Huidobro's experimental poetry project seeks to rearticulate poetry away from its supposed historical origins and to locate it, through his own work, and in his own words, into an unforeseen and unexpected future. In my analysis, the historical interruption at the core of the "new" as articulated by Huidobro's *creacionismo* – and thus its "futurity," to use Correa-Díaz's and Weintraub's term – specifically rejects the concept of putative origins lying at the very core of European historicism and that ultimately determines "political modernity" as Chakrabarty defines it. Part of the complexity in the process of cultural and linguistic translation articulated by Huidobro, and consequently by his aesthetic project, lies in the fact that *creacionismo* explicitly challenged the notion of putative origins as the sole source of aesthetic, creative, and poetic legitimacy, and consequently of literary value within a mono-national and monolingual geopolitical framework, including his own.[15]

At the same time, Huidobro's *creacionismo* allows us to trace and reassemble some of the associations that configured his experimental literature network during this period, examining, therefore, its geopolitical significance within the historical avant-garde as a critical category. To ignore these aspects of Huidobro's contributions to the avant-garde movement is to diminish the potential impact of his work outside of a primarily Spanish-language critical context, in particular for the construction of a larger and more complex comparative, global, and international examination of modernism and the historical avant-garde that this chapter, and the rest of this book, aim to address. In order to expand the complex transnational and translational dynamics at the heart of Huidobro's project and to explore his planetary engagement within a postcolonial framework, I will now turn to Huidobro's responses to the political, cultural, and literary traditions of Spain, as particularly related to its colonial legacies. I will examine Huidobro's challenge to the forms of European historicism he encountered in Spain through an analysis of his own socio-historical interaction with the contemporary avant-garde scene between 1918 and 1921, as well as in relation to his critical response to the Spanish literary tradition though his writings, in particular through his adaptation of the medieval epic poem *The Cid* in his *Mío Cid Campeador* (1929).

Huidobro and Spain: Converging Avant-Garde Networks and Divergent Histories

Prior to his arrival in Europe in 1916, Huidobro's encounter with Spain and Spanish culture was mainly filtered through his Jesuit religious education in Chile. Huidobro provides some insight into his early feelings towards Spanish culture and history in some of the essays included in *Pasando y pasando* (1914).[16] Huidobro's experience with Spanish culture dramatically changed after his trip to Spain in 1918, which followed a two-year stay in Paris. Once he was in Madrid, Huidobro's position swiftly changed from that of an outsider to that of a participant in the key circles of the Spanish literary scene of the time, where he soon achieved recognition as an influential literary figure. In a way, while Huidobro's knowledge of Spain prior to this visit was mainly connected to Spain's colonial history as transmitted through Spanish literary and cultural historiography – infused with Spain's own historicism and colonial legacy – Huidobro suddenly found himself making history in Spain.

Although many scholars have examined the impact of Huidobro's work in Spain, this historical account remains the subject of some controversy, in fact, part of a larger controversial dimension that is perhaps an avant-garde characteristic – as "embattled" in Perloff's critical sense of the term – that defines Huidobro's controversial life and work, for better or worse. A well-known problem with the reception of Huidobro's work, and a valuable place to begin an examination of his steady and radical planetary challenge to historicism, is the relation of *creacionismo* to European Cubism. As René de Costa has repeatedly stated, Huidobro's *creacionismo* constitutes a form of literary Cubism, "simplemente un nombre más dado al cubismo literario" (simply one more name given to literary Cubism), or, as he adds, "su manera personal de llamar al cubismo literario" (his [Huidobro's] personal way of referring to literary Cubism).[17] However, this now traditional interpretation of Huidobro's avant-garde poetic project is deficient in at least two ways. On the one hand, from this canonical approach to *creacionismo*, Huidobro's contribution to the historical avant-garde essentially amounts to a minor, derivative, and exotic footnote to the more central artistic movement constituted by the corpus of European Cubism. On the other hand, this canonical reading of Huidobro's work radically flattens what, in my reading, constitutes the postcolonial geopolitics of Huidobro's avant-garde project, as well as its specific historical and poetic particularities, that differ to a large degree from the development of Cubism in Europe as an avant-garde movement.

De Costa's interpretation stands as a canonical assessment of Huidobro's work within the field of Hispanic studies in general, and it thereby constitutes a rare common denominator within the otherwise divergent literary histories of the avant-garde both in Spain and in Latin America. In *Vanguardismo y crítica literaria en España (1910–1930)*, Andrés Soria Olmedo offers one of the most comprehensive studies of the period in Spain, which includes a detailed examination of Spanish literary history in relation to Huidobro's work. In his assessment of Huidobro, Soria Olmedo explicitly refers to de Costa's main premise, transforming it, however, into the maxim "creacionismo y cubismo no son independientes" (*creacionismo* and Cubism are not independent). Expanding this argument, the Spanish critic further asserts: "Algunos críticos hispanoamericanos, sobre todo, han defendido la originalidad absoluta de Huidobro en términos que a veces llegan a rozar el ridículo, y en los que no insistiremos" (I will not rehearse the claims of some Spanish American critics, in particular, who have defended Huidobro's absolute originality in terms that at times border on the ridiculous).[18] As this particular example shows, both Soria Olmedo and de Costa's canonical readings of Huidobro's *creacionismo* radically reduce and overly simplify the potential theoretical implications of Huidobro's work in the development of the historical avant-garde, particularly in relation to the production of a transnational and multilingual literary history of the period that can transcend national and monolingual constrains that have framed traditional literary histories. Moreover, if some Latin American critics have defended the originality of Huidobro's *creacionismo*, it is precisely because it constitutes an issue of the utmost relevance for the production of a literary history of the avant-garde in Latin America, as opposed to the lesser relevance of Huidobro's *creacionismo* for the purpose of constructing a national literary history of the period in Spain, as Soria Olmedo's argument clearly seems to suggest, at least from his own historiographic perspective. After all, the fact is that, as Vicky Unruh has observed in her influential and authoritative study *Latin American Vanguards*, Huidobro is "widely regarded as both the precursor and the founder of Latin American vanguardism."[19]

At the same time, it is important to recognize how critics have applied and adapted de Costa's interpretation of Huidobro's *creacionismo* as a form of literary Cubism within a Latin American literary history of the avant-garde. For example, Gloria Videla, in her influential *Direcciones del vanguardismo hispano-americano*, also relies on de Costa's critical reading of Huidobro's *creacionismo* in relation to European Cubism to affirm an intimate connection between his ideas with Cubism: "El creacionismo huidobriano está, pues, estrechamente vinculado con el cubismo" (Huidobro's *creacionismo* is thus closely related to Cubism).[20] However, in my argument the controversial question of the relation of Huidobro's work to both Parisian Cubism and its embodiment of "European modernity" for the critical consideration of *creacionismo* as an avant-garde poetics does not hinge on Huidobro's alleged originality (or lack thereof). By viewing *creacionismo* as a mere version or copy of Cubism, ultimately, we lose sight of Huidobro's crucial role in the complex networks and dynamics of displacement and circulation of modern poetics that appear to be central for a reconceptualization of the fields of comparative poetics and international modernisms, as argued here.

A related instance of the larger question of the impact in Spain of Huidobro's work is provided by Huidobro's alleged influence (or lack thereof) in the development of *ultraísmo*, generally considered the only "original" Spanish movement to belong to the historical avant-garde. It is widely acknowledged that Huidobro's arrival in Madrid in 1918 effectively triggered an avant-garde reaction of sorts among a group of young Spanish poets that included Cansinos-Assens, Guillermo de Torre, Gerardo Diego, and Juan Larrea – writers who enthusiastically embraced *creacionismo* when they first encountered it during the second decade of the twentieth century. As Videla, one of the main experts on the development of the *ultraísta* movement on both sides of the Atlantic, has argued, "Su visita a Madrid en 1918 fue la chispa que encendió en España la voluntad de un 'ultraísmo literario'" (His visit to Spain in 1918 was the spark that ignited in Spain the will of a "literary ultraísmo").[21] The *creacionista* impulse, and Huidobro's influence, evident in the early work of both Diego and Larrea – an issue that has generally been ignored due to the tendency to read these poets canonically as members of the later Spanish "Generación del 27" – appears to be related, among other factors, to the problematic literary histories of the avant-garde produced by de Torre, who consistently minimized the importance of Huidobro's work in relation to the historical avant-garde (both in Spain in particular and in the rest of Europe more generally). The gradual detachment between de Torre and Huidobro resulted largely from what Huidobro, as he expresses in his letters to de Torre, considered to be a spurious dissemination in Spain of the original "secret" of his *creacionista* poetics:

> Maldita mil veces la hora en que pasé por España y os revelé una parte de mi *secreto* tan querido y tan digno por su verdad y su pureza y mayor respeto. Unos me han estropeado con la falsificación y la confusión con respecto a la poesía misma y los otros queriendo robarme lo que era mío para ponerlo en la cabeza de Apollinaire, de Reverdy o de cualquier otro imbécil.
>
> (Be damned a thousand times the time I spent in Spain, when I revealed a part of my *secret* so beloved and revered due to its truth, purity, and loftiest esteem. Some have damaged me with counterfeiting and confusion regarding poetry itself and the others have wanted to steal what was mine to put it on the head of Apollinaire, Reverdy, or any other fool.)[22]

While Diego and Larrea remained extremely close to Huidobro and to *creacionismo* for a number of years, de Torre's original reaction of overwhelming admiration for Huidobro's contribution to the avant-garde in Madrid eventually turned awry, and he soon distanced himself from the Chilean poet and his strand of avant-garde poetics. This eventually bitter relationship with de Torre became one of the many widely documented and openly acrimonious disputes that Huidobro established with many of the leading avant-garde poets of his generation on both sides of the Atlantic, among them Pierre Reverdy, Pablo Neruda, and César Moro.[23]

It is obvious that by 1920 Huidobro's relationship with Spain in general, and the Spanish avant-garde literary scene in particular, was rapidly changing.[24] The gradual divergence and conflict between

Huidobro and de Torre would soon become an open literary rivalry for a prominent place in the historical avant-garde, in part because de Torre soon emerged as one of the founding members, practitioners, and literary historians of *ultraísmo* as a movement in Spain.[25] De Torre's eventual response to Huidobro's steadfast claim about the centrality of his own work within the avant-garde in Europe appears in his *Historia de las literaturas de vanguardia* (1965). In this panoramic history of the period, de Torre explicitly both rejects *creacionismo* as an avant-garde movement worthy of being categorized as such and drastically minimizes Huidobro's influence on both the Spanish and the European avant-garde. In fact, de Torre places Huidobro within the section of his *Historia* dedicated to *ultraísmo* as one of the four precursors to the Spanish avant-garde movement, together with Spanish writers Rafael Cansinos-Assens, Ramón Gómez de la Serna, and Juan Ramón Jiménez. What is striking about de Torre's historiographic decision to minimize the importance of Huidobro in his *Historia* of 1965 is that it constitutes a serious revisionist move in relation to his prior history of the period produced forty years earlier (i.e., *Literaturas europeas de vanguardia*, 1925). In contrast, in his earlier work de Torre in fact dedicates a complete section of his study of European avant-garde movements to *creacionismo* itself (always for him as a "modalidad" [modality] of Spanish *ultraísmo*), as well as to a rather detailed examination of Huidobro's conceptualization of poetics, his poetry, and his literary rivalry with Pierre Reverdy.

However, what is crucial here is that de Torre's about-face on the relevance of Huidobro's work ultimately aims to erase the specificity and particularity of *creacionismo* from the literary history of the historical avant-garde that he happens to be writing. In this context, the maxim "First in Europe, then elsewhere" used by Chakrabarty to define the European-centred logic of historicism proves immensely useful as a way of critically framing the actual conditions in which Huidobro's work was conceptualized within the historical avant-garde by some of his European contemporaries, such as de Torre. Indeed, Huidobro's condition as a foreigner and outsider – "su condición de extranjero, de 'metèque' [*sic*]"[26] – was specifically highlighted by de Torre in his own critical assessment of Huidobro's unwavering claims for a central role within the historical avant-garde, which de Torre ends up describing as a "pretentious" effort to "vindicar desesperada aunque tímidamente—pues en Francia no le consentirían enturbiar las fuentes—sus precedencias" (desperately albeit timidly vindicate his precedence and preeminence – since in France they wouldn't allow him to muddle the sources).[27] Thus, by placing Huidobro's *creacionismo* as a derivative poetics that he objectifies as a modality of Spanish *ultraísmo* through a deeply Eurocentric and historicist historiographic exercise, de Torre is suppressing (or trying to) the radical challenge to the logic of historicism at the heart of Huidobro's *creacionismo*, or, to use de Torre's problematic description, "muddling of the sources." Thus, as examined here, de Torre's historiographic effort to suppress Huidobro's rebellious stance against and challenge of the various historicist impulses that tried to objectify *creacionismo* as a derivative and unoriginal poetic project, in the case of de Torre subject to Spanish *ultraísmo*, articulate a form of historical thinking that dramatically reduces the geopolitical tensions triggered by the sudden emergence of Huidobro's work within the European literary scene. I submit that it is fundamental to save Huidobro's original contribution to the historical avant-garde from being buried in canonical literary histories of the period by emphasizing the aesthetic and political aspects of his work that previous approaches to the period have not been able to explain adequately in its full complexity and critical implications. Overall, in his unabashed objectification of Huidobro as minor, derivative, *métèque*, and foreign, de Torre ultimately reproduces, arguably for what appear to be largely self-serving and nationalistic purposes, what Chakrabarty terms "the useful but empty and homogenous chronology of historicism":

> If historical or anthropological consciousness is seen as the work of a rational outlook, it can only "objectify" – and thus deny – the *lived* relations the observing subject already has with that he or she identifies as belonging to a historical or ethnographic time and space separate from the ones he or she occupies as the analyst … It stops the subject from seeing his or her own present as discontinuous with itself. Some relations of everyday transactions can now take on the character of "unvanquished remnants" of the past (to recall Marx's phrase). But that only reproduces ultimately … the useful but empty and homogenous chronology of historicism.[28]

Chakrabarty's critique of historicism and of the kind of historical consciousness it articulates is extremely useful in exposing how de Torre's *Historia* erases from his own historiographic project Huidobro's key role in facilitating and constituting a network of avant-garde poetics. The fact is that Huidobro was able to connect the writers in Madrid associated with the *ultraísta* movement with the Paris-centred group, as well as with other Latin American avant-garde collectives, a series of associations clearly responsible for creating a European avant-garde movement. In this way, de Torre's historicism denies, in his historiographic effort, the emergence of the series of "lived relations" that constitute the "social life" at the core of Huidobro's poetics, as Bruno Latour defines this concept in his understanding of social networks. Therefore, we need to carefully retrace and, in Latour's sense, "reassemble" the series of "lived relations" at the core of Huidobro's original effort to articulate his own avant-garde project and the different social assemblages that it produced in order to re-evaluate from a transnational and multilingual perspective Huidobro's place within the historical avant-garde.

The Poetics of Lived Relations and the Planetary Geopolitics of Huidobro's *Ecuatorial*

As mentioned above, a key to the development of Huidobro's "lived" associations, as they relate to the impact of his project in Spain, is connected to the work of Juan Larrea and Gerardo Diego. The two young Spanish poets, who had first met in 1913 while studying at the Universidad de Deusto, a Jesuit college in Bilbao, were extremely close friends when Huidobro arrived at the Spanish capital in 1918. David Bary, a scholar who played a major role in the dissemination of Larrea's work, describes how Diego shared with Larrea in 1919 some of Huidobro's poems he had brought with him to Bilbao that were circulating in Madrid at the time. For Larrea the experience of encountering and reading these poems "fue un acontemiento decisivo. Cambió su vida" (was a decisive moment that changed his life).[29] It is important to emphasize the fact that this "lived relation," as Chakrabarty terms it, that historically connects Huidobro, Larrea, and Diego between 1918 and 1920 constitutes as a whole the experimental literature network generated by the publication, circulation, and impact of Huidobro's poetry in Spain during 1919. In other words, each of Huidobro's poems that was read, transcribed, and shared by both Larrea and Diego in 1919 functions as an "actor" in the sense explored by Latour in his approach to actor-network theory: Huidobro's experimental poems facilitate the kind of assemblage able to connect the "lived experiences" of these three different writers to each other within a network of associations. As Latour has argued, "An actor in the hyphenated expression actor-network is not the source of an action but the moving target of a vast array of entities swarming toward it."[30] Based on Latour's conceptualization of an actor-network, it can be argued that the circulation of Huidobro's poems between 1918 and 1920 crucially disseminates a series of poetic "moving targets" through which "a vast array of entities" assemble and come together, in direct relation to each other.

One of the major "actors," in Latour's sense, during this historical period and within the establishment of this particular avant-garde network is in fact Huidobro's poem *Ecuatorial*, first published in Madrid as a chapbook in August 1918 and reprinted in 1919 in the July issue of the Madrid-based journal *Cervantes*. As Bary and Goic, among others, have argued, *Ecuatorial* was one of the most influential avant-garde poems published in Spanish between 1918 and 1919 on either side of the Atlantic. As a groundbreaking experimental piece, *Ecuatorial* had a tremendous impact on Larrea and Diego when they first encountered it, becoming the inspiration for two early *creacionista* poems by Larrea ("Cosmopolitano," 1919) and Diego ("Gesta," 1922). Even de Torre himself, in the aforementioned *Literaturas europeas de vanguardia*, dedicates a few pages to *Ecuatorial*, a poem that he describes as "una de las más hermosas y cabales realizaciones de lirismo genuinamente contemporáneo" (one of the most beautiful and exceptional realizations of a genuinely contemporary lyricism).[31]

Huidobro's *Ecuatorial* opens with the very moment in which the poetic voice literally opens its eyes and "starts singing" about the "lejanías desatadas" (unravelling distances) that are being contemplated at the very beginning of the poem:

Era el tiempo en que se abrieron mis párpados sin alas
Y empecé a cantar sobre lejanías desatadas

Saliendo de sus nidos
                    Atruenan el aire las banderas

LOS HOMBRES
          ENTRE LA HIERBA
                    BUSCABAN LAS FRONTERAS
Sobre el campo banal
                    el mundo muere
De las cabezas prematuras
                    brotan alas ardientes
Y en la trinchera ecuatorial
                    brizada a trechos

Bajo la sombra de aeroplanos vivos
Los soldados cantaban en las tardes duras

Las ciudades de Europa
                    Se apagan una a una

(It was the time when my wingless eyelids opened
And I started singing about unravelling distances

Coming out of their nests
Flags thundering in the air

MANKIND
AMONG THE GRASS
SEARCHED FOR THE FRONTIERS
On the banal fields
the world dies
From premature heads
sprout wings on fire
And in the equatorial trenches
cradled in intervals

Under the shadow of living airplanes
Soldiers sang on harsh afternoons

The cities of Europe
turn off one by one)[32]

As this opening section shows, the poetic act of singing is also an act of seeing for the poetic voice of *Ecuatorial*. What is sung within the first moments of the poem is an experimental conflation of images and geographical spaces populated by crawling men crossing borders, anthropomorphized airplanes, soldiers in trenches, and falling stars. More importantly, this series of poetic "events" configure a landscape in which European cities are dying out, thus unveiling a vision in which the old world seems to be disappearing. This apocalyptic sense of historical ending eventually correlates in the early moments of the poem with the feeling of a new world emerging, in which the ashes of the old history of banished kings ("reyes desterrados") as well as the soaring figure of Christ, are eventually transfigured into a new creative rearticulation of the world in which human, technological, geographical, and natural elements combine into a new complex poetic whole. It is precisely at this point in the poem, in a rather literal planetary turn, that the poetic voice is able to locate and announce its own geographic position right at the world's equator:

Por todas partes en el suelo
He visto alas de golondrinas

Y el Cristo que alzó el vuelo
Dejó olvidada la corona de espinas

Sentados sobre el paralelo
Miremos nuestro tiempo

S I G L O E N C A D E N A D O E N U N Á N G U L O D E L M U N D O

(Everywhere on the ground
I have seen wings of swallows
And the Christ who took flight
Forgot his crown of thorns

Sitting on the parallel
Let us look our time

A C E N T U R Y C H A I N E D T O AN ANGLE OF THE W O R L D)[33]

The planetary dimension of this transfigured vision of the world is emphasized through Huidobro's striking poetic image of the "parallel" line of the equator as the structural axis of the poem. Thus, as the poetic vision in *Ecuatorial* progresses from this moment in the poem, its voice moves along the imaginary line on the surface of the Earth that divides the planet into two hemispheres: "Sobre el sendero equinocial / empecé a caminar" (Over the equinoctial path / I began to walk; line 55). The zero degrees of latitude that mathematically locate the world's equator thus serve as an imaginary point of view that shapes, or organizes, the poem, with a series of significant temporal and spatial implications. The planetary reaches of the poem and the series of geographical areas connected as the poem unfolds are in this sense breathtaking. A particularly relevant example of this planetary reach of *Ecuatorial* is seen in the following fragment:

El anunciador de estaciones
Ha gritado

Primavera
Al lado izquierdo
30 minutos

Pasa el tren lleno de flores y de frutos

El Niágara ha mojado mis cabellos
Y una neblina nace en torno a ellos …

Un paquebot perdido costeaba
Las islas de oro de la Vía Láctea

La cordillera andina
                    Veloz como un convoy
Atraviesa la América Latina

(The announcer of the seasons
Has shouted
                    Spring
                    To the left side
                        30 minutes

The train full of flowers and fruits goes by

The Niagara has wetted my hair
And a mist is born around them …

A lost steam ship was coasting
The golden islands of the Milky Way

The Andean Mountains
                    Fast as a convoy
Move across Latin America)[34]

As this example shows, Huidobro employs this "zero-degrees" perspective to connect simultaneously different parts of the world within the realm of the poem. The poetic voice constantly moves the reader along the four cardinal points connecting both north and south (Niagara Falls, the Andes), as well as east and west (California, London), while incorporating a series of juxtaposed references that relate seafaring to European colonialism and the exploitation of Africa, and gold-diggers in California with poor beggars in London, to name a few of the poem's many geographic and historical references. At the same time, the geographical reach of the poem attributes a crucial social dimension to its poetic vision of the world. This social dimension hinges on the contrast that the poetic voice constructs between a horizontal movement that rapidly and simultaneously covers different parts of the world (Congo, various European cities, Egypt, key areas across the Americas), and the temporal stasis of the poem in the year 1917. The latter emphasizes the historicity of the different events recounted in the poem, as it incorporates a series of large social problems within the larger planetary vision that it offers. This fixed historical time, in contrast to the wide-ranging spatial and geographic mobility of the poem, marks a split temporality that mirrors the hemispheric divide on which the poem is articulated into what, for the poetic voice, now constitutes a "divided century" ("siglo dividido"). Thus, while the apocalyptic nature of the vision incorporates different geographic areas, it does so synchronically, so that the events entering the poetic vision occur at the same time and in the same moment in history. By synchronically incorporating different geographical areas, and their particular social realities in relation to each other, Huidobro's *Ecuatorial* is not only a poem of planetary proportions, but also a poem that aims to break the continuity of history into two different planetary halves, both spatially and temporally.

This historical and temporal rupture allows the poetic vision unfolding in *Ecuatorial* to unveil a new creative potential able to liberate the "chained century" into an unknown future. As this analysis of the broken temporality and historicity of *Ecuatorial* shows, Huidobro conceived *creacionismo* as a poetic project able to articulate a different sense of history via the language of poetry itself in a way that radically challenges the historicist centrality of Europe as the only gravitational centre of such a new understanding of history, and thus of the new creative event entailed by his avant-garde project. Indeed, as Huidobro argues in his manifesto "La poesía," the value of poetry resides precisely in the new event it can constitute within the "distance" that exists between what can be empirically determined – "lo que vemos" (what we see) – and what we can imaginatively conceive – "lo que imaginamos" (what we imagine):

> La Poesía es el vocablo virgen de todo prejuicio; el verbo creado y creador, la palabra recién nacida. Su vocabulario es infinito porque ella no cree en la certeza de todas sus posibles combinaciones. Y su rol es convertir las probabilidades en certeza. Su valor está marcado por la distancia que va de lo que vemos a lo que imaginamos. Para ello no hay pasado ni futuro.
>
> (Poetry is the word pure of prejudice; the word created and creating, the newborn word. Its vocabulary is infinite because it does not believe in the certainty of all its possible combinations. And the role of poetry is to convert probabilities into certainty. Its value resides in the distance between what we see and what we imagine. There is no past or future for it.)[65]

This distance between the known and the imaginable where Huidobro locates his poetic project is intimately connected to the distance between divergent forms of history that Chakrabarty sees at the core of

European historicism. As shown here in relation to Huidobro's avant-garde project, this distance is essentially configured by two divergent forms and conceptualizations of history: on the one hand, we have the historicity of Huidobro's own poetic project that is determined by a series of "lived" associations, to use Chakrabarty's expression, that are configured by the personal, geographic, literary, and material assemblages connected to the historical emergence of his work as a key moment within the transnational circulation of avant-garde poetics; on the other hand, Huidobro's project is confronted by the historicist attempts, such as that of Guillermo de Torre, to objectify these synchronic "lived" associations – leading to the different experimental literature networks connected to Huidobro's project – by a historicist attempt to construct a history of the European avant-garde, in which Huidobro's poetics tended to be marginalized and considered "foreign," "derivative," and ultimately "unoriginal."

Huidobro's *Hazaña*: Postcolonial Translation and the Avant-Garde Poetics of *Mío Cid Campeador* (1929)

Huidobro's commitment to both his poetic vision and his challenge to the historicist logic of the European avant-garde remained undeterred during what was arguably his most productive period. Between 1929 and 1931 Huidobro not only completed and published his masterpiece *Altazor* but also published a remarkable series of influential works that included, among others, *Temblor de cielo*, *Cagliostro*, and the novel *Mío Cid Campeador*, a work that has rarely been studied as part of Huidobro's overall avant-garde *oeuvre*. *Mío Cid Campeador* is in fact best defined as a hybrid text that combines elements of a poem, a novel, and a potential screenplay, constituting an excellent example of the geopolitical dimension of Huidobro's avant-garde project from both a transnational and a postcolonial perspective, particularly in relation to Spanish national culture.[36]

The project of *Mío Cid Campeador* was originally conceived by Huidobro as a result of an encounter with Douglas Fairbanks.[37] The Chilean writer wrote this work inspired by a conversation he had with the filmmaker in 1927, more precisely in the Hotel Crillon in Paris, and possibly by the remote prospect of having his *hazaña*, or heroic hybrid text, turned into a Hollywood movie. Unfortunately for Huidobro, Fairbanks's interest in the Cid soon faded and the project ultimately failed to materialize. Thus, what originally emerged as an attempt to turn the Castilian Cid into a Hollywood hero for one of Fairbanks's historical action movies of the silent era ended up becoming Huidobro's own *hazaña*, or heroic deed, another key component of the historical and poetic expansion of his avant-garde project, as well as another example of his effort to interfere with the historicist logic his avant-garde project encountered.

Huidobro's *Mío Cid Campeador* can be studied from many different perspectives connected to the historical avant-garde, as well as to international modernist studies, including as a modernist rewriting of literary history, as an avant-garde historical novel, and in relation to the history of cinema, to mention three potential approaches. It is important to consider how the actual process of adaptation in *Mío Cid* entails a form of translation – both as a creative transformation of an original text that is essential to the literary history of Spain and of Spanish national identity, and as an act of cultural translation connected to his *creacionista* project. If, according to film theorist Francesco Casetti, an adaptation constitutes the translation of an original work into a new "communicative situation," we need to analyse what Huidobro's *Mío Cid Campeador* communicates differently in relation to the original medieval epic poem, and what this new reconfiguration is trying to communicate in itself.[38]

The *Cantar de Mio Cid* is the earliest extant medieval epic poem composed in Castilian and is thought to have been produced around 1140. The medieval poem narrates the heroic deeds of the historical figure Rodrigo Díaz de Vivar, a nobleman in the court of King Alfonso VI during the Al-Andalus period in the eleventh century. In his critical edition of the poem, originally published in 1911, the Spanish philologist Ramón Menéndez Pidal, perhaps the key scholar in the institutionalization of the *Cantar de Mio Cid* within Spanish literary history, argues that this epic poem "es el primer monumento de la literatura española" (is the first monument of Spanish literature).[39] Echoing the approach of the nineteenth-century historian and literary critic Marcelino Menéndez Pelayo, who saw in the *The Cid* "el ardiente sentido nacional que, sin estar expreso en ninguna parte, vivifica el conjunto" (burning national feeling that, without being explicit anywhere, enlivens the entire group),[40] Menéndez Pidal emphasizes from a traditionalist perspective the nationalist content of the poem:

> Además el poema del Cid, apartándose de la hostilidad regional que respiran otros poemas castellanos, extiende su respeto y su amor a *quant grant es España*: mira a ésta unida en su mayor parte por el imperio de Alfonso sobre *portogaleses, gallizianos, leoneses* y *castellanos*; la considera también toda bajo el nombre de *la limpia cristiandad*, empeñada en la común guerra contra los moros y honrada en sus diversas familias reales por la sangre del Cid: *oy los reyes de España sos parientes son.*

> (Besides, the *Song of My Cid*, moving away from the regional hostility that transpires in other Castilian poems, extends its respect and love for *quant grant* is Spain: it addresses a Spain mostly united by the rule of Alfonso over the Portuguese, Gallicians, Leonese, and Castilians; it also regards it as a whole in the name of a pure Christianity used in the common war against the Moors, and honours its various royal families through the Cid's blood: "Today the kings of Spain are his relatives.")[41]

A key feature that connects Huidobro's *Mío Cid Campeador* with the critique of historicism that lies at the core of *creacionismo* is the way in which Huidobro himself incorporates Menéndez Pidal's historicist recuperation of the Cid, and its "burning national feeling" as the "first monument of Spanish literature," into his own avant-garde project.[42] Significantly, by transforming the figure of the Cid into a key manifestation of his avant-garde poetic project as a *creacionista* image, Huidobro radically subverts the historicist logic of Spanish intellectuals such as Menéndez Pidal, writing in the first three decades of the twentieth century during the reign of King Alfonso XIII. At the same time, and in line with his controversial avant-garde ethos, Huidobro in his adaptation is not only subverting the historicist drive of Spanish national history, carefully developed by Menéndez Pidal less than two decades earlier, but ultimately claiming his own legitimacy as translator and interpreter of the Cid himself – which in Huidobro's case amounted not just to the poem, but to the historical figure of Rodrigo Díaz de Vivar. Huidobro's letter to Fairbanks that prefaces *Mío Cid Campeador* is followed by a fascinating foreword in which the Chilean writer literally translates himself into his own version of the medieval Castilian epic poem in two main "heroic" ways, which together flesh out the avant-garde nature of his own *hazaña*: first, in another example of the avant-garde self-aggrandizing that characterizes Huidobro, he claims to be, in an act that borders on Borgesian metafiction, a direct descendent of the Cid himself based on heraldic information he apparently found in an encyclopaedia; second, and in addition to employing a dubious and self-mythologizing heraldic genealogy – which also highlights the problematic myth of idealized and normative masculinity that pervades his work – Huidobro translates himself into his own version of this epic poem through an idiosyncratic use of literary language.[43]

Moreover, an exceptional feature of Huidobro's *Mío Cid Campeador* is his attempt to make his language in the poem sound explicitly "foreign." To be more precise, Huidobro wants his own version of the heroic journey of the Castilian Cid to be uttered not in contemporary Spanish form, but rather to sound "American," that is, Spanish American, as well as French. From the opening lines, we see that Huidobro wants to radically defamiliarize, as it were, the very language of the poem from its own "original," putative or native language. He seeks, in his own words, to "invade," that is, to occupy and transform, the Castilian diction of this paradigmatic Castilian poem – arguably the central literary work at the core of the Spanish nationalist and imperial ideology – into a new version of itself:

> It seems to me a very good thing that languages should invade one another as much as possible –should fly like airplanes over frontiers and custom-houses and land in anybody's territory. Perhaps, thanks to this mutual invasion of languages, we shall arrive some day at one international language, and then the only disadvantage that Poetry suffers among the other arts will disappear. Moreover, it is not to be denied that Castilian is a pretty heavy language, stiff, and that a little nimbleness and flexibility will do it no harm.[44]

In other words, what Huidobro is trying to accomplish in this work is, literally, to subvert the very colonial logic that has been ideologically built around the "stiff" language of the original medieval poem. We see that he explicitly aims to avoid an ethnocentric reiteration of the original (as embodied in modern Spanish, for example) in order to give rise to a kind of international lingua franca in a new Spanish version consistent with his dream of universality for his avant-garde poetics of *creacionismo*. Moreover, the kind of "little nimbleness and flexibility" used by Huidobro in his adaptation of the Castilian epic into his own *Mío Cid Campeador* not only alters the diction of the original into a new linguistic form, but ultimately ends up articulating a radical avant-garde cultural translation of the features of medieval Castile and of the figure of the Cid as one of the key historical, ideological, and linguistic sources of Spanish national identity. The following passage from Huidobro's work highlights some of the translational aspects that characterize his *hazaña* from both a linguistic and a historical perspective:

> España se hace un solo eco para repetir:
> —¡Viva el Cid Campeador!
> El nombre sube, sube al espacio, se condensa, se electriza y vuelve a caer sobre la tierra en lluvia de heroísmos.
> —¡Viva el Cid Campeador!
> Una bandada de golondrinas pasa volando, pesca el nombre al vuelo, y va a repetirlo por todos los rincones del mundo
> Mío Cid, Mío Cid, van chillando las golondrinas.

> España se agranda de todas las lenguas de esta palabra.
>
> Así el nombre Cid brota repentino de los poros de la tierra y se encuentra instalado sobre todos los labios, cantante como un árbol de luz. Nace, crece, sube al cielo, se multiplica, se hace selva, invade las llanuras, cruza los ríos, transpone las cordilleras, cubre a España, salta las fronteras y los mares, llena a Europa, desborda del mundo, crece, crece, asciende, asciende, y se para arriba en el cénit, hinchando esperanzas.
>
> Historia y Geografía se obsesionan con su nombre. Cid hacia el norte, Cid hacia el sur, Cid hacia el este, Cid hacia el oeste. La rosa de los vientos huele a Cid Campeador. …
>
> El heroico nombre, enredado en laureles, forma un nido de águila en el punto más lato de la historia, dando a la historia vibraciones de poema. Allá en la eternidad, anidando en las cuerdas de un laúd.
>
> CID, CID, CID.[45]

> The multitude was but one throat, shouting: "Long live the Cid Campeador!" All Spain was but one echo to repeat: "Long live the Cid Campeador!" The name rose up, rose up into space, was charged and condensed and feel again in a heroic rain: "Long live the Cid Campeador!" A flight of swallows flying overhead caught up the name on the wing, and carried it to all the corners of the world. "My Cid, my Cid," the swallows sang as they flew; and Spain grew by leagues as she heard the word. So the name Cid issued suddenly from the pores of the earth and found itself upon all tongues, singing like a tree in the sun. It was born, and grew, and ascended into Heaven; multiplied, and was one with the forests, invaded the plains, crossed the mountains, covered Spain, leapt the frontiers and seas, filled all Europe, burst the boundaries of the and grew and ascended and stayed only at Hope's zenith. History and Geography were obsessed with the name – Cid to the north, Cid to the south, Cid to the east, Cid to the west, borne by the wind like a rose … That heroic name, garlanded with laurels, is an eagle's nest on the highest peak of History, sending through History a surge of song; and there it remains through all eternity, nestling in the strings of a lute.[46]

Huidobro enacts here a form of linguistic translation and adaptation of the original Castilian poem that subverts its previous critical interpretations precisely by challenging the historicist logic that pervaded the canonical reception of the poem within Spanish literary history. The figure of the Cid becomes in Huidobro's hands not so much the source, or historicist origin, of the "burning national feeling," as Menéndez Pelayo argues, but rather an energizing creative force of tremendous proportions. Huidobro creates through the figure of the Cid a planetary force that pervades the entire natural world, one capable of spreading from Spain to the four corners of the world and, most significantly, capable of altering the course of history. It is also important to note the reappearance in this passage of the poetic figure of the "golondrina" (swallow) within the planetary emergence of the Cid in the poem, perhaps the most consistent *creacionista* image in Huidobro's poetic project, as we saw earlier, and one that connects works as diverse as *Ecuatorial*, *Mío Cid Campeador*, and, most prominently, *Altazor*, as well as *Temblor de cielo*. The natural, transnational, and lyric dimensions of the swallow as a poetic image makes it perhaps the most important manifestation and unifying principle of the planetary and anti-historicist drive at the core of Huidobro's avant-garde project.

Thus, Huidobro's version of the Cid embodies an idea of Spain very different from that which Menéndez Pidal describes. Huidobro's version of the Cid embodies a form of Spain that does not constitute the manifestation of a force of colonial empire resulting from the Cid's "imperial rule" over different Iberian cultures, as Menéndez Pidal argues, but rather a more utopian, larger, freer, and more expansive force. In this sense, Huidobro's conflation of the images of the Cid and Spain constitutes a key *creacionista* poem-object, an experimental poetic form fully determined and conceptualized by the creative and anti-historicist impulse at the core of the avant-garde poetics of the Chilean writer. Within Huidobro's vision these two figures are constituted as creative principles within the poem, mirroring in fact the poetic logic of radical creation that emerges in other works of Huidobro's *creacionismo*: "crece, crece, asciende, asciende, y se para arriba en el cénit, hinchando esperanzas" ("and grew and ascended and stayed only at Hope's zenith").[47]

A key final aspect of the postcolonial dimension of form of planetary engagement at the core of *Mío Cid Campeador* emerges at the end of Huidobro's *hazaña* when Huidobro's Cid dies tragically, as, for Huidobro, does Spain:

> Murió el Cid. ¿Oís lo que digo? ¡Murió el Cid Campeador! ¡Cómo me zumban los oídos! Se hace el vacío en el vacío, se hace el caos en el caos. Se me rompe la pluma.
>
> España pierde el sentido y se desmaya entre las demás naciones, que no pueden consolarla. Su poesía, su exaltación, su cuerda mas vibrante, su vida extraordinaria y alucinante, su supervida recia y generosa, su esencia, su símbolo, ha muerto.
>
> Se oye el ruido de una lágrima que resbala por el infinito. Después un silencio profundo se hace sobre la creación.[48]

> The Cid was dead. Do you hear what I say to you? There is a drumming in my ears, emptiness within emptiness, chaos within chaos; and my pen is broken. Spain fell swooning into the arms of her sister nations, but there was none of them who could console her. Her poetry, her exaltation, her most vibrant chord, her life peerless and glamorous, her superman strong and generous, her vital essence, her living symbol, was dead. There was the sound of a tear that slid into the infinite; and then a profound silence fell upon creation.[49]

The death of the Cid here also constitutes for Huidobro the poetic death of Spain. What is remarkable about Spain's poetically dying together with the epic hero of Huidobro's *hazaña* is that it is a death that occurs before it is historically and politically configured as a modern nation. Thus, by dying together with the figure of the Cid, the poetic essence of Spain as an experiential realm of creative potential literally collapses for Huidobro before it can exist as political reality, that is, as part of the ideological and political project of a Spanish nation state that can be historicized and institutionalized as such. Instead of positing the figure of the Cid as the putative origin and historicist essence of what Spain will later become historically, Huidobro imagines the figure of the Cid to embody a form of creative potential that Spain could never reach, given the tragic death of the medieval epic hero within Huidobro's *hazaña*. Ultimately, by collapsing the figures of the Cid and Spain in relation to each other, and each of their respective temporalities, Huidobro is driving his radical critique and challenge to the form of historicism at the heart of Spanish national culture through his planetary adaptation of the Castilian medieval poem.

What is striking here is that Menéndez Pidal's version of the past through the literary figure of the Cid, and the related homogenous and traditionalist notion of Spanish imperial identity attached to it, was being institutionalized by Primo de Rivera's regime in Spain at precisely the same time that Huidobro was working on *Mío Cid Campeador*, as explored in the coda of this book. This same traditionalist understanding of Spanish identity described by Menéndez Pidal and promoted by Primo de Rivera's regime during the last years of Alfonso XIII's reign would then be ideologically and politically imposed after the Spanish Civil War by Francisco Franco's fascist dictatorship, a regime that would adopt the figure of the Cid to promote the "birth" of the Spanish national spirit and of its imperial dimension in terms similar to those used by Menéndez Pidal. As opposed to this hegemonic traditionalist understanding of the past, Huidobro's *Mío Cid Campeador* radically rearticulates this past in order to highlight the important role played by Spain as a topos and point of contact for avant-garde cultural production during this period, as well as in terms of the significance of the notions of Castilla (Castile) and Spain as avant-garde literary or imaginary tropes within and outside the realm of Spanish culture during this historical period.

Huidobro's *Creacionismo* and the Planetary as Utopia

As I have shown in this chapter, Huidobro's *Mío Cid Campeador* and *Ecuatorial* constitute key parts of an avant-garde project that invites his readers – past, present, and future – to connect in unexpected ways a series of events and experiences that still have not been sufficiently studied in relation to each other: for example, connecting Huidobro with Douglas Fairbanks, and thus connecting the generally divided fields of anglophone and non-anglophone modernisms, as well as Latin American and Spanish approaches to the historical avant-garde, while at the same time connecting the imperial history of Spain with postcolonial responses to this colonial legacy in ways that defy the logic of canonical historiographic methods and disciplinary boundaries. As part of this project, Huidobro's particular literary responses – clearly rooted in the writer's Latin American and Chilean origins – to the political, cultural, and literary tradition of Spain, and his overall critique of its historicism relevantly suggests a commitment to disrupting and interfering with the Eurocentric approaches to the avant-garde that have marginalized authors located outside of Europe and the Anglo-American context. From this perspective, and despite its many polemical and controversial dimensions, Huidobro's work is of particular relevance when studying the politics and poetics of the historical avant-garde as a critical category in relation to Spanish and European cultural production during this period, as well as to contemporary forms of literary history within the particular framework of this chapter, and the larger argument of *A Planetary Avant-Garde*. At the same time, Huidobro's critique of historicism at the core of *creacionismo* provides insight into the complex relation that exists between his deep commitment, evident throughout his entire literary career, to the kind of transnational geopolitics manifested in the form of planetary engagement I have explored here, as well as the "futurity" and utopic nature of his own avant-garde poetic vision.

By constantly occupying an unstable and mobile location between Europe and Latin America, as well as constituting an important transnational link between different experimental literature networks, Huidobro's *creacionismo* opened many paths and venues of artistic exchange that allowed for the circulation of modernist and avant-garde poetics wherever Huidobro and his work went. I have shown the value of tracing again these paths, particularly in their transnational dimensions, for a fuller understating of Huidobro's place within the historical avant-garde, and of different approaches to his experimental poetics. My overall attempt to locate Huidobro's place within the historical avant-garde has been, as Latour suggests, to "reassemble" a series of networks by "following the actors themselves" in order to "learn from them what the collective existence has become."[50] This is a critical process of reassembling and connecting, as we have seen in Huidobro's work, different sites of avant-garde cultural production as a process of cultural and linguistic assemblage and translation operating simultaneously at both a local and a transnational level. Huidobro's *oeuvre* therefore presents us with a body of work that emphasizes the importance of the act of translation, as a poetic, literary, and historical movement within and between different traditions and cultures in order to gain a more open and complex picture of the historical avant-garde.

Ultimately, Huidobro's *creacionismo* explicitly seeks to respond from his own positionality to the various forms of historicism that lie at the core of the historical avant-garde as a critical category, which happened to be in development during the first three decades of the twentieth century. Indeed, as Bürger has argued, it is precisely the self-awareness of the historicity of the historical avant-garde, and of its "attack" on "the institutionalized commerce of art" that establishes it as a "historically concrete and theoretically exact" critical category, as has been suggested by Jochen Schulte-Sasse.[51] I have shown, however, that Huidobro's project politically intends to assume this "avant-garde attack" as a historical process that is not intrinsically "foreign" to him, and consequently to his Latin American condition. As one such project, Huidobro's work exemplifies the kind of geopolitical engagement that I describe as "planetary" in this book and that the Chilean writer carries out first and foremost through the series of "lived" transnational and translational associations, to use Chakrabarty's term, that historically ground the poetics of *creacionismo*. Therefore, by asserting his legitimacy as a member of the historical avant-garde in his own terms, Huidobro's avant-garde project challenges the historicist logic of origins that has traditionally defined this period and critical category through the form of planetary engagement at the core of his experimental project.

As argued in this chapter, Huidobro's place within the historical avant-garde can thus be conceived as being articulated by poetic and historical assemblages whose sources are both outside and inside Europe, and whose branches expand and cross as they extend through Europe and the Americas. The implication of his work can direct our attention towards a higher transnational realm of connectedness, and also to an unforeseen and unexpected future that lies well beyond what a historicist conception of history – literary or otherwise – could effectively model. As a planetary critique of historicist cultural origins, Huidobro's avant-garde project expresses a horizon of possibilities, or an "experience of the impossible" similar to that suggested by Spivak in her original conception of the planetary:

> The "planet" is, here, as perhaps always, a catachresis for inscribing collective responsibility as right. Its alterity, determining experience, is mysterious and discontinuous – an experience of the impossible. It is such collectivities that must be opened up with the question "How many are we?" when cultural origin is detranscendentalized into fiction.[52]

From this perspective, we see that Huidobro's avant-garde project supports the geopolitical disruption of "cultural origins" as the source of aesthetic and poetic legitimacy within the historical avant-garde precisely by envisioning a radical "experience of the impossible," to use Spivak's words in her conceptualization of the planetary. Huidobro precisely projects this "experience of the impossible" into a utopic future through the experimental poetics of *creacionismo*. While Huidobro's planetary proposition of a space outside geography and a time outside history invokes an essentially utopian vision that arguably exists only within his own, ultimately self-centred, poetic project – such as the poetic image of the epic Díaz de Vivar radically transformed into an avant-garde manifestation of Huidobro's *creacionismo* – it is a geopolitical proposition that deserves to be legitimately considered in its complexities and tensions as central to a more nuanced and non-Eurocentric re-evaluation of the historical avant-garde from a comparative and multilingual perspective.

Chapter Three

Away from Montmartre: Blaise Cendrars, Tarsila do Amaral, and the Travel Notes of the Historical Avant-Garde

Blaise Cendrars's poetry collection *Feuilles de route* (a work that has been translated into English as both "Ocean Letters" and "Travel Notes") documents his round-trip transatlantic journey between France and Brazil during a nine-month period in 1924.[1] The Swiss-born Cendrars (Frédéric-Louis Sauser, 1887–1967) embarked on his journey to Brazil at a time when he was already well known across Europe as one of the key writers of the European avant-garde in general, and within the Parisian cultural scene in particular. By 1924, Cendrars was a widely recognized, almost legendary figure through his work as a poet (*La prose du Transsibérien et de la Petite Jehanne de France* [1913]), prose writer (*Profond aujourd'hui* [1917]), editor (he was one of the co-directors of the publisher Éditions de la Sirène), filmmaker, and ballet producer (*La création du monde*, 1923), among the many artistic endeavours he engaged in before and after his participation as a soldier in the French army in World War I. While Cendrars's 1924 poetry collection has received considerably less critical attention than his widely regarded poetic masterpiece *Prose of the Trans-Siberian*, *Feuilles de route* underscores a fundamental moment within the emergence of key forms of planetary engagement during the historical avant-garde. Parallel to his journey to Brazil, and as Cendrars's *Feuilles de route* gradually unfolds as a sequence of poems, there emerges a complex network of experimental poetics that appears to be paradigmatic, while not unique in itself, of a more complex exploration of the geopolitical dimensions of the "non-organic" avant-garde form, to use Bürger's terminology. As a collection of experimental poetry that was literally produced through a direct encounter with the geography, society, culture, and history of Brazil, Cendrars's *Feuilles de route* – and the network of experimental poetics articulated around this work – helps unveil a complex instance of planetary engagement that radically expands the geopolitical dimension of the historical avant-garde.

The first edition of Cendrars's 1924 poetry collection was published as *Feuilles de route*, vol. 1, *Le Formose*, published in a limited run of eight hundred copies by Au Sans Pareil, the Parisian press founded by 1919 by René Hilsum, and which included only "Le Formose," the first part of the longer collection that Cendrars's would later publish as *Feuilles de route*. The relevance of Cendrars's *Feuilles de route*, and particularly its first edition, for an examination of planetary engagement within the context of this book is twofold: on the one hand, it is a work that displays Cendrars's own poetic "discovery" of Brazil as a new realm for the expansion – temporal as well as geographical – of his own Paris-centred conception of avant-garde poetics; on the other hand, Cendrars's collection registers the emergence of Brazilian *modernismo* at a crucial moment in which its leading figures were explicitly trying, from a postcolonial position, to move away from Eurocentric hegemonic canons and models of literary history, stemming mainly from Brazil's colonial history under the Portuguese Empire. One of the key planetary implications related to *Feuilles de route* is the fact that the collection manages to inscribe Cendrars's own travelling experience within and in relation to the history – cultural and literary – of both modern Brazilian literature and the historical avant-garde from a transnational and transcontinental perspective. In this sense, it is very important to contextualize Cendrars's poetic response to his journey to Brazil as a literary and cultural process that operates as part of a much larger network of experimental poetics that both supersedes and contains Cendrars's own work through a wider series of relations among diverse avant-garde artworks, writers, and aesthetic movements connecting the European avant-garde with the early development of Brazilian *modernismo*. Hence, it is not coincidental that *Feuilles de route* happens to be dedicated to Cendrars's friends in Brazil: "mes bon amis de São Paulo," as well as "aux amis de Rio-de-Janeiro," two groups of influential Brazilian artists that, together with the other dedicatee, Leopold de Freitas "du Rio-Grande-do-Sul," comprise an all-male list of key figures of the Brazilian modernist movement, which included Paulo Prado, Mário de Andrade, Sergio Millet, Oswald de Andrade, and Sérgio Buarque de Holanda.

Excluded from this dedication, as will be further explored in this chapter, is the visual artist Tarsila do Amaral (1886–1973), one of the most influential members of the Brazilian modernist movement. However, while Tarsila, as she is generally known within Brazilian literary and art history, does not appear in Cendrars's dedication to his Brazilian "amis," her name is indeed included in the cover ("Dessins de Tarsila" [Illustrations by Tarsila]) of the first edition of the collection, *Le*

Formose. Tarsila authored the illustration included on the book's cover, a sketch of Tarsila's famous and controversial painting *A Negra* (The Black Woman, 1923), as well as the seven illustrations to the series of poems included in its first edition.[2] The rest of Tarsila's illustration in the first edition of *Feuilles de route* are part of a series of sketches of rural areas of Brazil across the region of Minas Gerais that Tarsila produced on a highly influential collective trip that took place during Cendrars's 1924 journey. In fact, in later editions of Cendrars's *Feuilles de route*, as well as reprints of Cendrars's work in various anthologies and translations, Tarsila's illustrations of the first 1924 edition have generally been removed entirely or in part, considerably limiting the impact of her role as the illustrator and Cendrars's collaborator in this work.[3] While she is generally unacknowledged as an essential part of Cendrars's project in *Feuilles de route*, I argue in this chapter that Tarsila's collaboration with Cendrars in 1924, and her own creative involvement in the illustration and production of its first edition, are of paramount importance for a new critical assessment of this key network of experimental poetics within a planetary understanding of the historical avant-garde.

By reassembling the particulars of this avant-garde transatlantic network, this chapter also recuperates for a comparative understanding of this period the influential *Pau Brasil* movement that Tarsila would champion in collaboration with her then partner Oswald de Andrade (1890–1954), as well as with Mário de Andrade (1893–1945), two other key Brazilian modernists who collaborated with Cendrars during the 1920s and who, like Tarsila, repeatedly travelled back and forth across the Atlantic during this period, including key stays in Paris.[4] As I argue in the following, a new critical reconsideration of this specific moment in the larger history of the avant-garde now appears both possible and timely, particularly in relation to the recent re-evaluation of the work of Tarsila in the United States and Europe. While the importance of the contributions of Brazilian *modernismo* to the historical avant-garde in their own right are beginning to be acknowledged outside of Brazil and Latin America – as evidenced by the critically acclaimed exhibitions of Tarsila's work (*Tarsila do Amaral: Inventing Modern Art in Brazil*) held at the Art Institute of Chicago and MoMA in 2017 and 2018, respectively, and their extremely positive media reception across the United States[5] – there is a considerable need to critically reconsider this particular network within a comparative and transnational scholarly examination of the historical avant-garde, beyond the hegemonic centre-periphery historicist models traditionally used for its scholarly study. Part of the purpose of this chapter is to explore the significance of Tarsila's collaboration with Cendrars in *Le Formose*, in relation to both the Eurocentric logic of Cendrars's influential avant-garde project and the local articulation of modernist poetics in Brazil during the same period.

Travel Notes I: Cendrars's Avant-Garde Waybill and the Roadmaps of Colonial History

Cendrars's poetry travelogue to Brazil in *Feuilles de route* is divided into three main sections, which correspond to the main stages of his first trip to the country in 1924. Section 1, titled "Le Formose" – which was, as noted above, the only one included in the first edition of the collection (*Le Formose*, 1924), and is the main focus of this chapter, per Cendrars's collaboration with Tarsila in this edition – covers the first stage of his journey via train from Paris to Le Havre, and then on the steam ship *Formose* from Le Havre to Brazil across the Atlantic.[6] As for the other two parts of *Feuilles de route*, published in later editions, the second (and shortest) section is titled "São Paulo," and focuses on Cendrars's arrival and stay in the Brazilian city as the central part of his journey; while the series of poems comprising the third and final section, given the simple numerical title "III," encompass Cendrars's return to France on the steam ship *Gelria*, which concluded his nine-month voyage.

As its title suggests, *Feuilles de route* can be read, more or less literally, as a series of poetic travel notes, constituting a form of modernist "postcard haikus," as Richard Sieburth has relevantly described them.[7] At face value, Cendrars's poetic project developed in *Feuilles de route* thus appears to be an avant-garde poetic documentation through different vignettes of moments encountered throughout his journey across the Atlantic and within Brazil. In fact, the collection as a whole closely relates to Cendrars's actual experiences during his 1924 Brazil journey, mostly through a series of brief and objectively driven poetic pieces describing his impressions of various cities, people, and specific moments or events of his journey. Upon closer examination of their formal features, some of the poems included in *Feuilles de route* also display a more lyric expression, in which Cendrars presents a series of subjective viewpoints or poetic "close-ups" that explore a complex series of emotions and feelings as related to his experiences travelling to and across Brazil. Connecting these two modalities of poetic representation, at the core of Cendrars's literary encounter with Brazil is the modernist technique that Christoph Wall-Romana has defined as "cinepoetry." Perhaps the most relevant "cinepoetic" element in *Feuilles de route* can be described in terms of what Wall-Romana refers to as a "clipped almost telegraphic style," a formalist-oriented description that parallels

Sieburth's description of Cendrars's poems in *Feuilles de route* as "postcard-like" poetic compositions.[8]

At the same time, intrinsically connected to what Wall-Romana formally describes as the "cinepoetic" dimensions of Cendrars's poetry – whether analysed as objectively or subjectively driven pieces – lies an implicit process of mapping and inscribing Cendrars's round-trip journey to Brazil as a central moment in the development of his overall avant-garde poetic project. From this perspective, Cendrars's *Feuilles de route* presents a poetic mapping of his journey to Brazil that is constituted not only geographically (parallel to the sailing route taken by the SS *Formose* along the Atlantic coastline of Southern Europe and West Africa towards Brazil, and the return journey back to France aboard the SS *Gelria*), but also as a process configured temporally. From this dual perspective, the very path of Cendrars's sea journey to Brazil correlates with various spatial and historical routes that both precede and, at times, overlap with the spatio-temporal development of his own poetic writing. Thus, the "cinepoetic" and experimental form of the collection as a whole is structured upon the geographical and temporal realms that are connected through the journey. For example, as the *Formose* is about to depart the coast of France, Cendrars's collection records an overlapping series of spatio-temporal experiences that are particularly imbricated in the poem "Claire de lune," Cendrars's fifth piece in the collection:

> On tangue on tangue sur le bateau
> ...
> Une jeune Argentine accoudée au bastingage
> Rêve à Paris en contemplant les phares qui dessinent la côte de France ...
> Le bruit de ma machine à écrire l'empêche de mener ce rêve jusqu'au bout[9]

The poetic representation of the moving sound of the typewriter in "Claire de lune" marks the rhythm of the passage of time as a form of writing able to relate the different experiences of Cendrars's own transatlantic journey. Marked by the typewriter's sounds, "qui sonne au bout de chaque ligne et qui est aussi rapide qu'un jazz,"[10] Cendrars's poems in *Feuilles de route* gradually and cumulatively establish a complex process of recording of time in which the present moment emerges as a temporality parallel to the act of poetic composition, which gravitates around the experience of the lyric "I" or poetic self in relation to the experience of travel.

As Carrie Noland has shown, Cendrars's characteristic use of the first-person poetic voice, or lyric "I," emerges in direct relation to and tension with the various forms of technology to which his avant-garde project responds. This tension constitutes one of the key formal features of Cendrars's experimental poetics, with Noland describing him as a "modern lyricist at odds with the very dynamism he emulates": "His ambiguous position with regard to modern technology reflects a tension peculiar to the lyric's confrontation with the machine."[11] In *Feuilles de route*, this poetic tension, and the related first-person experience at the core of the project, appears through the poetic figuration of mechanical typing as a form of writing that marks the temporality of travelling – a temporality intrinsically related to the process of poetic composition and its mechanical inscription, as well as the very form of the sequence of poems that configure Cendrars's collection.

Feuilles de route displays from the get-go a multiplicity of temporalities that lie at the core of Cendrars's conception of avant-garde poetics and experience of modernity. As part-travelogue recording his experiences to and from Brazil, which ranges from a self-reflexive tone, at times self-ironizing, to a purely documentary mode, Cendrars's collection displays a fascination with the kind of "marking of time" that, as Kimberley Healey has shown in relation to modernist Francophone travel literature, is provided by new and technologically driven forms of travel, writing, and conceptions of history:

> Speed, marking time through writing, and historical relativity are also three different ways of plotting or marking time. The three corresponding visual images of time are a fluid line of speed and motion, a series of linguistic markers or milestones that map specific points in time, and larger fields of historical time that can be ordered in a linear manner.[12]

Cendrars's cinepoetic "travel notes" can also be seen, quite literally, as "linguistic markers or milestones that map specific points in time," as Healey suggests. From this perspective, the avant-garde tension and formal complexity of *Feuilles de route* resides primarily in how the three sections of the collection are able to embody through its experimental form multiple dimensions of time and space connecting the textual temporality of Cendrars's poetry with the historical, geographical, and temporal dimensions of the "documented" journey. Thus, this spatio-temporal experience of transatlantic travel ultimately forms part of a larger formal and aesthetic project, which Cendrars describes in the poem "Claire de lune" as "Mon idée."[13] A key feature of the striking sense of simultaneity at the core of Cendrars's travel notebook that connects the three main modernist markings of time described by Healey is that it can exist as such only through the linguistic experience of Cendrars's poetic voice as the link between the various temporal dimensions imbricated in his collection. Thus, for Cendrars, the geographical route travelled across the Atlantic by the SS *Formose* is connected in *Feuilles de route* to an experience of time linking the present with a historical past, or, rather, with an idea of a history that is rearticulated, and at times re-enacted, by the poetic voice through the very process of writing.

It is precisely in the dual sense explored above regarding Cendrars's "travel notes" – namely, as poetically mapping the spatio-temporal expansion across the Atlantic of his version of avant-garde poetics, while registering the emergence in Brazil of a divergent conceptualization of experimental art and literature embodied in Brazilian *modernismo* – that the other two potential translations of the French term *feuille de route* in English – "road map" and "waybill" – become highly relevant for the present analysis of Cendrars's 1924 collection. Thus, *Feuilles de route* can quite literally be said to constitute a "road map" of the transatlantic expansion of Cendrars's own version of avant-garde poetics – in the sense of "an outline or representation of something," as well as "a plan or strategy intended to achieve a particular goal" – while at the same time constituting a poetic "waybill," in the sense of a "description of goods … entrusted for shipment to stated destinations."[14] From this double semantic perspective, *Feuilles de route* highlights Cendrars's mapping of his Paris-centred conception of avant-garde poetics (explicitly marking the spatio-temporal route of his own poetic journey to Brazil as a "road map" of exploration and discovery), as well as marking the various "goods" configuring his own avant-garde "waybill" that he is "importing" and thus bringing with him across the Atlantic through his journey. Given his status as a key representative of the European avant-garde, the various avant-garde "goods" entailed by Cendrars's "waybill" in *Feuilles de route* are not just configured by the series of poems comprising the collection, but are also constituted by the various forms of modernity and aesthetic rupture with the past emerging through the network that connects Cendrars and his literary project with the group of Brazilian modernists configured by Tarsila, Oswald de Andrade, and Mário de Andrade, as the key members of a larger circle. The circulation of these avant-garde "goods" across their network – both material (such as the poems and artworks examined in this chapter) and symbolic (such as the forms of modernity these works represent) – appears to have been central both to the production of *Feuilles de route* as a collection and to the reception of both Cendrars and his poetics in Brazil by the local press, as well as experienced, in different ways and not without tension, by the members of the Brazilian modernist scene at the time.

As portrayed in *Feuilles de route. I. Le Formose* (the first section, "Le Formose," in later editions of *Feuilles de route*), Cendrars's journey to Brazil initially appears to constitute an attempt to temporarily disconnect from life in Europe. Both the objective and the subjective forms of "cinepoetic" writing described above can be seen equally at work in the first few poems comprising Cendrars's "travel notes." In these early poems, Cendrars describes the initial stages of his sea journey to Brazil in brief poetic sketches of the main coastal areas and port cities he is travelling through prior to crossing the Atlantic (namely, Le Havre, Bilbao, A Coruña, the coast of Portugal, the Canary Islands, and Dakar). At the same time, Cendrars describes the sea journey in terms of a process of personal and aesthetic regeneration, as the Swiss-born writer imagines, in rather exoticized and racially charged terms, a more exuberant and natural world in the tropics. These early poems in the collection tend to emphasize the process of poetic writing located, for Cendrars, at the core of the form of mapping of the route to Brazil taken by the SS *Formose*, as well as the kind of personal regeneration he envisioned as central to the journey itself.

A good example of these dynamics at work in the first section of *Feuilles de route* is the poem "En route pour Dakar." Aboard the SS *Formose*, rather literally en route to Dakar, Senegal, and about to begin its passage across the Atlantic, Cendrars figures Brazil in this poem as a paradisiacal realm of peaceful futurity in which he can eventually forget his past experiences in Europe. Brazil, or, rather, the prospect of arriving in Brazil, presents for Cendrars a future temporality in which the poetic voice, as a version of Cendrars himself, hopes to forget what appears to be a recent traumatic memory explicitly related to the Great War ("Adieu Europe que je quitte pour la première fois depuis 1914").[15] The poem thus marks a temporal rupture and farewell from the coldness and steeliness ("L'air est froid") of a known European experience – also embodied in the European immigrants of diverse nationalities depicted in the poem, and with whom Cendrars shared his transatlantic journey to Brazil – and towards a desired and exoticized foreign future: "Je veux tout oublier ne plus parler les langues et coucher avec des nègres et des nègresses des indiennes des animaux des plantes."[16]

As displayed in "En route pour Dakar," Cendrars presents a poetic figuration of the Lusophone Latin American nation that exoticizes and objectifies Afro-Brazilian and Indigenous men and women in problematic ways through their equation in the poem with the natural world of "animals and plants" ("des animaux des plantes"). In contrast to his psychologically rich descriptions of the groups of white Europeans in this poem and the rest of this section of the collection – they are all shown to miss the city of Paris ("qui regrettent Paris"), for instance[17] – his objectification of Brazil's Afro-descendant and Indigenous populations in this poem reflects Eurocentric categorizations of non-European communities that are closely related to similar racial prejudices present during early modern European colonialism. In this sense, Cendrars's avant-garde poetic mapping in this collection is articulated in a present moment that mirrors the historical past of European colonial explorers, while also remaining aware of its own temporal configuration through a series of observed moments registered regularly, almost compulsively, by his own poetic writing.

Overall, the different dimensions of the journey itself converge around the figure of Cendrars's poetic voice – the gravitational centre of *Feuilles de route* as a poetic project – as well as Cendrars's effort, both figuratively and literally, to break away from his own past. "En route pour Dakar" ultimately collapses these different temporalities by shifting the objective drive of the first few stanzas into a striking and deeply subjective close-up, zooming into the lyric's voice psyche at the very instant that concludes the poem:

> Et devenir dur comme un caillou
> Tomber à pic
> Couler à fond[18]

This poetic process of subjective immersion at the end of "En route pour Dakar" constitutes a striking and crucial poetic image at the core of Cendrars's collection as a whole. On the one hand, the image mirrors a similar figuration of self-immersion in Cendrars's earlier Futurist-inspired manifesto of 1917, *Profond aujourd'hui* (Profound Today), in which Cendrars describes a material dissolution of the self underwater: "The skin becomes gelatinous, transparent, iridescent like the flesh of an anemone. The centers of sensitiveness become polarized. Sponge of the depths, the brain breaths gently."[19] At the same time, the poetic process of "couler à fond" as a process of "sinking" represented in "En route pour Dakar" not only figures a dissolution of the self parallel to the one described in "Profound Today," but also entails a sense of openness to the various temporalities that coalesce within the collection.

Thus, as Cendrars tries to temporally record this subjective temporality in "En route pour Dakar," the related synchronic temporality of his actual journey to Brazil powerfully overlaps in the collection with the diachronic dimension of history, a temporal tension between past and present that is collapsed in the poem. The colonial implications of Cendrars's journey in *Feuilles de route* just highlighted become in fact more concrete as the rest of the collection unfolds: as his poems gradually describe the journey along the Atlantic from the northwest coast of the Iberian Peninsula into the Western coastline of Africa towards Dakar, it does not go unnoticed to Cendrars that the very route followed by the SS *Formose*, and consequently by himself and his writing, happens to be the same sailing route used by the early modern Iberian colonial explorers, as he states in the poem "Sur les côtes du Portugal": "Du Hâvre nous n'avons fait que suivre les côtes comme les navigateurs anciens."[20]

Furthermore, later in the collection, Cendrars invokes the early modern "discovery" of Brazil in a brief, six-line poem titled after the Portuguese navigator and explorer Pedro Álvares Cabral, referred to as "Álvarez" by Cendrars in the poem, which commemorates Álvares Cabral's departure from Lisbon in the year 1500 and his arrival in Brazil ("et le Brésil fut découvert"[21]). By explicitly invoking the colonial history of Portugal as part of his own "travel notes," Cendrars inserts himself into the chronological line of early modern European colonialism of the Americas from a diachronic perspective, while articulating a subject position that re-enacts in its very present the past historical experience of arguably the best-known Portuguese navigator in the early modern Portuguese Empire. Thus, if his journey to Brazil entails for Cendrars a sinking to the bottom of the self in the hope of a renewal for his own avant-garde poetics and European-centred aesthetic project, it does so as a journey that explicitly and self-consciously mirrors the imperial legacy of Iberian colonialism, embodied in the figure of Álvares Cabral. In a book published in 1922 commemorating the centenary of Brazil's independence from Portugal in 1822, the historian Jaime Cortesão – also director of the National Library of Portugal at the time – asserts that Álvares Cabral's maritime journey across the Atlantic embodies the two defining events in Portuguese history, namely the establishment of a Portuguese economic empire in Asia and the effective beginning of the colonization of Brazil: "Iniciou Pedro Álvares Cabral os dois actos políticos mais grandiosos de toda nossa história,—o imperio económico de Oriente e a colonização do Brasil" (Pedro Álvares Cabral inaugurated the two most grandiose political events of all our history: the economic empire in Asia and the colonization of Brazil).[22]

Generally considered within Portuguese colonial historiography to be the "discoverer" of Brazil, the arrival of Álvares Cabral to the coast of Brazil in the year 1500 led to the creation of a colonial empire that would soon spread across four continents, and which was based mainly on the Portuguese control of key commercial routes to Asia, as well as the establishment of the slave trade across the Atlantic that led to millions of African people being enslaved for over four hundred years. Cortesão's mythologizing, neo-imperial, and nationalistic interpretation of Portuguese colonial history in 1922, and, more specifically, of Álvares Cabral's role as a key navigating figure in the imperial conquest and worldwide expansion of Portugal, dramatically clashes with the understanding of the same dynamics of empire as analysed by contemporary historians of world empires, such as Jane Burbank and Fredrick Cooper. As Burbank and Cooper have shown, these same dynamics of empire, as pertains particularly to Portugal, are intimately connected to the state-sanctioned violence, racism, and brutal exploitation of both resources and people across Africa and the Americas through the establishment of a complex system of sailing routes and commercial networks that also included Southeast Asia, as well as various European markets: "Portugal, with its enclaves in Africa and resources and experience gained from coercion and commerce across oceans and continents, seized by conquest a large territory in the Americas, then profited from linkages of African labor, American land, and European markets."[23]

Writing during 1924, just two years after the centennial of Brazilian independence, Cendrars is specifically invoking in *Feuilles de route* a parallel spirit of modern exploration and discovery closely related to the imperial and colonial ethos at the core of Cortesão's historiographic recuperation of the figure of Álvares Cabral. It is thus highly important in this context to highlight how the figure of Álvares Cabral embodied for Cortesão in 1922 a traditionalist and historicist notion of the "birth" of Brazil as part of a Portuguese national epic impulse within a colonial, imperial, and commercial project: "Sim, bem longe das inspirações ou caprichos do acaso, o Brasil nasce de nós, na plenitude do sentido e do ritmo, como um primeiro canto de epopeia" (Yes, far from the inspirations or caprices of chance, Brazil is born of us, in a fullness of meaning and rhythm, as a first canto of an epic poem).[24] Evoking the paradigmatic case of the early modern epic poem – perhaps as a reference to Luís de Camões's *Os Lusíadas* (1572) – as a literary form central to the writing and "singing" of national histories, Cortesão describes what, for the Portuguese historian, constituted in 1922 the creative and spiritual origins of the process of early modern colonization characterizing nothing less than "the birth of Brazil from us."[25]

From this perspective, Cendrars's invocation of the figure of Álvares Cabral in *Feuilles de route* is not an anachronistic instance or nostalgic reference to a colonial past, but rather appears to be central to the growing neo-colonial impulse that characterized certain institutional and cultural policies developed during the first three decades of the twentieth century in Portugal, as well as other parts of Europe.[26] As António de Oliveira Salazar argues in "Princípios fundamentais da revolução política" (Fundamental Principles of the Political Revolution) – a speech given in 1930 in which he provides some of the main political and ideological foundation of his dictatorial regime, the *Estado Novo*, established after the military coup that brought an end to the First Portuguese Republic – Portugal's claim to its overseas possessions is related to what Salazar defines as a "categorical imperative" connected to Portuguese early modern colonial expansion:

> Na nossa ordem política, a primeira realidade é a existência independente da Nação Portuguesa, com o direito de possuir fora do continente europeu, acrescendo à sua herança peninsular, por um imperativo categórico da História, pela sua acção ultramarina em descobertas e conquistas, e pela conjugação e harmonia dos esforços civilizadores das raças, o património marítimo, territorial, político, e espiritual abrangido na esfera do seu domínio ou influência.
>
> (In our political system, the first reality is the independent existence of the Portuguese Nation, with the right of territorial possession outside of the European continent and the growth of its peninsular heritage by the categorical imperative of History through its overseas achievements in discoveries and conquests, and through the combination and harmony of its civilizing efforts on the various races, and the maritime, territorial, political, and spiritual heritage that encompass the sphere of its domain and influence.)[27]

The colonial and imperial ethos of Salazar's principle of political revolution is based, in part, on a consideration of Portuguese overseas territorial possessions not just as a contemporary categorical imperative of Portugal as a nation state in 1930, but also as a categorical imperative determined by its own colonial history.[28]

As shown in the recuperation of the figure of Álvares Cabral by Cendrars discussed above, and parallel to Cortesão's mythic reimagination of this historical figure, Cendrars is poetically "singing" through his "cinepoetic" style what appears to be the emergence or "birth" of Brazil as a key signifier within his own avant-garde poetic project. What is a stake here is indicative not necessarily of a neo-colonial impulse at the heart of Cendrars's project as such, but rather of a more complex and larger historicist instance in which Cendrars, as a key representative of the European avant-garde, locates his own avant-garde project in relation to a larger history of European colonization – a historical positing in which modern Brazilian culture and history are not only "mapped" within Cendrars's poetic vision, but ultimately commodified as depending on a Eurocentric geopolitical perspective and source of signification.

These geopolitical and historicist dimensions at the core of Cendrars's *Feuilles de route* – and its colonial implications, examined above – are further highlighted at the end of the 1924 edition of the collection (section 1 in later editions of *Feuilles de route*), through a series of poems marked by an overwhelming and exhilarating sense of ontological instability and epistemological uncertainty. In these pieces, the poetic voice appears partly unable to process the "foreignness" encountered once the SS *Formose* reaches mainland Brazil. In fact, after he arrives in the port city of Santos and takes a train to the city of São Paulo, Cendrars's poetic mapping of this part of his journey in *Feuilles de route* depicts the natural exuberance of Brazil as an overwhelming and unsettling experience. For example, in the poem "Ignorance," Cendrars describes in highly exoticizing terms the overwhelming presence of various forms of Brazilian vegetation, which he specifically highlights in the last section of the poem:

> Qu'il n'y a aucune trace de culture
> Puis je ne sais plus rien de tout ce que je vois
> Des formes
> Des formes de végétation …[29]

This is a poetic encounter with a cultural and natural otherness embodied in a complex series of forms of vegetations and plants ("des palmiers," "des cactus," "un fruit aphrodisiaque") that, while creating a sense of epistemological loss, hinted at in the self-ironic title of the poem, are ultimately understood by Cendrars as a lack of "culture." There is thus a tension between Cendrars's self-reflexive acknowledgment of his own ignorance when confronting what he sees once he arrives in Brazil with the ideological construction of "culture" that is understood by default as belonging to the sense of European history and geopolitics that Cendrars himself represents and embodies within his own avant-garde project. However, once Cendrars makes it to the city of São Paulo, the poetic voice appears to grow more confident in relation to its own centrality within both the reality encountered and Cendrars's own poetic vision as represented in his collection. This particular contrast can be seen more concretely in the last poem of this first section, "Sào-Paulo" (the last poem in the original first edition of *Feuilles de route*, vol. 1, *Le Formose*). As presented in the poem, the city of

São Paulo constitutes a more familiar urban and industrialized space, providing the poetic voice with a series of more legible cultural and technological forms that facilitate the kind of "mapping" characteristic of the previous navigational part of the collection. Thus, the arrival in São Paulo represents a crucial moment within the temporality of *Feuilles de route* in which the poetic voice, while trying to repress and control the foreignness encountered ("Je crois être en gare de Nice"[30]), also highlights the unsettling nature of a spatio-temporal realm outside of a purely European geopolitical centre. For Cendrars, arriving to São Paulo's train station allows him an encounter with a more relatable and legible city space parallel to modern urban structures in European cities, such as London and Nice. The poem is thus articulated through a moment of epistemological and ontological self-recognition in relation to Cendrars's appreciation of São Paulo's modernity as well as to his own assertion of himself as the central figure in *Feuilles de route*, as highlighted in its last two lines, "Bonjour / C'est moi."[31] This ending of "Sào-Paulo" recalls here the earlier self-reflexive poems in the collection, as well as Cendrars's self-assumed "pioneering" role in his journey to Brazil and his own centrality within his own avant-garde project in the terms examined earlier in this chapter. However, it is only through this double process of self-recognition that Cendrars is able to acknowledge, for the first time within the structure of *Feuilles de route*, the presence of the key figures of Brazilian modernism he encountered on his journey ("Je trouve tous mes amis"[32]).

Travel Notes II: On Avant-Garde "Origins," Tarsila's Brazilian Modernism, and Delaunay's *Tour Eiffel* in São Paulo

The arrival of Cendrars in São Paulo in 1924 was covered by the main local newspapers of the time, and was also registered in the publications and personal archives of some of the key figures of Brazilian *modernismo*, as extensively documented by scholars Aracy Amaral, Alexandre Eulalio, and Adrien Roig.[33] However, Cendrars's encounter with the various cultural and social circles of São Paulo at such a crucial time in the development of Brazilian *modernismo* requires a further critical reconsideration related to the understanding of the historical avant-garde presented in this book beyond a more traditional European-centred perspective. On a primary level, Cendrars's arrival took place after the groundbreaking and influential *Semana de Arte Moderna* held in São Paulo's Municipal Theatre from 10 to 17 February 1922, as well as the publication of Mário de Andrade's poetry collection *Pauliceia Desvairada* (Hallucinated City), also in 1922.[34] These two events taking place in 1922 clearly mark an artistic and cultural modernist revolution in Brazil that preceded Cendrars's arrival and its potential impact across the Brazilian cultural scene of the period in many ways: while the *Semana de Arte Moderna* has been critically recognized as a central event in the development of modernism and the avant-garde outside Europe, which included the participation of most of the writers and artists who welcomed Cendrars in Brazil, Mário de Andrade's *Pauliceia Desvairada* (composed between 1921 and 1922 and published by Casa Mayença in São Paulo in 1922) constitutes an experimental response to modernity and modern urban experience that is uniquely Brazilian, not only in its modernist focus on the poetization of modern life in the city of São Paulo, but also in its aesthetic form and linguistic expression, as well as in terms of its economic, cultural, and historical references.[35] As Justin Read has shown, and in contrast to Cendrars's own understanding of the city in *Feuilles de route*, Mário de Andrade presents São Paulo as a vibrating metropolis displaying the very tensions of modern life, particularly in terms of the city's own socio-economic complexities: "If anything, the São Paulo of *Paulicéia desvairada* is a meeting ground between socio-economic classes, above and beyond the meeting of cultures."[36]

A second reason for a critical reconsideration of this specific avant-garde network in this context – and perhaps one of its most pressing – lies in the fact that the emergence of modernism in Brazil has been traditionally analysed by European and Anglo-American art and literary historians as a derivative movement that emerged only through prior contact with European avant-garde poetics and artists such as Cendrars. This traditional perspective has generally been embraced by critics on both sides of the Atlantic when describing this specific network of avant-garde artists. This is the case with Aracy Amaral, who has described Cendrars and his Parisian circle as key to the development of the new local focus that characterized Brazilian modernism, and who has interpreted this network in terms of what he refers to as the "discovery of Brazil … in Paris": "La curiosidad por el dato local … se intensifica en la década de los veinte interesada en exotismos en el círculo artístico parisiense. Es lo que se denomina el descubrimiento de Brasil…en París" (The curiosity for the local detail … intensifies itself during the decade of the 1920s with the interest in exoticisms of the Parisian circle. It is what is called the discovery of Brazil … in Paris).[37]

A particularly relevant and recent example of this historiographic problem is provided by the influential art historian and critic Juan Manuel Bonet in a revisionary study of Tarsila published as part of the catalogue of a highly influential 2009 retrospective exhibition of Tarsila's work at the Fundación Juan March in Madrid – an exhibition that can be seen as a direct precursor to Tarsila's Art Institute of Chicago / MoMA exhibitions of 2017 and 2018. Bonet, former director of both the Reina Sofía Museum of Modern Art in Madrid and the Instituto Cervantes, two extremely influential state cultural institutions in Spain, explicitly claims that the "rediscovery" of Brazil – as one of the main sources of the experimental poetics developed by Tarsila, as well as key Brazilian members of the *modernista* group – was directly dependent on the guiding influence of European artists of the period.[38] Referring in particular to Cendrars's impact on Tarsila's work, Bonet describes their collaboration as a form of strict dependency based on the guiding influence of Cendrars, who, like other European artists of the period, such as Darius Milhaud, is understood by Bonet as paving the way for Brazilian modernism to emerge: "De nuevo, como había sucedido en el caso de *Saudades do Brasil* hay que decir que es un extranjero, en este caso un poeta de otra lengua, quien marca el camino del redescubrimiento del país" (Again, as happened in the case of *Saudades do Brasil*, it must be said that it is a foreigner, in this case a foreign-language poet, who paves the way for the rediscovery of the country).[39]

Bonet's claim essentially posits the notion that a group of Brazilian modernists, including artists and intellectuals of the stature and influence of Tarsila, Oswald de Andrade, and Mário de Andrade, among others, required the (repeated) contact and actual presence in Brazil of key European figures who could "pave the way" for the "rediscovery" of their own country, culture, and aesthetic traditions. Not only does this critical assertion minimize the radical originality of the reinterpretation of Brazilian culture and history carried out by this group of Brazilian *modernistas* in the 1920s, but it also seems to ignore the problematic Eurocentric and colonial undertones of such a claim, particularly when voiced as recently as 2009. In other words, similar to Cortesão's neocolonial and almost mythical historiographic interpretation of early modern Portuguese colonialism centred around the figure of Álvares Cabral, Bonet's interpretation of this historical moment in Brazil rearticulates and reproduces a neocolonial logic at the core of Cendrars's parallel avant-garde roadmap and waybill of cultural discovery in *Feuilles de route* – and thus its mirroring of Eurocentric historicist claims regarding the notions of "cultural origins" and "territorial expansion" in relation to the development of the historical avant-garde.

Overall, Bonet's approach does not take into account the particular transnational and transcontinental dimensions of specific avant-garde poetic projects such as Tarsila's, or the complexities of their own historical and cultural relations to larger processes and networks operating beyond "Europe" as a geopolitical reality. More importantly, also implicit in Bonet's claim is the idea that it is only due to the physical presence in Brazil of key European avant-garde artists, such as Cendrars, that this "rediscovery" of Brazilian culture by the *modernistas* could be materially and symbolically exported back to Europe, and thus made legible outside the local or national confines of Brazilian literary and art history. Thus, while Bonet's critical interpretation takes Cendrars's role at face value as the essential component – its own categorical imperative, as it were – of this particular network of experimental poetics, it also minimizes the role of the Brazilian artists in the very same process of "rediscovery." Overall, it constitutes a critical interpretation of the notion of the "rediscovery" of Brazil that minimizes the sense of cultural appropriation and commodification in Milhaud's and Cendrars's respective "discoveries" of Brazilian culture during this period.

Within this context, both historical and critical, a fascinating moment marking the development of Tarsila's modernist poetics and its correlation to Cendrars's work can be historically traced back to his stay in São Paulo in 1924, particularly through the reappearance in Brazil of a key avant-garde artwork, namely Robert Delaunay's famous painting *Champs de Mars: The Red Tower* (1911; figure 3.1). Delaunay's *Champs de Mars*, held at the Art Institute of Chicago since 1953, was originally bought by Tarsila in 1923 while she was living in Paris, and soon after became one of the main works in her collection held in São Paulo.[40] In an event coinciding with Cendrars's stay in São Paulo, Tarsila exhibited Delaunay's painting at the Conservatório Dramático e Musical on 12 June 1924, in an exhibition that also included a public lecture by Cendrars, which would later be published as his essay "The Eiffel Tower."[41]

Delaunay's *Champs de Mars* thus constitutes here a key actor – in both historical and formal terms – within the larger avant-garde network explored in this chapter: the reappearance in São Paulo of Delaunay's highly influential experimental painting not only adds another dimension to the correlation between the works of Cendrars and Tarsila parallel to the publication of *Feuilles de route*, but also underscores a crucial tension between their respective understandings of avant-garde poetics, and their respective origins, as well as historical and cultural sources. Cendrars knew Delaunay well during the period in which *Champs de Mars* was produced, and had previously collaborated with him and his wife, Sonia Delaunay (formerly Sonia Terk), on various projects, most famously through her illustration of Cendrars's masterpiece *Prose of the Trans-Siberian*.[42]

In his São Paulo lecture of 1924, Cendrars highlights his own role in the events leading to the production of Delaunay's groundbreaking

Figure 3.1. Robert Delaunay, *Champs de Mars: The Red Tower* (1911–23). Oil on canvas, 63 ¼ × 50 ⅝ in. (160.7 × 128.6 cm). Joseph Winterbotham Collection, 1959.1.
Source: The Art Institute of Chicago / Art Resource, NY.

artwork, primarily by describing the time he spent together with Delaunay: "In the years 1910, 1911, Robert Delaunay and I were perhaps the only ones in Paris talking about machines and art and with a vague awareness of the great transformation of the modern world."[43] Moreover, and following the road-mapping logic that characterizes *Feuilles de route*, as described above, Cendrars presents his São Paulo audience with a first-person account of the production of Delaunay's work in what appears to constitute, in Cendrars's own words, no less than the Parisian "birth" of the historical avant-garde:

> Delaunay is increasingly drawn by what is taking place, there outside, and the infinitely minute play of light he studied in a sunray he now sees as gigantic, enormous in the luminous ocean welling over Paris ...
>
> It was then I met him.
>
> I talk to him about New York, Berlin, Moscow, about prodigious centers of industrial activity spread out over the whole surface of the earth, about the new life being formed, about universal lyricism, and that tall youth, who never left Paris and was only interested in questions of form and color, had guessed all that while he was contemplating the Tower, deciphering the first colored billboards that were beginning to cover houses, watching the birth of mechanical life in the streets before his eyes ...
>
> As soon as I could go out, I went with Delaunay to see the Tower. Here is our trip around and in the Tower.[44]

Similar to the poetic voice in *Feuilles de route*, Cendrars's account of this historical event in his Delaunay lecture presents himself again as the primary witness to the production of an experimental artwork whose form of modernity is conceptualized in historicist terms – not only as an original artwork in itself, but ultimately as an avant-garde "origin" that can be exported by Cendrars to other parts of the world as part of his larger "waybill" of avant-garde goods, in the sense examined above. In other words, Cendrars's retelling in 1924 of what appears to constitute an act of witnessing the birth in Paris of the avant-garde in 1911 provides him with the power – both material and symbolic – to ascribe value, not only to his own work, but to Delaunay's painting as well. As presented to his São Paulo audience, this shared historical experience with Delaunay emerges as an intrinsic component of Cendrars's positioning of himself as the central figure in both the avant-garde revolution in the arts and the original and radical sense of modernity embodied, in this case, in Delaunay's groundbreaking painting.

What is crucial here is that Cendrars's own narrative on the birth of the avant-garde on display in his 1924 São Paulo lecture "The Eiffel

Tower" is part of his larger rearticulation of a Eurocentric logic of progress and modernity as the categorical imperative of his own avant-garde poetic project.[45] However, this categorical imperative inherent in Cendrars's project is in tension with other critical understandings of both Delaunay's revolutionary artwork and the "origins" of the avant-garde, such as, for example, Tarsila's own critical interpretation of Delaunay's *Champs de Mars*. From this perspective, finding Delaunay's *Champs de Mars* in Brazil during his 1924 trip constitutes for Cendrars a challenge to his self-assumed centrality within the network, as well as a key turning point in the divergent paths of Cendrars's and Tarsila's respective poetics, as explored in this chapter.[46]

In Tarsila's critical essay "Delaunay e la Torre Eiffel," originally published in *Diário de São Paulo* on 26 May 1936, the Brazilian artist describes some of the key formal features of Delaunay's painting and its impact in relation to her own work, as well as its importance as a part of her own painting collection. While highlighting it as one of the most discussed works of her collection – "Entre los cuadros de mi colección de pinturas modernas, la *Torre Eiffel*, de Robert Delaunay, es el más discutido, el que mas aviva la curiosidad" (Among the works in my modern collection of paintings, the *Eiffel Tower*, by Robert Delaunay, is the one most discussed, that draws more curiosity)[47] – Tarsila also recollects Cendrars's particular response in 1924 when he found Delaunay's influential work in her possession:

> El lienzo de 1911 es como un torbellino, la Torre, dinámica, fragmentada como si fuese vista al pasar en tren rapidísimo o un aeroplano, aparece en medio del cuadro. Inmensa, dominándolo todo, achatando los edificios de siete pisos plantados en París en la neutralidad del gris oscuro. Ese es el cuadro de mi colección, el de 1911, la decantada Torre tan conocida, tan reproducida en revistas de arte. El poeta Blaise Cendrars, al encontrarla aquí en São Paulo, tuvo un gesto de alegría y sorpresa, su imaginación hirvió al descubrir una grieta en una esquina del lienzo y describió la actitud indignada de Jean Cocteau ante las palabras pronunciadas en nombre del pasado contra el símbolo del espíritu moderno.
>
> (The painting of 1911 is like a whirlwind, with the Tower, dynamic and fragmented as if seen from a fast train or airplane, appearing in the middle of the painting in its full dynamic force – immense, dominating it all, collapsing the seven-story buildings of Paris with the neutrality of a dark grey. That is the painting in my collection, that of 1911, the tilted Tower so well known, and reproduced in art magazines so many times. The poet Blaise Cendrars, upon finding that painting here in São Paulo, had a

> gesture of joy and surprise, with his imagination boiling upon discovering a crack in a corner of the canvas. He described Jean Cocteau's indignant attitude at the words voiced in the name of the past against the symbol of the modern spirit.)[48]

Tarsila is here referring to two main aspects in relation to Delaunay's *Champs de Mars* as part of her collection in São Paulo: while highlighting Delaunay's avant-garde rearticulation of traditional approaches to the pictorial representation of perspective, Tarsila also describes Cendrars's response when seeing the painting in the hands of Tarsila in 1924, and his first-person account of encountering Delaunay's work during the first decade of the twentieth century in Paris.

On the one hand, Tarsila's formal analysis of Delaunay's work highlights its dynamic fragmentation of perspective, and the innovative experience of modernity represented in this painting, providing a critical interpretation that underscores Delaunay's radical collapse of traditional representations of time and space as central, and never alien, to Tarsila's own work and understanding of avant-garde poetics.[49] For Tarsila, Delaunay's experimental conceptualization of visuality is grounded on a more abstract approach to colour beyond the representation of a specific object or meaning that highlights the very materiality of the artwork, a notion in line with the *Pau Brasil* period of Brazilian modernism (which will be explored further in the final section of this chapter):

> La pintura, para él, debe resumirse en colores, el dibujo no existe, la aplicación de un color junto a otro formará una línea sin intención de limitar la superficie, sin darle una determinada forma que signifique alguna cosa, que represente un objeto. El interés está en la técnica, en la materia.
>
> (Painting, for him, consists of colour, in an exclusion of drawing in which the application of one colour next to another configures a line without limiting a surface, or providing a certain shape that may mean something, or represent an object. The interest is in the technique, in matter.)[50]

On the other hand, Tarsila's comments underscore Cendrars's specific response to finding Delaunay's work in São Paulo: a sense of relative shock and surprise when finding the painting in Tarsila's possession that is further developed in the lecture that Cendrars gave parallel to the 1924 exhibition of the painting. In contrast to Cendrars's understanding of this key moment of the historical avant-garde represented in Delaunay's *Champs de Mars*, Tarsila presents the ideas of simultaneity, as well as the new experience of traditional representations of time and space not as external, or "foreign," to her own experience of modernity, but rather as intrinsically related to a new rearticulation of Brazilian art.

In other words, Tarsila's own poetic project and interpretation of the avant-garde – which will become central to the Brazilian modernist revolution and the *Pau Brasil* movement – can, and perhaps should, be considered as central to the historical avant-garde as Delaunay's and Cendrars's respective works and conceptualizations of experimental poetics. In fact, contrary to Cendrars's self-centred and Paris-based interpretation of avant-garde origins, Tarsila's development of an avant-garde understanding of modernity, as described in a retrospective essay from 1950, took place primarily in Brazil prior to her 1923 stay in Paris, in a process deeply connected to her own local sense of both history and a "heightened" visual representation:

> Parece mentira … mais foi no Brasil que tomei contato com a arte moderno (o mesmo se deu, aliás, com Graça Aranha), e, estimulada pelos meus amigos, pintei alguns quadros onde a minha exaltação se comprazia na violência do colorido. Depois de permanência em São Paulo, voltei a Paris e o ano de 1923 foi o mais importante na minha carreira artística.
>
> (It may not seem true … but it was in Brazil that I made true contact with modern art [the same happened with Graça Aranha]. It was there, encouraged by my friends, where I produced some paintings in which my exaltation was indulged in the intensity of colour. After a stay in São Paulo, I returned to Paris, and the year 1923 was the most important in my artistic career.)[51]

Ultimately, for Tarsila, these very same central avant-garde features also emerge in Brazil as part of an overall act of resistance to previous traditional forms of knowledge and history that, in my reading, is central and not marginal, simultaneous and not belated, to the same aesthetic revolution embodied in Delaunay's painting in her possession, as well as its divergence from Cendrars's avant-garde project articulated in *Feuilles de route*.

Travel Notes III ("et le Bresil fut découvert" / "por ocasião da descuberta de Brasil"): Cendrars's "Discovery" of Brazil, Oswald de Andrade's *Pau Brasil*, and the Diverging Routes of an Avant-Garde Network

In order to further examine the various implications of the forms of planetary engagement articulated by this specific avant-garde network, and as a conclusion to this chapter, I refer to another crucial event that emerges as closely related to both Tarsila's and Cendrars's work during this period: the publication of Oswald de Andrade's foundational poetry collection *Pau Brasil*, perhaps the essential work in the articulation of Brazilian *modernismo*, and arguably one of the most crucial moments in the development of the Latin American avant-garde. As Carlos Jáuregui has argued in his influential study of cultural anthropophagy across Latin America, *Canibalia*, Andrade's revolutionary *Pau Brasil* collection is central not only to an understanding of the early period of Brazilian *modernismo*, but also to the influential *antropofagia* movement that would be initiated by Andrade with the publication of the *Manifesto Antropófago* in 1928.[52] Andrade's *Pau Brasil* is divided into nine different sections, providing, as a whole, an innovative poetic journey across the history, geography, and culture of Brazil, always from Andrade's own understanding of the "discovery of Brazil" as the foundation of an avant-garde poetics.[53]

Within the specific focus of this chapter, Andrade's *Pau Brasil* collection plays a crucial role within the overall tension and divergent understanding of experimental poetics at the core of the network connecting Cendrars's work to the development of Brazilian *modernismo*. It is important to highlight that Andrade's *Pau Brasil* was first published in 1925 by the Parisian publisher Au Sans Pareil, which also published the first edition of Cendrars's *Feuilles de route*, a publisher with whom Cendrars also collaborated as an editor. In its first edition, which also included a prologue by Paulo Prado from 1924 and a series of illustrations by Tarsila preceding each of the nine sections, Andrade's *Pau Brasil* was originally dedicated to Cendrars with the following epigraph: "A Blaise Cendrars por ocasião da descuberta de Brasil" (To Blaise Cendrars, because of the discovery of Brazil).[54] While this dedication to Cendrars in *Pau Brasil*, and the related reference to a sense of cultural "discovery" of Brazil, may seem like a small anecdote and ironic gesture, it is particularly relevant within the larger critical and historical context of the development of Brazilian *modernista* and *antropofagia* movements and its relation to Cendrars's work and the European avant-garde.

On a primary level, Andrade's sense of "discovery" of local culture as the foundation for a new avant-garde poetics presented in his influential collection emerges as a parallel but radically different poetic project than the one articulated by Cendrars in *Feuilles de route*, as examined above.[55] This radical sense of avant-garde revolution as a new "discovery" of Brazil is specifically expressed by Andrade in the manifesto that precedes the poems included in *Pau Brasil*, and which sets the tone for the rest of the collection. The manifesto was originally published in

1924 as the "Manifesto da Poesia Pau-Brasil," in which Cendrars also happens to figure prominently, as shown in this particular fragment:

> País de dores anônimas. De doutôres anônimos. Sociedade de náufragos eruditos.
>
> Donde a nunca exportação de poesia. A poesia emaranhada na cultura. Nos cipós das metrificações.
>
> Século vinte. Um estouro nos aprendimentos. Os homens que sabiam tudo se deformaram como babéis de borracha. Rebentaram de enciclopedismo.
>
> A poesia para os poetas. Alegria da ignorância que descobre. Pedr'Álvares.
>
> Uma sugestão de Blaise Cendrars: —Tendes as locomotivas cheias, ides partir. Um negro gira a manivela do desvio rotativo em que estais. O menor descuido vos fará partir na direção oposta a vosso destino ...[56]
>
> (Country of anonymous pain. Of anonymous doctors. Society of learned castaways.
>
> Where poetry was never exported from. Poetry tangled in culture. In the creepers of metrification.
>
> The twentieth century. A blast in learning. The men who knew everything collapsed like rubber Towers of Babel. They burst from so much encyclopedism.
>
> Poetry for poets. The bliss of an ignorance that discovers. Pedr'Álvares.
>
> A suggestion from Blaise Cendrars: Have your locomotives ready, depart! A black man cranks the handle of the rotational divergence in which you exist. The slightest slip will make you head in the direction opposite your destination.)[57]

Not only does poetry appear as central to the process of cultural rediscovery envisioned by Andrade in this manifesto, but it also entails a radical departure from tradition as a way of rearticulating the sense of planetary alterity and divergence within the Brazilian modernist movement, to which I will return at the end of this chapter, particularly in terms of the complex racial politics connecting both Andrade's and Tarsila's work during this period.

As embodied in *Pau Brasil*, Andrade's reimagining of a new poetic modernity highlights the sense of urgency at the core of the need to establish itself against the dominance of European literary models and forms of literary history, while also highlighting Cendrars's impact on Andrade's own conception of modernist poetics. In particular, the explicit invocation of the historical figure of Pedro Álvares Cabral in the *Pau Brasil* manifesto ("Pedr'Álvares") unveils Cendrars's and Andrade's divergent positionalities in relation to the sense of the "discovery of Brazil" in this context. While Cendrars invokes Álvares Cabral in *Feuilles de route* as a mirror image of his own epic journey of poetic discovery to Brazil from a Eurocentric geopolitical position, as shown above, the same figure is seen by Andrade in *Pau Brasil* as a marker of a much larger and complex process of cultural rearticulation of Brazil as a postcolonial nation-state whose modernity is in direct tension with the European socio-cultural models imposed by Portugal across its colonial empire.

Thus, the poetic recuperation of the figure of Álvares Cabral within their network of experimental poetics signifies both a historical event within the "categorical imperative" of the European neocolonial impulse traceable in Cendrars's *Feuilles de route*, on the one hand, and a reimagining of poetic tradition within the perspective of Andrade as a representative member of Brazilian *modernismo*, on the other. In other words, while Cendrars's poetry collection aims to map out his own "discovery" process of Brazil – as central to the expansion of his poetic project, as well as to his process of self-discovery and rejuvenation – Andrade presents a parallel but differing reading that explicitly resists such a Paris-centred "discovery," mapping, and potential "exportation" of Brazil back to Europe as conceptualized by Cendrars. In this sense, Andrade's own modernist invocation of Álvares Cabral highlights a form of local creative impulse that builds upon – challenging and overcoming – traditional forms of knowledge intrinsic to Brazilian history and cultural identity in 1924, in stark contrast to Cendrars's reading of Brazilian culture as still representing, in that same year, an absent sense of "culture," as in the poem "Ignorance," examined above (i.e., "Qu'il n'y a aucune trace de culture"[58]). As Stephanie D'Alessandro has remarked, the mention of Álvares Cabral in Andrade's *Pau-Brasil* manifesto entails a rejection of an understanding of Brazilian culture as a mere "product imported from Europe": "He implied this by referring to the first Portuguese navigator, Pedro Álvares Cabral, to describe the sky. Instead, he called for the production of uniquely Brazilian work that – like the prized pau brazil (brazilwood) tree itself – could only come from Brazilian soil."[59]

Cendrars's and Andrade's differing positionalities, and the related tension connected to their respective understandings of the "discovery" of Brazil, are also explicitly highlighted in the complex publication history of Andrade's *Pau Brasil* collection, particularly in Andrade's later removal of Cendrars's name from its epigraph, simply leaving it as "por ocasião da descuberta de Brasil."[60] While the original inclusion of

Cendrars's name in the epigraph suggests a sense of collective process of discovery – related to a shared avant-garde aesthetic vision and poetics that connects Cendrars's European avant-garde logic and Andrade's modernist commitment to a new Brazilian literature – the later removal of Cendrars's name from the dedication seems to have been aimed at avoiding the appearance of having a sole European "discoverer" of what for Andrade constitutes a much larger process of modernist cultural rearticulation. In this sense, the significant removal of Cendrars's name emphasizes an attempt to assert a local creative source through an important sense of cultural agency for this collective effort of rediscovery at the core of the *Pau Brasil* movement within the larger history of Brazilian *modernismo*.

Overall, there appears to be a fundamental difference in the actual understanding and experience of this very network of experimental literature and art connecting Cendrars and Brazilian *modernismo* as conceptualized primarily by Tarsila do Amaral and Oswald de Andrade – in terms of both the historical actors involved and how their avant-garde network has been critically understood and historicized a posteriori. This difference is, in my analysis, related to Bruno Latour's distinction between a conceptualization of the network as a "result" and an understanding of the network as a "process," previously examined in the introduction. For Latour this double sense of the network is a crucial distinction, as he argues here:

> The distinction between the two senses of the word network would be the same if she were interested in railroads: following the tracks is not the same as investigating the French national railroad company. And it would still be the same if, taking the word more metaphorically, she wanted to investigate "networks of influence": here, too, what circulates when everything is in place cannot be confused with the setups that make circulation possible.[61]

Latour's analogy of the dual conception of the railroad as network provides an apt framework for the current analysis of the avant garde network of experimental poetics examined in this chapter. Latour's conception helps highlight Cendrars's dependency on the very networks of spatial and material travel and circulation of culture already established, and which made his own journey to and across Brazil in 1924 materially possible. At the same time, in considering Latour's paradigm, Cendrars also appears to be mostly uninterested in investigating in much detail that same network as an actual process connected to the social and historical conditions of existence – intrinsically related to the process of the Portuguese colonization of Brazil – of the very people and institutions that facilitated his own arrival in the city of São Paulo and his stay in Brazil during 1924.

It is thus not surprising that Cendrars's collection barely makes any specific reference throughout *Feuilles de route* to the work, or the artistic and cultural significance of the key artists he encounters in Brazil. Other than the dedication of the book mentioned above, his only reference to the members of the Brazilian *modernista* collective is when he describes them as "mes amis" (my friends) in a few instances in the collection, and a final reference to Oswald de Andrade's "blues" or sadness ("Oswald qui a le cafard"[62]) when Cendrars leaves São Paulo in the first poem of section 3 of *Feuilles de route*, "Depart." Thus, as opposed to experiencing the network as a process that connects a complex series of overlapping actors (artists, works, personalities, poetics, histories, material means of transportation, etc.), Cendrars is mostly invested in the (rather personal) result of the actual network as it facilitates his own encounter with Brazil, as shown in *Feuilles de route* – belatedly and after the fact, as pointed out by Latour in relation to the "result" sense of his dual understanding of a network. From this perspective, the main relevance for Cendrars of the actual network in which he is participating is essentially the result that allows him to get where and what he was originally looking for in Brazil (i.e., its cultural and poetic incorporation into his own avant-garde project).[63]

On the other hand, this same network is experienced in a very different way by Tarsila and Oswald de Andrade, as well as many of the Brazilian artists who welcomed Cendrars to Brazil in 1924. In contrast to Cendrars's experience of this network, documented in *Feuilles de route,* their experience appears to be understood as a more complex and collective process, in terms of their poetic remaking of Brazilian cultural and literary forms as a larger critical response to the social, economic, and historical conditions of Brazil as a postcolonial society, in relation to both Portugal's colonial history and European forms of historiography and literary traditions. As shown here, by incorporating the reflections and works produced by the Brazilian *modernista* collective as part of the same period and network, even in incomplete form, we are able to present a richer and more complex understanding of this artistic and historical process, and consequently of the historical avant-garde as a whole – one that emerges beyond a question of particular (and alleged) European-centred origins, sources, and influences.[64]

Ultimately, the examination of this avant-garde network unveils a fluid and collaborative process that can be best described in terms of what Mário de Andrade originally referred to as a "correlation" when relating his first impressions of the collaboration between Tarsila and Cendrars. As Mário de Andrade highlighted in his review of the first edition of *Feuilles de route*, published in the modernist journal *A Revista* in 1925, there is a parallel simplified construction of the image connecting the work of Cendrars and Tarsila, in their respective art forms, at the core of their inter-artistic collaboration:

> A nova coleção de poesias de Blaise Cendrars vem comentada pela ingenuidade construtiva do traço solido e tranquilo de Tarsila do Amaral. Não se pode deixar de notar a correlação que existe entre a arte da pintora brasileira e a do poeta francez. Ha em ambos a calma architectonica da linha precisa. Feuilles de Route são desenhos simplificados das paisagens por onde Cendrars passou.
>
> (The new collection of poems by Blaise Cendrars is illustrated by the constructive ingenuity of the solid and quiet trace of Tarsila do Amaral. One cannot avoid pointing out the correlation that exists between the art of the Brazilian painter and the French poet. There is in both the architectonic calmness of the precise line. *Feuilles de route* is composed of simplified designs of the landscapes through which Cendrars passed.)[65]

On a primary level, Mário de Andrade's reference to this "correlation" between the poems by Cendrars and the illustrations by Tarsila specifically highlights Tarsila's authorial role in relation to Cendrars's poetry collection. By emphasizing the formal similarities between the work of both artists, Andrade underscores the importance of a shared experience of experimental form at the core of this correlation – a correlative figuration based on the "calmness of the precise line" that can be connected both to the "cinepoetic" dimension of Cendrars's poetry and to the sense of simultaneity of perspectives and "intensity of color" at the core of Tarsila's conception of painting during this period. Andrade's critical recognition of this correlation at the level of experimental form directly connects the avant-garde artwork itself with the experience of encountering a landscape – in other words, as a planetary figuring of aesthetic form that emerges at its core through an encounter with and experience of alterity in the world.

Moreover, as Andrade's conception of this correlation highlights, there is a conscious collective impulse in their respective experiences of this network that, as shown in this chapter, connects Cendrars's avant-garde project to the forms of planetary engagement embraced by the Brazilian *modernista* movement in the early 1920s. Some of these key collaborative and relational features are also highlighted by Tarsila in the following passage from a retrospective essay on the development of the *Pau Brasil* and *Antropofagia* periods of Brazilian *modernismo*:

> Em 1924 (depois de alguns anos de Europa), numa viagem a Minas em companhia de um grupo de intelectuais, impressionei-me com ambiente, realmente tradicional. Nas casas coloniais de Ouro Preto, São João del Rei, Tiradentes, Sabará, Mariana e outras cidades, fui encontrar as cores vivas, azul, rosa, amarelo, que tanto me falavam à sensibilidade no meu tempo de menina e que me diziam serem caipiras e feias. Emancipada pelo cubismo que importara de Europa, vinguei-me da coação de tantos anos, transportando essas mesmas cores, vivas e limpas, para a minhas telas, que se transformaram em Brasil. Criei uma pintura simplesmente brasileira, sem nome. Em 1925, um ano depois, Oswald de Andrade lançava o *Pau-Brasil*, livro que teve grande repercussão e influências no país. Esse livro foi ilustrado por mim ... Convém notar que Oswald de Andrade, (em companhia de Mário de Andrade, Blaise Cendrars e outros) fazia parte do grupo que partiu de São Paulo para Minas ao redescobrimento do Brasil.
>
> (In 1924 [after a few years in Europe], on a trip to Minas with a group of intellectuals, I was struck by a truly traditional environment. In the colonial houses of Ouro Preto, São João del Rei, Tiradentes, Sabara, Mariana and other towns, I found the bright colours – blue, pink, yellow – that spoke so deeply to the sensibility of my time as a child and that they had told me were *caipira* and ugly. Liberated by the cubism I had imported from Europe, I took revenge on the coercion of so many years, transporting those same bright and clean colours that, in my canvases, became Brazil. I created a simply Brazilian form of painting, without a name. In 1925, a year later, Oswald de Andrade launched *Pau Brasil*, a book that had great repercussions and impact in our country. This book was illustrated by me ... It is worth noting that Oswald de Andrade [accompanied by Mário de Andrade, Blaise Cendrars and others], was part of the group that left São Paulo for Minas Gerais to rediscover Brazil.)[66]

Tarsila's description of this process, as well as the mention of the influential trip of their avant-garde group to Minas Gerais, which also included Cendrars – a foundational trip that figures prominently as well in Andrade's *Pau Brasil*, particularly in the section "Roteiro das Minas" – highlights not only the sense of collective artistic agency that emerged parallel to their experience of travel and discovery, but also the rediscovery of a poetics that had already emerged for Tarsila prior to her journeys to Europe ("que tanto me falavam à sensibilidade no meu tempo de menina que me diziam serem caipiras e feias").

It is precisely the formal and political dimension of these forms of planetary engagement that seems crucial to examine in order to unveil the sense of tension and, ultimately, divergence in the paths followed by Cendrars and Tarsila within their network of experimental poetics.[67] This tension – understood as both correlation and divergence – at the core of their respective understandings of avant-garde poetics can in fact be seen in the illustrations by Tarsila included in the first edition of Cendrars's *Feuilles de route*, which are closely related to the aforementioned 1924 trip to Minas Gerais with Cendrars. The first five illustrations (on pages 14, 18, 23, 34, and 56 of *Le Formose*) represent a series of abstract landscapes, in Tarsila's characteristic style during this period, constituted by "postcard-like" sketches of small rural homes and natural areas – which appear to mirror the "cinepoetic" descriptions included in the early series of poems through which Cendrars's describes the journey to Brazil in the collection.

However, the sixth illustration by Tarsila (included in page 64) – which corresponds to the section of the poetry collection in which Cendrars describes the actual encounter with the city of São Paulo as represented in the collection – clearly departs from the sketch-like simplicity of the previous five illustrations. This image by Tarsila is characterized by a multiplicity of smaller images juxtaposed with each other, and is marked at the bottom right corner with the words "Serra da Mantiqueira" and "Rio Parahyba," which, in contrast to the other illustrations, explicitly locate the image in relation to the Mantiqueira Mountains (a mountain range spanning the states of São Paulo, Minas Gerais, and Rio de Janeiro in south-eastern Brazil) and the Paraíba do Sul River. Tarsila's sixth illustration in *Le Formose* is overall configured by a series of fragmentary sketches of different local figures (human, natural, and architectonic) that are juxtaposed with each other.[68] At the same time, the illustration also includes a series of words in Portuguese related to some of the images represented in the picture – "hortensias" (hydrangeas), "campo" (field), "girasol" (sunflower), "palmeiras cauda de pavão" (peacock-tail palm trees) – which clearly contrast with the lack of words in her previous illustrations, and, for that matter, with the absence of the Portuguese language in the rest of the poetry collection by Cendrars. Overall, this image by Tarsila powerfully sketches and locates, within the textual and poetic realm of Cendrars's own avant-garde "mapping" of Brazil in *Le Formose*, the significance of the very people, buildings, and objects that collectively comprise the local specificity of this geographic and cultural region of Brazil. Through this illustration, together with the other five included in *Le Formose*, Tarsila thus manages to inscribe within Cendrars's own avant-garde "travel notes," and from a radically Brazilian modernist stance, precisely the same sense of local specificity that lies at the very core of her own understanding of avant-garde poetics.

From this perspective, Tarsila's own sense of correlation between the collective development of a new modernist aesthetics related to an experience of local travel and landscape across Brazil appears to be connected to the notion of "errant modernism" developed by Esther Gabara. Gabara's conceptualization of Latin American modernism in general, and Brazilian *modernismo* in particular, focuses on the medium of photography and its representations of landscape, particularly in relation to an uneven experience of modernity simultaneously portrayed through a series of "photographic landscapes that *err*."[69] Gabara's definition of the logic of errancy, in relation to the work of Mário de Andrade in particular, is in this sense applicable to the correlation between collective travel and a modernist "visual" rediscovery of the local at the core of the experimental poetics network connecting Cendrars with Tarsila and Oswald de Andrade, and the development of the *Pau Brasil* movement:

> Modernist erring contains two movements: the first judgment locates an original error, which must be corrected by an intervening act; the second finds the first intervention to be already wrong and proclaims an aesthetic result of error itself ... Errant abstraction maintains the place of figurative landscape, even as it distorts its content and appearance.[70]

The sense of correlation explored in this chapter as part of a shared network of experimental poetics is precisely articulated upon the double movement of "modernist erring" described here by Gabara. In the case of Tarsila, this "modernist erring" is related to the finding of an error ("the bright colours ... they had told me were *caipira* and ugly") that can be turned through experimental form into a new "aesthetic result" able to radically alter Brazilian cultural and aesthetic traditions ("those same bright and clean colours that, in my canvases, became Brazil"). It is the occurrence of this transformational modernist strategy that facilitates an overlapping of differing perspectives, as well as a Brazilian response on Tarsila's part – clearly divergent from Cendrars's – to the larger questions on the experience of modernity, experimental form, and the very historicity of the avant-garde. This complex process of erring, in Gabara's sense, is directly related to the formal correlation that leads up to a new aesthetic manifestation of modernist poetics – differing from Cendrars's – as a form of planetary engagement that is central, and not marginal, to the historical avant-garde when understood as a transnational and transcontinental process that can diverge, and not just derive, from the work of European authors during this period.

In sum, based on the approach and analysis developed in this chapter, the experience of the network as process radically exceeds the particular result originally sought by Cendrars when he embarked on his journey to Brazil in 1924. As shown here, Cendrars's "waybill" to Brazil articulated by *Feuilles de route* as a whole ultimately aims to return and revert back – "bien loins de Montmartre" (far away from Montmartre), the key line that the poetic voice repeats throughout Cendrars's *Prose of the Trans-Siberian* – to the Parisian centre of this poetic vision by explicitly incorporating Brazil, always seen by Cendrars as source material for his own avant-garde project, and as part of a much larger process of cultural translation and commodification to be exported for his European audience and their eventual consumption. The temporality of this neocolonial logic, which collapses more than four hundred years of the complex history of European colonialism of the Americas, is perhaps best exemplified by the explicit invocation of Christopher Columbus in one of the poems included in the final section of *Feuilles de route*, which almost closes the series of poems, and which was written while Cendrars was finally making his way back to Europe aboard the SS *Gelria*. In the poem "Christophe Colomb," Cendrars solemnly concludes: "Ce que je perds de vue aujourd'hui en me dirigeant vers l'est c'est ce que Christophe Colomb découvrait en se dirigeant vers l'ouest."[71]

Ultimately, the main critical implication of closely following Cendrars's lead in his poetization of the journey to Brazil documented in *Feuilles de route*, and of claiming him, as both Bonet and Amaral do, as a necessary European artist for the cultural "rediscovery" of Brazil "in Paris" for figures such as Tarsila and Oswald de Andrade, is that it overly simplifies the network of experimental poetics that emerges during Cendrars's trip to Brazil in 1924, as well as the series of critical, historical, and poetic implications related to this network. As this chapter has shown, this is a critical over-simplification that reduces not only the complex, collaborative, and fluid nature of relations inherent to their network, but also its material, historical, and spatio-temporal conditions. It also assumes, perhaps too readily and at face value, that the historicist assertion of an alleged "European" origin for the avant-garde embodied, in this case, in Cendrars's avant-garde project – and its related sense of both an intrinsic modernity and a historicity, as highlighted by Bürger, that has become hegemonic within critical studies of the avant-garde – constitutes a notion that is never politically countered or resisted during the same historical moment by avant-garde artists from and across different parts of the world outside Europe. These are extremely influential artists who, as shown here in the case of Brazilian *modernismo*, are explicitly and actively involved in the very same networks and aesthetic experimentation related to the emergence and development of the historical avant-garde in their own terms and geopolitical contexts.

As opposed to the mapping process at the core of Cendrars's *Feuilles de route* examined in the first section of this chapter, it is the sense of correlation, in the sense highlighted by Mário de Andrade, that appears as the essential formal feature of the larger network of experimental poetics. While the two are parallel on a formal level, the divergence in the poetics of Cendrars and Tarsila becomes manifest in the political implications and respective understandings of history as both dimensions pertain to the question of planetary engagement, particularly in relation to Iberian colonialism, as explored in this book. In other words, the question of planetary engagement unveils a sense of political divergence that transcends the traditional questions of origins, tradition, and influence at the core of the historicity of the avant-garde, as posed by Bürger.

One of the values of this particular sense of planetary engagement is how it can help establish the historical positionality of the Brazilian avant-garde in their own terms as central to the larger history and theory of the historical avant-garde, as a political dimension that is central to the very understanding of experimental form within this very network, as the following remarks by Sergio Millet on Tarsila's work highlight: "Su obra … no es únicamente valiosa como realización artística, de las más originales que hemos visto en Brasil, sino tambien como realizacion poética y como documentación, por muy paradójica que sea, de la adolescencia de nuestro país (Her work … is not only valuable as an artistic achievement, of the most originals that we have seen in Brazil, but also as a poetic achievement and as a documentation, as paradoxical as it may be, of the adolescence of our country).[72]

It is in this sense that one of the key contributions of Brazilian *modernista* project articulated by figures such as Tarsila and Oswald de Andrade is to provide a new political understanding of Brazil's own history as a postcolonial nation trying to disarticulate and move away from the institutional and cultural legacies of Portuguese colonialism and imperialism. Inherent in this process towards aesthetic independence is also an effort to provide through experimental form a new geopolitical understanding of the avant-garde itself as a transnational movement that transcends a purely European historiographic model and understanding of its own history. As shown in this chapter, these two related claims (an aesthetic or poetic understanding of alterity, and a transnational understanding of the local vis-à-vis a larger sense of history and empire) go hand in hand, as part of this same network, and are central to the notion of planetary engagement explored in this book.

There is no doubt that, in the contemporary moment, their contributions require further consideration, particularly in relation to the question of race and the legacy of slavery in Brazil as represented in the key avant-garde works by Tarsila and Oswald de Andrade. Tarsila's work commodified and objectified the figures of Afro-descendant men and women as part of her own aesthetic project as a visual artist, as in the particular case of the painting *A Negra*, included on the cover of *Le Formose*, as well as in her sixth illustration in the collection examined above. The case of her painting *A Negra* is particularly problematic since not only is it a portrait of an Afro-descendant woman portrayed with highly deformed physical features, but also, as Tarsila acknowledges, it was in fact an experimental painting representing one of the descendants of slaves living on her own family's estate. At the same time, Oswald de Andrade's influential *Pau Brasil* manifesto also objectifies Afro-descendants as part of his modernist poetic vision: in the passage quoted earlier in this chapter, an unnamed Black male figure initiates through his anonymous work and effort the very sense of alterity and motion that pervades the impactful planetary image of "the rotational divergence in which you exist" at this crucial moment of the manifesto: "Un negro gira a manivela do desvio rotativo em que estais. O menor descuido vos fará partir na direção oposta a vosso destino" (A black man cranks the handle of the rotational divergence in which you exist. The slightest slip will make you head in the direction opposite your destination).[73] As argued by scholars and critics in both the US and Brazil in relation to the recent exhibitions and retrospectives of Tarsila's work in particular, and Brazilian *modernismo* in general, these retrospectives to some degree avoid critically tackling and considering, as part of their important revisionist effort in recuperating the figure of Tarsila, the difficult and painful politics of race and the legacy of slavery as they appear as part of this crucial moment of the Brazilian modernist movement.[74]

Overall, the forms of planetary engagement traced in this chapter in the work of Tarsila and Oswald de Andrade in relation to Cendrars's work demonstrate a resistance to a Eurocentric reading of their network, as well as an attempt to reconsider through their work their own historical and postcolonial positionality, and their unique contributions to a transnational revolution in the arts embodied in the historical avant-garde. As shown here, as opposed to a traditional interpretation of the network as result, an understanding of the network as process facilitates the emergences of a series of other relations, artworks, events, and outcomes beyond both Cendrars and the European avant-garde as the hegemonic centre of our understanding of this network in particular, and the historical avant-garde in general, as well as beyond the authorial control of Tarsila and Oswald de Andrade in their visual and poetic reimaginings of Brazilian culture. This is a network whose history and actors require further critical attention; one whose main sources, artworks, and voices merit wider examination; one that is not yet completely understood in its complexity; and one whose various ramifications and implications, inclusions and elisions, and included and silenced voices deserve to be further explored for a more complete and nuanced understanding of the historical avant-garde.

Chapter Four

The Spectre of Translation: Angela Manalang Gloria, José Garcia Villa, Claro Recto, and the Comparative Poetics of Modernism in the Philippines

In a key passage of his critical exploration of nationalism in Southeast Asia in *The Spectre of Comparisons*, Benedict Anderson powerfully recuperates a crucial moment within José Rizal's *Noli me tángere*. Anderson, searching for words in 1963 to express the feeling of "vertigo" after listening to then president of Indonesia, Sukarno, presents in this passage a complex instance of cultural, historical, and epistemological anxiety. As Anderson details, it was almost twenty-five years after listening to Sukarno, and only after reading a passage from the 1886 masterpiece by José Rizal – generally considered the father of nationalism in the Philippines – that he is finally able to name his own anxiety as a form of "double vision":

> For the first time in my young life I had been invited to see my Europe as through an inverted telescope ... I did not find a good name for this experience till almost a quarter of a century later, when I was in the Philippines and teaching myself to read Spanish by stumbling through José Rizal's extraordinary nationalist novel *Noli Me Tangere*. There is a dizzying moment early in the narrative when the young mestizo hero, recently returned to the colonial Manila of the 1880s from a long sojourn in Europe, looks out of his carriage window at the municipal botanical gardens, and finds that he too is, so to speak, at the end of an inverted telescope. These gardens are shadowed automatically – Rizal says *maquinalmente* – and inescapably by images of their sister gardens in Europe. He can no longer matter-of-factly experience them, but sees them simultaneously close up and from afar. The novelist arrestingly names the agent of this incurable double vision *el demonio de las comparaciones*. So that's what it was in 1963, I said to myself: the spectre of comparisons.[1]

Anderson's critical recognition that the only way to name the vertigo of seeing "Europe as through an inverted telescope" happens to be precisely through Rizal's "spectre of comparisons," or rather "el demonio de las comparaciones" in the original, constitutes a fascinating case for comparison. Anderson interprets Rizal's fictional articulation of this instance of "double vision" as a comparative interpretation of a Manila city scene in *Noli me tángere,* which had previously seemed natural to the novel's protagonist, Juan Crisóstomo Ibarra y Magsalin. As originally articulated in his novel, Rizal's literary representation of "double vision," in the terms highlighted by Anderson, describes the effects of the hero departing for the European metropole and then returning to Spain's Southeast Asian colony, which he views with a renewed political agency and perspective. As Anderson argues, Rizal's description of the protagonist's return from Europe presents the old Manila scene as a "mechanical" reproduction of its European models: "He can no longer matter-of-factly experience them, but sees them simultaneously close up and from afar."[2]

In the particular passage of *Noli me tángere* to which Anderson refers, the narrator of Rizal's novel presents Ibarra as he is re-experiencing Manila following his return from a formative journey to Europe, in a re-encounter with his homeland that mirrors Rizal's own return after his European sojourn between 1882 and 1887.[3] This contemplative moment in the novel not only recalls the protagonist's own childhood memories in the Philippines, but also recuperates and juxtaposes ("maquinalmente" or "mechanically") a series of memories of Ibarra's adult experiences in the neighbourhood of Lavapiés in Madrid, Spain, which are now recollected in relation to his present experience of the Philippine capital. Thus, as his protagonist is contemplating Manila's botanical garden, Rizal uses the figure of "el demonio de las comparaciones" in order to denote Ibarra's own memory of European botanical gardens, "en los países donde se necesitaba mucha voluntad y mucho oro para que brote una hoja y abra su cáliz una flor" (in countries that need plenty of will and plenty of gold for a leaf to sprout, and for a flower to open its calyx).[4]

While for Rizal this act of comparison is grounded in a complex sensorial, almost synesthetic, amalgamation of smells, sounds, and voices experienced in two different continents that bring a series of past memories into the present, Anderson's related act of comparison emphasizes a visual sense of replication inherent in the colonial botanical garden in relation to its European models: "These gardens are shadowed automatically – Rizal says *maquinalmente* – and inescapably by images of their sister gardens in Europe."[5] By switching the emphasis in the actual object of comparison, Anderson establishes a comparative relation focused on the ghostly apparition of an image, which he reads as a mechanical reproduction of a European colonial model imposed onto the Southeast Asian colony. Moreover, Anderson's authorial choice to translate Rizal's original phrase "el demonio de las comparaciones" into the English "the spectre of comparisons" is not inconsequential. While the Spanish term *demonio* literally means "demon" or "devil" and generally has strong religious and cultural implications, Anderson's use of the word "spectre" (which is semantically closer to the Spanish terms *espectro* or *fantasma*) reveals a different kind of ghostly and haunting connotation.[6]

It is precisely this semantic difference between the original and its translation that establishes Anderson's comparative critical reading here, using Rizal's original fictional description as part of Anderson's own translated sense of "double vision." While there is a level of untranslatability in Rizal's singular expression in Spanish (which itself could be regarded as a version of the traditional saying "Las comparaciones son odiosas" [comparisons are odious]), Anderson's English translation clearly steers the original implications of Rizal's words into a new critical paradigm and interpretive community.[7] From this perspective, Anderson's "spectre of comparisons" as the translation of Rizal's original "demonio de las comparaciones" articulates a comparative connection that is structured through four key steps: (i) a failure of one's own language to denote an event that no longer seems familiar; (ii) the recognition of the linguistic articulation of the same failure in a different linguistic form (i.e., Rizal's passage); followed by (iii), the translation of the foreign term into one's own language and new interpretive community; and, finally, (iv) the recognition of the value of critical comparison as a way to potentially overcome such an original failure of one's own language (i.e., seeing Europe through Southeast Asia, or vice versa).

Thus, within Anderson's acts of both comparative reading and English translation, Rizal's original words suffer a complex process of linguistic and critical transfiguration. While ushering the use value of Rizal's original comparison into a new historical period, Anderson dramatically transforms and displaces – semantically, culturally, and critically – Rizal's Spanish original into a new version of itself. As a result, Rizal's original is suddenly able to operate in a new theoretical and geopolitical context, as Anderson succinctly argues: "So that's what it was in 1963, I said to myself: the spectre of comparisons."[8] Thus, while Anderson's "spectre of comparisons" is not necessarily related to the dizzying socio-economic material differences between the Spanish metropole and its Southeast Asian colony, as seen by Rizal in the late 1880s, it is intrinsically connected to the "kind of haunting" that he famously locates at the core of the "imagined reality" of modern nationalism, roughly a hundred years after Rizal.[9] As widely acknowledged, the central tenet of Anderson's critique of modern nationalism is particularly developed in his celebrated work *Imagined Communities* (1983), where he explores various instances of the "ghostly *national* imaginings" that, he argues, saturate modern nations.[10] Anderson's reading of Rizal, and of his own critical effort to articulate a postcolonial nationalism in the Philippines, is clearly framed within his overall approach to modern nationalism as a spectral and ghostly imagining.

Anderson's comparative strategy in his conceptualization of Rizal's "demonio de las comparaciones" as the "spectre of comparisons" opens up the kind of "ghostly schema" that Jacques Derrida describes as central to his reading of Karl Marx's conceptualization of commodities in his *Spectres of Marx* (a work originally published in 1993, five years before the first edition of Anderson's *Spectres of Comparison*). For Derrida, the "ghostly schema" manifests itself in the process through which the spectral dimension of commodities, entailing a symbolic transformation of the materiality of things, unveils the conceptual difference between the notions of "spirit" and "spectre":

> If one keeps to use-value, the properties (*Eigenschaften*) of the thing are always very human, at bottom, reassuring for this very reason ... It is quite different when it [wood as thing/table] becomes a commodity, when the curtain goes up on the market and the table plays actor and character at the same time, when the commodity-table, says Marx, comes on stage (*auftritt*), begins to walk around and to put itself forward as a market value ... The ghostly schema now appears indispensable. The commodity is a "thing" without phenomenon, a thing in flight that surpasses the senses (it is invisible, intangible, inaudible, and odorless); but this transcendence is not altogether spiritual, it retains that bodiless body which we have recognized as making the difference between specter and spirit. What surpasses the senses still passes before us in the silhouette of the sensuous body that it nevertheless lacks or that remains inaccessible to us.[11]

Hence, the emergence of a "spectre of comparisons" or "demonio de las comparaciones," as respectively voiced by Anderson and Rizal, refers to the figure of an act of comparison established by what Derrida describes as "the silhouette of the sensuous body that it nevertheless lacks or that remains inaccessible to us." In Rizal's and Anderson's conceptualizations, the present moment is seen in terms of the "ghostly schema" of a critical act of comparison that transforms the material specificity of the here and now into a spectral version of itself. Further, by turning

Rizal's Spanish "demonio" into its English "spectre," Anderson considerably reduces the material and sensorial implications of Rizal's original figuration of this moment of double vision in his 1886 novel; it therefore constitutes an act of interlingual translation through which Anderson is able to switch the emphasis in the actual object of comparison in Rizal's original phrase. In so doing, Anderson is ultimately commodifying Rizal's original recognition in the novel and its "spirit," in Derrida's terminology, into a spectral version of itself through an act of translation that becomes a form of transfiguration.

The paradoxical positionality of both Rizal's original "double vision" in Spanish and its translation and transfiguration into English by Anderson appears to be articulated upon the same kind of "'thing' without phenomenon, a thing in flight that surpasses the senses" that Derrida places at the core of the "ghostly schema" inherent in Marx's theorization of commodities.[12] In the rest of this chapter, I argue that the paradoxical positionality of both Rizal's original "double vision," on the one hand, and the kind of "ghostly schema" described above in terms of its problematic translation and transfiguration into English by Anderson, on the other, constitutes a paradigmatic critical framework for Filipinx literature during the first three decades of the twentieth century. This historical period is marked by the United States' occupation of the Philippines through the jurisdiction of the Insular Government of the Philippine Islands, established by the United States government between 1901 and 1935, which quickly followed the Philippine Revolution against Spain (1896–8) and the Spanish-American War of 1898.[13] This colonial rupture was carried out by the United States through a complex combination of economic and political policies and strategies, among them the sudden imposition of the English language and Anglo-American educational traditions in a socio-historical context that, prior to that point, had been entirely dominated by Spanish language and culture, as well as by Catholic religious traditions that were at the core of the colonial ideology of the Spanish Empire.

I argue, therefore, that a crucial aspect of the form of "double vision" operating in the work of key authors from the Philippines writing during the United States occupation is that while it is intimately related to Rizal's own "demonio de las comparaciones" – as part of a reaction to the Spanish Empire, and the imposition of the Spanish language and cultural and religious institutions during its colonial control of the Southeast Asian archipelago – it is also determined by the new political, linguistic, and cultural system enforced by the United States in the Philippines since 1898. In other words, in the early part of the twentieth century, Filipinx literature experienced a cultural rupture that was intrinsically connected to a double historical transformation in which one colonial ideology and hegemonic system was abruptly replaced by another in the span of less than four years.

We therefore need to look more closely at the series of influences of the two hegemonic powers that shape a deeply complex and painful historical process that determines the development of Filipinx culture and history in this period. I provide a comparative critical examination aiming to connect the local impact and various literary manifestations of this historical process within Filipinx modernist and experimental poetry of the early twentieth century, within a larger understanding of the legacy and logic of empire during the historical avant-garde from a transnational and multilingual perspective.[14] More specifically, I explore below how the early experimental poetry of Filipinx writers José Garcia Villa (1908–97) and Angela Manalang Gloria (1907–95), and their respective use of the English language and anglophone modernist poetics, contrasts with the work of Spanish-language poets, particularly as embodied in the work of Claro Recto (1890–1960), one of the most influential writers and intellectuals of the so-called "Golden Age" of Spanish-language Filipinx literature in the twentieth century. These three influential Filipinx writers articulated closely related but differing modernist poetics, carrying out an incorporation of various forms of Spanish American *modernismo*, on the one hand, and of anglophone modernism, on the other, while responding in divergent ways – in terms of language, poetics, gender, and politics – to both the colonial legacy of the Spanish Empire and the early twentieth-century imperialism of the United States. In my analysis, the literary and historical implications of the divergent careers and poetics embraced by these three key Filipinx writers precisely during the period of the historical avant-garde demonstrates the impact of their respective transnational literary networks as they led to differing constructions of modernism and postcoloniality within the same multilingual cultural context in the Philippines. Moreover, their respective manifestations of modernist poetics during this period, particularly when read comparatively within this historical context, shed light on the "unsettled and asymmetrical forces of modernity" that, as Adam Lifshey describes in relation to Spanish-language Filipinx poetry after 1898, operate beyond their original shared local context in the Philippines. In what follows, I examine the multilingual and geopolitical dimensions of early twentieth-century Filipinx poetry within a planetary framework by comparing the conflicting conceptualizations of modernist and experimental poetics in the early work of Recto, García Villa, and Manalang Gloria, specifically focusing on their divergent and at times opposed political positions.

United States Imperialism and the Question of the Spanish Language in the Philippines after 1898

In order to contextualize the response to Spanish colonialism and US imperialism articulated by modernist Filipinx poets during the first three decades of the twentieth century – and the various forms of anxiety this dual imperialism generated – it is important to examine the central role played by the Spanish language within key literary and cultural circles of this period in the Philippines. While, according to Vicente Rafael, only a very small fraction of the Philippine population was ever completely fluent in Spanish during the entire period of Spain's colonial rule,[15] the impact of Spanish language and literature before, during, and after the Philippine Revolution was considerable and extremely influential from a cultural and social perspective. As the language of the local elite – as Rafael argues, "limited to an elite, mostly mestizo (Chinese and Spanish) minority with access to a university education in Manila and Europe"[16] – Spanish was the language of the *ilustrado* leaders prior to and during the Revolution, as well as that of Rizal's highly influential works. Consequently, Spanish was also the language used by the descendants of the *ilustrado* intellectuals and their families, who were, in many instances, deeply critical of the United States' colonial occupation after 1898.

Moreover, the use of Spanish by different members of the elite class in the Philippines during key periods of the transition from Spanish to US colonial rule is connected to what the historian Renato Constantino has described as a deep ambivalence towards the Spanish language and cultural institutions during the last decades of the Spanish colonial empire:

> The native and *mestizo-sangley ilustrados*, like the Filipino-Spaniards, had an ambivalent attitude toward Spain and their native country. Their education was Spanish, and the mental conditioning they received was Castilian. They regarded Spain as their mother country, aping their superiors and aspiring to be like them. Yet despite their wealth, they were not and could never be Spaniards. The Spaniards tolerated them as allies, but the racial barrier and the economic restrictions on their position, made them conscious of their inferior status ... They were therefore pro-Spanish and at the same time anti-Spaniard.[17]

It is important to emphasize the unstable nature of this linguistic and cultural ambivalence in the Philippines regarding the use of Spanish during this period by the Hispanized elite. There always remained a distance and a separation between the Spanish-born members of the political and religious colonial administration of the Philippines ("peninsulares") and the local population (in its various categories, as set out by Constantino above). Despite this fact, however, Spanish – as the main linguistic medium and primary symbolic system of the colonial regime – did constitute a key component of the elite's perception of itself, not only in relation to the colonial metropolis, but also in relation to the majority of the native population of the Philippines at the time, which did not have regular access to Spanish. At the same time, Catholicism remained an intrinsic part of Spanish colonial identity, not only in the self-definition of the elite before and after the Philippine Revolution, but also as a key aspect of the *ilustrado* Revolution itself.[18]

Considered within a wider cultural and multilingual paradigm, a critical reconsideration of the role played by Spanish-language literature after the Philippine Revolution helps to clarify the sense of "ambivalence" that Constantino identifies within the Hispanicized elite of the period, particularly in terms of the sense of "double vision" at the core of Filipinx modernist poetry, produced in both English and Spanish during this period. As argued by Martin Joseph Ponce, anglophone literature in the Philippines originally emerged in response to the cultural and linguistic framework provided by Spanish-language and vernacular literatures: "Whatever the Anglophone writers thought of the Philippine languages during the first decades of U.S. colonialism, it is certainly the case that Anglophone literature acquired its political power and cultural status in relation to Spanish and vernacular literatures."[19]

The early Spanish-language poetry of Claro Recto exemplifies this relationship. A jurist, politician, and member of the Philippine Senate and House of Representatives for more than thirty years, Recto was appointed associate justice of the Philippine Supreme Court by President Franklin D. Roosevelt in 1935. As members of a wealthy *ilustrado* community from the southern cities of Tiaong and Lipa, in the province of Batangas, Recto's family was heavily Hispanized, as described in detail by Constantino in his biography of Recto, *The Making of a Filipino* (1969). Moreover, after receiving his Bachelor of Arts degree from the Jesuit-founded Ateneo de Manila in 1909, Recto studied law at the Catholic University of Santo Tomás, generally considered the oldest existing university in Asia, which received the Royal Seal by the Spanish Crown in 1785. In her study of Philippine scholarship at the end of the Spanish Empire, moreover, Megan Thomas argues that the University of Santo Tomás was a unique academic institution in that it helped to develop the intellectual and scholarly context that precipitated the *ilustrado* Revolution, which would ultimately topple the Spanish colonial regime.[20]

Constantino's account of Recto's early life suggests that, as a graduate of the University of Santo Tomás, he displayed the kind of "ambivalence" towards Spanish political and cultural institutions that was characteristic of the *ilustrado* community, embracing Spain as an essential part of his own heritage and identity ("the Recto family was strongly drawn to Spain and to its culture"[21]) while acknowledging his distance and exclusion from Spanish culture, given his condition as a colonial subject who could never be considered an equal by the *peninsulares*. At the same time, as Constantino notes, Recto developed a parallel but nonetheless differing ambivalence towards the US occupation after the Revolution:

> Recto was confronted with this ambivalence towards the Americans in his social milieu and felt it in his own personal life. On the one hand, he had strong prejudices against the Americans because his mother, Doña Micalea, had been arrested and imprisoned by them for giving aid to the revolutionary forces under General Miguel Malvar … On the other hand, the leaders respected by Recto and his family had already collaborated. They had accepted the new conditions, had been won over by the new thinking.[22]

This twofold ambivalence towards both Spanish and American culture, as particularly related to the notion of a comparative "double vision" explored in this chapter, can be explicitly traced in Recto's key poetry collection *Bajo los cocoteros (Almas y panoramas)* (Under the Coconut Trees [Souls and Panoramas]), originally published in 1911 by Librería Manila Filatélica.[23] Recto's *Bajo los cocoteros* is a collection of early poems, written between 1909 and 1911, divided into fourteen different sections that combine nationalist and political pieces with more lyrical and meditative poems. The lyrical sections of *Bajo los cocoteros* – with section titles such as "Sinfonía de las rosas" (Symphony of Roses), "Del libro del amor" (From the Book of Love), and "Las flores del terruño" (Flowers from the Land), among others – are closely connected in form and tone to the *modernista* poetry of Latin American authors such as the Nicaraguan Rubén Darío (1867–1916) and the Mexican Amado Nervo (1870–1919), while Recto's more political series of poems in the collection share the revolutionary and anticolonial (as well as anti-imperial) ethos that also pervades the work of other writers associated with the *modernista* movement, such as the Cuban José Martí (1853–95).[24]

The formal and political connections between Recto's *Bajo los cocoteros* and Spanish American *modernismo* are striking.[25] From a formal perspective, and especially in the more explicitly lyrical poems in the collection, Recto's work shares the heightened sense of musicality and figural exoticism of *modernismo*, including its strong aestheticism and a careful concern with formal sophistication, while directly responding to the specific forces of modernity locally affecting and altering Philippine history. Significantly, in his prologue, the Filipino writer and politician Fernando María Guerrero (also a graduate of the Ateneo de Manila and the University of Santo Tomás) emphasizes the newer and innovative dimension of Recto's poetry, describing the contemporary value of his voice as a lyric poet who demonstrates the modern sensibility of Spanish American *modernismo*:

> ¿Se ha modernizado el poeta? Sí, si por modernismo se ha de entender la tendencia contemporánea de convertir la Poesía en reflexión integral de lo subjetivo y lo objetivo, de lo formal e ideológico, para adaptarla plenamente lo mismo a los aspectos de la realidad visible que a los más ocultos matices y vibraciones del sentimiento.
>
> (Has the poet modernized himself? Yes, if by *modernismo* one understands the contemporary tendency of turning Poetry into an integral reflection on the subjective and the objective, on the formal and the ideological, in order to fully adapt it both to the aspects of visible reality and to the most hidden nuances and vibrations of feeling.)[26]

An important feature of Guerrero's theorization of Recto's poetry in terms of *modernismo* as a contemporary poetic tendency is his reference to *La poésie contemporaine (1884–1896)* by the French critic E. Vigié-Lecocq. *La poésie contemporaine* was an influential critical work in which Vigié-Lecocq theorizes key features of late nineteenth-century French Parnasian and Symbolist models. In particular, the French scholar discusses in his study of modern French poetry the treatment of nature, love, mysticism, decadent and symbolist art, and technique and language in the work of poets such as Charles Leconte de Lisle, Stéphane Mallarmé, Paul Verlaine, Arthur Rimbaud, and José María de Heredia – precisely the same poetic models that influenced the original development of the first stage of Latin American *modernismo* (particularly as embodied in Rubén Darío's prominent poetry collection *Azul*, originally published in Valparaíso, Chile in 1888).[27]

More specifically, Guerrero refers to the poetic style that Recto displays in his more lyrical poems in this collection, namely "Rosas de carne" (Carnal Roses) and "Rosas de Eros" (Roses of Eros), poems with strong formal and conceptual connections to *modernismo*. In "Rosas de carne," Recto fleshes out a lyrical condemnation of carnal and sensual love, paradoxically emphasizing what, to him, appears as the intoxicating and irresistible power of these "carnal roses" that "everyone craves," rhetorical figures expressed through richly sensorial poetic language. The poem, opening with two chained irregular octaves, creates a complex rhyming pattern (*abbabccd*, *defefgeg*) that generates an enhanced sense of poetic rhythm and musicality:

"Rosas de carne"
        ¡Oh, rosas de lascivia!
Yo sé que os extenuáis de emociones supremas
cuando en sus corolas deposita sus gemas
el bienhechor rocío, entre la noche tibia.
        Fuísteis como diademas
en las frentes de Lais, de Salomé, de Aspasia,
de las *cocotes* de Europa y bayaderas de Asia,
y de las margaritas que enfloraron América …

("Carnal Roses"
        Oh, lascivious roses!
I know you are extenuated by supreme emotions
when the beneficent dew deposits
in your corollas its gems in the warm night.
        You were like diadems
on the foreheads of Lais, Salome, Aspasia,
of the *cocotes* of Europe and *bayaderas* of Asia,
and of the daisies that flowered America …)[28]

As these opening lines show, "Rosas de carne" is pervaded by a kind of *modernista* synesthetic play with various sensations, while evoking a mythical and exotic past. The poem constitutes an exploration from a patriarchal and masculinist poetic voice of a form of female sensual and sexual power intrinsically connected to forces of nature operating beyond human and rational control, a form of normative order that is characterized through a series of male figures in the poem. As articulated by Recto, the poetic voice expresses its moral opposition to the dizzying and intoxicating carnal roses, which are gendered in the poem as female not only linguistically, but also metaphorically, being characterized by Recto as the "diadems" of women from classical antiquity, and as female dancers from various parts of the world.

Moreover, the formal connection of Recto's poetry in *Bajo los cocoteros* to Spanish American *modernismo* is also emphasized thematically in "Rosas de carne" by the appearance in the central moment of the poem of the figure of the swan ("cisne"), perhaps the paradigmatic poetic symbol of Spanish American *modernismo*:[29]

Habéis mirado al Cisne, prodigador de halagos,
ensangrentar su pico en los muslos de Leda,
sobre la mansedumbre de los dormidos lagos.

(You have watched the Swan, bestower of compliments,
bleed its beak in the thighs of Leda,
over the gentleness of the slumbering lakes.)[30]

Placing this central *modernista* figure at the core of his exploration of carnal sensuality in *Bajo los cocoteros*, Recto here makes explicit reference to the poetry of Rubén Darío, namely his use of the figure of the swan in his influential collection *Cantos de vida y esperanza* (originally published in 1905). In his poem "Leda" and the fourth poem included in the section "Los cisnes" – dedicated to the Spanish *modernista* poet Juan Ramón Jiménez – Darío famously reinterprets the Greek mythological story in which Zeus, in the form of a swan, rapes Leda, daughter of Thestius and wife of Spartan king Tyndareus:

Tal es, cuando esponja las plumas de seda,
Olímpico pájaro herido de amor,
Y viola en las linfas sonoras a Leda,
Buscando su pico los labios en flor.

Suspira la bella desnuda y vencida,
Y en tanto que al aire sus quejas se van,
Del fondo verdoso de fronda tupida
Chispean turbados los ojos de Pan.

(So it is, when the silk feathers become a sponge,
The Olympic bird, wounded of love,
Violates Leda in the sonorous waters,
Its beak looking for her lips in bloom.

The beauty sighs, naked and defeated,
And while her complaints are gone into the air,
From the greenish background of bushy foliage
Pan's eyes shine in agitation.)[31]

As critic Cathy Jrade observes, for Darío, the mythical figure of the swan "becomes a symbol of universal harmony in all its forms, including artistic creation and sexual love."[32] For Darío, Jrade argues, the figure of Leda is the female counterpart of the mythological power of Zeus, embodied in the image of the swan, and therefore key to Darío's own conceptualization of the sexual act, which, according to Jrade, "is celestial in its ecstasy as well as its origin, but also epitomizes the unity of all life."[33]

Unlike in Darío's celebration of a mythical form of a universal manifestation of sexual love in his Leda poems, the poetic voice in Recto's "Rosas de carne" blames the female carnal roses for passively witnessing the action of the swan. It is as if, by witnessing the event, they somehow bear responsibility for the swan's sexual aggression against the mythological figure of Leda. Recto here uses the same linguistic and poetic figure of the swan's beak ("pico") originally used by Darío ("Buscando su pico los labios en flor"), but with very different implications ("ensangrentar su pico en los muslos de Leda"). In his own poetic rearticulation of the original image by Darío, Recto emphasizes in "Rosas de carne" the animality and bodily nature of the figure of the swan and its brutal and violent action. As the poetic voice states in the last two lines of "Rosas de carne," these feminine roses are desired by various types of male figures (which from Recto's masculinist stance range from artists to pious men of faith). In what emerges as a deeply heteronormative and religiously driven critique of various forms of scientific and material progress, these "carnal roses," while described as tempting in the poem, ultimately embody for Recto a force unable to satisfy a spiritual or inner need:

> Rosas carnales, malas, iguales que vuestra ciencia,
> No os quiero, vuestro encanto no cura mi dolencia.
>
> (Carnal roses, as evil as your science,
> I do not want you, your charm does not cure my pain.)[34]

By favouring the "roses of Eros" as opposed to the "carnal roses," which are described in the poem as "evil as your science," Recto inverts the sense of pagan and mythological forms of sensuality in both Darío's poem and his *modernista* poetics in their full violence and brutality, into a less sensual and more traditional Christian poetics of spiritual love (as related especially to the sense of religious mysticism specifically mentioned by Recto in the poem). These particular figurations of sexuality highlight how, for Recto, the feminine danger of such "carnal roses" contrasts with the more spiritual "roses" that emerge in the subsequent piece in the collection, the poem "Rosas de Eros." For Recto, in contrast with the "carnal roses" in the previous poem, the "roses of Eros" embody an eternal and less distressed form of love that, through Recto's patriarchal lens, appears as more docile and pure in relation to what he views as a spiritual form of love: "Es que sois muy buenas / como vuestras hermanas / las rosas vesperales / y las místicas rosas" (You are very good / like your sisters / the vesperal roses / and mystical roses).[35] From this perspective, Recto's rewriting of Darío's poetic treatment of the figure of the swan articulates a translation and recreation of Darío's *modernista* original within the particularities of Recto's own local cultural, ideological, and historical context.

Within the larger historical and literary context explored in this chapter, Recto's Hispanicized – both linguistically and ideologically – construction of femininity in these two *modernista* poems included in *Bajo los cocoteros* displays a deep sense of male anxiety at a time in which gender roles in the Philippines were rapidly changing due to the sudden cultural changes set in motion by the US occupation.[36] As Sianne Ngai has argued, anxiety in general, and male anxiety in particular, demonstrates a "spatial dimension" in how it deploys itself as "something projected onto others ... as a quality or feeling the subject refuses to recognize in himself and attempts to locate in another person or thing."[37] Ngai's conceptualization of male anxiety helps us understand Recto's poetic treatment of femininity in *Bajo los cocoteros* as constituting an affect that, by projecting "embodiments of negativity," is not only deployed outside itself, but more importantly, and at the same time, also represents "a form of distanciation that plays some role in the affect's general prominence in cultural narratives of intellectual life," as Ngai argues.[38] In this sense, Recto's poetic rendering in *Bajo los cocoteros* of different notions of male anxiety, female sexuality, femininity, and gender roles – embodying, as in these two lyrical poems, a carnal rather than a spiritual form of "rose" in relation to a patriarchal and heteronormative male sexual or spiritual quest respectively figured by the Filipino poet in his 1911 collection – reflects opposing ideological and social conceptualizations of gender and sexuality within this same historical context in the Philippines. As Denise Cruz has shown in *Transpacific Femininities*, the ideal of the Filipina woman held by the male Hispanicized *ilustrados* in the early twentieth century included a "desire to discipline and check what they saw as Filipinas' aberrant sexual behaviors, especially in the wake of education, new opportunities for women, changing codes of conduct, and the influx of popular culture from the United States."[39]

Recto's poetic representation of his critical stance and anxiety regarding the cultural and political changes related to the US occupation of the Philippines are considerably more explicitly in other poems in the collection. Thus, in *Bajo los cocoteros*, Recto conveys his anti-imperial politics in a series of nationalist, autobiographical, and historical poems (roughly half of the total poems in the collection) that consider the sources of the Philippine nation and culture, the celebration of Rizal as a patriotic hero, and the imperial colonization by the United States. A particularly striking example is the poem "En aquellos días" (In Those Days), in which the poetic voice recalls events connected to Recto's own childhood that coincided with the aftermath of the Spanish-American War. Recto describes events related to the US occupation of the Philippines, the painful loss on behalf of the motherland (*patria*), and the "peace" that ensued, as in the following verses:

En aquellos días
Eran aquellos … ¿te acuerdas?
luctuosos y aciagos tiempos,
en que el bolo decidía
la causa de nuestro Pueblo.

Eras niña todavía,
Yo, más niño aún. Y huérfanos
Éramos. Nuestro buen padre
Ya entonces había muerto …

La paz se anunció … ¿era paz? …
Volvimos a nuestro pueblo,
y encontramos ¡con qué pena!
El patrimonio desecho.

Los odiosos enemigos
hicieron grandes saqueos
Todo fue botín de guerra
del nuevo Atila extranjero.

(In those days
Those were the days … do you remember?
Mournful and unlucky times,
In which the *bolo* knife decided
The cause of our People.

You were a still girl
Myself, then just a child. And we were
Orphans. Our good father
Dead by then …

Peace was announced … was it peace? …
We returned to our village,
And found, with so much sadness!
Our wasted heritage.

The hateful enemies
And their massive looting.
Everything was a spoil of war
For the new foreign Attila.)[40]

In this heavily autobiographical poem – structured in twenty octosyllabic quatrains with assonant rhyme in the even verses – Recto explores not only the war-like conditions related to the US occupation of the Philippines, but also the more subjective and personal loss related to this complex history of recolonization by a new foreign power.[41] The poetic voice addresses a loss, both personal and national, in which various familial figures (a mother, brother, and sister) are emotionally joined to each other through the death of the father and the lyric expression of a pain that is intrinsically connected to the loss of the homeland, a land precariously defended with *bolo* knives and conquered by the brutality of a new imperial "Attila." While the days of war and struggle are over, the entire familial and national heritage of the motherland has been literally and figuratively "wasted," as the poetic voice makes clear.

Recto's *modernista* poetics are thus determined by two different colonial empires, represented in the above poem by the two foreign Attilas – namely, the legacy of the Spanish Empire (and its linguistic, literary, cultural, and religious implications) and the historical reality of the US occupation in 1901, along with its political and cultural aftermath. In this shifting and ambivalent context, moreover, Recto considers the status of the Spanish language, personally and nationally, to be an issue of utmost importance. This is something also explored in Recto's essay collection *Monroismo asiático* (Asian Monroeism, 1929), in which he insists, "Consideramos el castellano como cosa nuestra, propia" (We consider Castilian to belong to us).[42] Therefore, his use of the Spanish language not only allows Recto to retranslate in his own terms the form of Spanish American *modernista* poetics that revolutionized

Spanish-language poetry across the world during the last two decades of the nineteenth century, but also articulates a form of political resistance to the new colonial occupation endured by the Philippines after the *ilustrado* Revolution.

As shown here, Recto's version of *modernista* poetics articulated in *Bajo los cocoteros* constitutes a complex process of cultural translation and poetic transfer. Through the poems included in the various sections of the collection, Recto reconceptualizes the experience of modernity represented by the poetics of Spanish American *modernismo* not only as a response to the hegemony of the Spanish Empire in the Philippines, but also as an intrinsic part of Philippine national identity and resistance regarding US colonialism. As Recto further elaborates in *Monroismo asiático*, the use of Spanish in the Philippines at that time formed part of what he describes as the "spiritual legacy" of Filipinx culture and history, the language having been purified of what Recto refers to as its imperial "material dross" during the Philippine Revolution.[43]

Parallel to the cases of Rizal and Anderson, Recto creates through his own version of *modernista* poetry a critical reconfiguration of a particular historical experience through a double act of comparison in which the development of a local history is necessarily seen in relation to a larger cultural engagement able to acknowledge a rapidly shifting political overlay of divergent colonial and imperial ideologies across world history. As in Anderson's translation of Rizal's original "demonio de las comparaciones," Recto's articulation of an act of "double vision" – in this case through his own version of Spanish-language *modernista* poetics in *Bajo los cocoteros* – demonstrates how once the ability to name a previously known experience is lost, the only way to voice this anxiety may be through a different linguistic and critical configuration able to assign new meanings and hermeneutic values to rapidly changing historical conditions and identities.

Transcreating Anglophone Modernist Poetry in the Philippines: Garcia Villa's and Manalang Gloria's Early Experimental Poetics

The power of literature, in this case modernist poetry, to respond to the experience of colonialism continued to pervade Filipinx culture during the second and third decades of the twentieth century. The final section of this chapter explores how Anglo-American modernism, as mainly filtered through the colonial educational system imposed by the United States in the Philippines, impacted the development of Filipinx literature as the Spanish language gradually lost its use and symbolic value for the local Philippine elite. This is particularly evident for the period following the founding of the anglophone University of the Philippines in 1908 by the US colonial government, as part of a broader process over the first half of the twentieth century in which American colonial policies effectively shaped and determined a wide range of economic, educational, and social Philippine institutions. In this sense, Epifanio San Juan Jr. has shown that American English, as the new colonial language, effectively supplanted both Spanish and the various local vernaculars as the "primary symbolic system" in the Philippines:

> Writers and intellectuals then constituted the most effective mediation or relay between the colonizing power and the subjugated populace. The first Filipino writers in English (e.g., Paz Marquez-Benitez, Jose Garcia Villa) were educated in the University of the Philippines founded in 1908; their writings were first published by the college journals. The idiom of American English displaced both Spanish and the vernaculars as the primary symbolic system through which Filipinos represented themselves, that is, constituted themselves as colonial subjects with specific positions or functions (rights, duties) in the given social order.[44]

The early work of José Garcia Villa powerfully exemplifies this larger linguistic and cultural shift highlighted here by San Juan. Villa's early modernist writings, which he produced while still living in the Philippines, eventually led to his successful literary and professional life in the United States after his arrival in 1929 to study at the University of New Mexico, with his long prestigious career as a writer and scholar in the US including Guggenheim, Bollingen, and American Academy of Arts and Letters awards. Villa also served as a prominent poetry editor for the independent publisher New Directions in the late 1940s, as well as an adviser on cultural affairs to the president of the Philippines in 1968.

Villa's early work in the 1920s played a crucial role in a larger shift within Filipinx literature and poetics away from both the Spanish-language colonial literary paradigm and the politics of Tagalog nationalism.[45] The central relevance of Villa within this shifting context relates primarily to the fact that he has generally been considered to be the originator of Filipinx modernist English-language poetry. Thus, while San Juan refers to him as "the inventor of Modernist writing in English in the Philippines,"[46] Ponce describes the publication in 1929 of Garcia Villa's early poetry collection "Man-Songs" in the *Philippines Herald Magazine* as marking what he refers to as the beginning of "Anglophone Filipino modernism":

> Anglophone Filipino modernism begins with a scandal. In the spring of 1929, a series of poems called "Man-Songs" appeared in the *Philippines Herald Magazine* under the name O. Sevilla. The pseudonym apparently did little to screen the poet's identity since, shortly after the third installment, José Garcia Villa was brought to court and fined 50 pesos for allegedly "polluting public morals."[47]

While the overt sexuality and queer eroticism that characterizes Villa's "Man-Songs" led to Villa's suspension from the University of the Philippines after its publication in 1929, that same year Villa was able to win a short-story contest and used the prize money to travel to the United States for the first time.[48] For the young Villa, his experience in the Philippines as an emerging writer reflected and was affected by the competing forces of the different languages, ideologies, forms of education, and temporalities he encountered in the 1920s. Villa's central role in the development of modernist anglophone poetry in the Philippines reflects a deep commitment to experimental poetry as a medium of artistic expression, as well as his own complex positionality within this larger historical and cultural context, in terms closely related to the sense of cultural and historical "vertigo" or "double vision" at the core of Philippine modernity traced in the work of Anderson, Rizal, and Recto in this chapter.

A parallel sense of "vertigo" permeates Villa's early poetry, in particular the series of poems that Villa himself refers to as "the best of the work done in early youth."[49] While some of Villa's early poems were published in local journals and magazines in the Philippines during the 1920s and early 1930s, they were first collected and reprinted as "Early Poems" in Villa's 1958 collection *Selected Poems and New*, published in New York by McDowell, Obolensky.[50] The tension between these various cultural and linguistic influences emerges in Villa's work as a form of anxiety embodied in key thematic and linguistic features that characterize his early poetry. For example, Villa's early poem "One hemisphere the heart," numbered 222 in his *Selected Poems and New*, thematizes the problem of a split identity that is "parted" into two "hemispheres," a manifestation of affect or feeling that also appears figured in the poem as an ambiguous lack of clear vision:

> One hemisphere the heart,
> Another the mind,
> The two one World
> But one is blind— …[51]

Here, the poetic voice expresses a sense of ontological uncertainty and imbalance connected to a halving of experience into two different hemispheres, voicing a struggle to form one "World." In this early poem, the possibility of a better integrated and more holistic experience appears to be split by a preceding tension rooted in a patriarchal figure, "One Father / Who willed a world so parted."[52] The poem therefore poses the question of balance within a split world, lyrically voicing the tensions and complexity of an experience intrinsically divided into two. Villa's early poem thus illustrates in complex ways how the related sense of anxiety expressed by the poetic voice is intrinsically connected to an open and fluid, yet unsettled, identity determined in part by different historical forces at odds with each other, as well as beyond one's agency or control. This complex dimension of both ontological fluidity and epistemological uncertainty at the core of Villa's early poetry is also powerfully expressed in the poem "Testament," included in Villa's 1929 "Man-Songs," particularly in the following line: "I cannot understand my own unorthodoxy."[53]

The sense of anxiety concerning one's place in the world emerging in Villa's early poetry appears elsewhere in his writings during this period as an anxiety of putative origins in general, and regarding the sources of anglophone modernist poetry in the Philippines in particular. As mentioned above, critics like Ponce and San Juan date the beginning of anglophone modernism to the publication of Villa's "Man-Songs." However, while Villa's 1929 collection is generally thought of as the first poetic manifestation of anglophone modernism in the Philippines, it is very important to emphasize in this context that for Villa himself, the origins of the new anglophone poetics of Filipinx literature lay not in his own early collection of poems, but rather in the work of Filipina poet Angela Manalang Gloria, who was also a student at the University of the Philippines in the late 1920s. Although Manalang Gloria is less well known today than Villa, his indebtedness to her early experimental poetry in English is clearly and powerfully expressed in his essay "The Best Poems of 1931," in which Villa explicitly credits Manalang Gloria with initiating and transforming the field of modernist Filipinx poetry in English:

> In last year's poetry there was most noticeable the trend towards the philosophic. The lyric note was low and hardly present. I think it is wise to state here that lyricism should not be abandoned: the song of the heart is as beautiful as the song of the wind – and rises higher. Filipino poetry was mainly lyrical until a few years ago. It was, in fact, too lyrical, nauseatingly lyrical. Consequently it was a period of very poor poetry. Not until the

> advent of Angela Manalang Gloria did Filipino poetry in English first rise to the level of true poetry. Miss Manalang (now Mrs. Gloria) raised Filipino poetry from the quagmire of vacuous sentimentalism to the dignity of true art … Miss Manalang is therefore, in my opinion, chronologically as well as [*sic*] magnitudinally, the first of our poets.[54]

As Villa states here, he considered Manalang Gloria to be the "first of our poets," and thus able to successfully articulate through her early work a radical change in poetics – from what he deemed to be the "nauseatingly lyrical" poetry of their predecessors – to a newly avant-garde poetry, closer to what Villa refers to as "the dignity of true art." As Jonathan Chua suggests (see n. 45 above), these new aesthetic, literary, and ideological categories at the core of both Manalang Gloria's and Villa's writings and conceptions of modern poetry in the 1920s reflected the anglophone literary and aesthetic models inherent in the American higher education system imposed at the University of the Philippines, from which both graduated in 1929.[55] While Villa would eventually retreat from his early enthusiasm and admiration for Manalang Gloria's poetry, what is crucially at stake in Villa's 1932 remarks is the recognition of her work as radically changing the direction of Filipinx writing in English, in relation to previous poetic traditions in the Philippines. By describing Manalang Gloria in 1931 as "the first of our poets," Villa is thus locating in her new and experimental poetry a fundamental aesthetic and ideological rejection of the work of previous, and almost exclusively male, Filipinx poets writing in either Spanish or Tagalog. In his remarks, furthermore, Villa views the latter tradition as constituting a lesser body of literature essentially detached from the higher order of the "philosophic" and "true poetry."[56]

According to Edna Zapanta Manlapaz – perhaps the most influential critic to reassess Manalang Gloria's poetry for contemporary readers and scholars – if her relatively brief *oeuvre*, comprising just over a hundred poems, mostly published in various periodicals and then later reprinted in the collection *Poems* (Manila, 1940), led to her consideration as an "indisputably major figure in Filipino poetry in English," it is because of Manalang Gloria's rediscovery by two groups of readers in the 1990s, namely "Filipino feminists in search of recorded testimony by forebears like Manalang Gloria who had had to define their womanhood within the same patriarchal society," on the one hand, and readers "revaluating modern Filipino poetry in English," on the other.[57] Indeed, Manalang Gloria's earliest poems, first published in the most important 1920s and 1930s English-language periodicals in the Philippines, were read by contemporary readers in light of the work of American women poets accessed primarily through literature courses at the University of the Philippines, and related literary publications during this period. It was in this academic and literary context that Manalang Gloria's work as a poet socially emerged as providing a new sense of womanhood to young Filipina women writers and readers at the time, as Manlapaz observes:

> Expectations of what a female poet looked like were no doubt shaped by the public personas of contemporary American women whose poetry Filipino students had been reading in their literature classes. Did she look like a modern flapper girl such as Edna St. Vincent Millay, who boasted in one of her most popular poems that she was burning her candle at both ends? Or was she like Marianne Moore, who wore her hair in long braids twisted like a crown upon her head, looking every inch like the librarian she was? Surely, she didn't look anything like Amy Lowell, a heavyset woman who smoked slim cigarillos? Perhaps, she looked more like the palely elegant "white queen," Elinor Wylie?[58]

As rearticulated by Manalang Gloria through her poetry, the poetic modernism of Moore, Lowell, Sara Teasdale, and Adelaide Crapsey was suddenly given a new poetic valence in the Southeast Asian archipelago. It was during the first phase of her writing career (1925–30) that Manalang Gloria's feminist poetics provided a new model for the emergence of Filipinx poetry in English, formally and philosophically, in the sense described by Villa above.

Manalang Gloria's early experimental poetry in English powerfully expressed the rapidly changing historical experience at the core of Filipinx culture and society under the United States in the 1920s. In this context, the incorporation of the poetics of anglophone modernism in particular in Manalang Gloria's early poetry not only offered a social model of "what a female poet looked like," but also provided an experimental literary form for the articulation of a new and freer poetic voice in Philippine society for women, who since Spanish colonization had been subjected to a patriarchal normative system that strictly defined both gender and social roles. A crucial feature of Manalang Gloria's early poetry, some of it written while she completed her college education, is her formal and conceptual connection to the modernist poetics of imagism, which was the primary poetic movement with which most of the American women writers read by Manalang Gloria and her contemporaries in the Philippines were associated.[59]

A relevant example of Manalang Gloria's early poetry is a series of three cinquains originally published in 1927 that connect with the modernist form of Crapsey's own experimental poetry.[60] From a purely formal perspective, this series of three poems closely follows the structure and tone of Crapsey's own modernist cinquains – indeed, the poetic form was originally invented and used by the American poet between 1911 and 1913 – which Crapsey originally published in the collection *Verse* in 1915. Crapsey's cinquains included in *Verse* are composed of three one- or two-syllable verses (generally the first two and the fifth verses), with longer third and fourth verses, generally of five to seven syllables each. A relevant example of Crapsey's experimental cinquains is the poem "The Warning":

> Just now,
> Out of the strange
> Still dusk … as strange, as still …
> A white moth flew. Why am I grown
> So cold?[61]

While Crapsey's cinquains tend to have a more standard syntactical structure (in which the entire cinquain constitutes one or two complete sentences, as in the above example), Manalang Gloria's experimental recreations of Crapsey's modernist poems present relatively shorter, more impactful syntactical juxtapositions. Manalang Gloria's "The Closed Heart" – one of the poems that comprise "Cinquains," a series of three cinquains that Manalang Gloria originally published as a series in the *Philippines Herald Magazine* on 30 October 1927 – provides a striking rearticulation of Crapsey's modernist experimental poetics:

> The Closed Heart
> Call not …
> Sharp bramble cast
> Deep shadows on the stone door
> Of my hall … O strange one, why linger
> Still there?[62]

These shorter syntactical fragments ("Call not," "why linger / Still there?") also highlight the visual intensity of the various images interconnected within each of these three cinquains, as in the central image of "The Closed Heart" in the verse "Deep shadows on the stone door." As shown here, Manalang Gloria's cinquains appear to be closer in her poetic figuration of visuality to the imagistic features of the poetry of Amy Lowell (1874–1925), another major modernist anglophone woman writer whose poetry Manalang Gloria also studied at the University of the Philippines. Consider Lowell's poetic articulation of imagism in the poem "Time," originally published in 1919 as part of her collection *Pictures of the Floating World*:

TIME
Looking at myself in my metal mirror,
I saw, faintly outlined,
The figure of a crane
Engraved upon its back.[63]

"Time" constitutes one of Lowell's attempts to translate traditional Japanese poetry freely, "to reproduce the perfume of a poem," as she argued, in order to further explore a modernist concern with the poetic image through the practice of literary translation.[64] In this sense, Lowell's modernist embrace of creative translations of Chinese and Japanese poetic forms in *Pictures of the Floating World*, and the experimental exploration of poetic images and lyric subjectivities emerging through this process of translation, is in fact part of Lowell's own take on (and separation from) Ezra Pound's influential conceptualization of imagism as a modernist poetics. As Andrew Thacker has importantly argued, referring to the transformation of the poetics of imagism by women poets, particularly by Lowell and H.D., their poetry expanded and altered the lyric valences and implications of the more normative model of modernist poetics envisioned by Pound into more fluid and open poetic manifestations: "These two female poets sought to redefine the 'hard light, clear edges' of Pound's aesthetic and extend Imagism into other varieties of what Lowell termed the 'sensuous sense of seeing,'" which ultimately aimed at the obliteration "of boundaries – between prose and poetry, masculine and feminine, homosexual and heterosexual."[65]

Overall, throughout her experimental poetry published in the late 1920s, Manalang Gloria transforms in her own terms the modernist poetics of imagism, as originally articulated by the key male figures of the movement, such as Pound, by successfully reinterpreting two main dimensions of Amy Lowell's radical expansion of imagism: a fascination with Asian and non-Western conceptualizations of the poetic image, and the intimately related exploration of a "sensuous sense of seeing" that exposed and problematized the restrictions and limitations of normative patriarchal models of representation and aesthetic experience at the core of canonical forms of anglophone modernism itself. What is particularly relevant in this context about Manalang Gloria's rearticulation of the poetics of imagism in her early poetry, especially in the series of poems originally published in the *Philippines Herald Magazine* in 1927, is how she is able to expand, and retranslate, from her own Southeast Asian geopolitical perspective as a woman poet in the Philippines, both the imagist concern with Asian literary traditions of poets like Crapsey and the sexual and gender politics at the core of Lowell's reformulation of imagism. A particularly relevant example of how Manalang Gloria rearticulates these two dimensions of Lowell's and Crapsey's versions of imagism is her poem "To a Mestiza," which she originally published in the *Philippines Herald Magazine* on 25 September 1927:

To a Mestiza
I found the silent meeting of the East
and West in the willowy glimmer of a Bicol
pool – in the beautiful being that is you.[66]

The sensuous imagery, characteristic of imagism, of this three-line poem is powerfully established through the "willowy glimmer" in its second line, here emphasizing the fluidity and calmness of the natural water pools in the Bicol Region of southern Luzon. At the same time, that image articulates a natural transition to the tranquil fusion (as a "silent meeting") of East and West embodied in the figure of the mestiza woman referred to in the title of the poem, and also addressed by the poetic voice in the last line of the poem as "the beautiful being that is you." By embodying the merging of the two main cultures and histories at the core of the Filipinx experience of modernity – represented in the poem as both silent and beautiful – the figure of the mestiza woman personifies in Manalang Gloria's poem a sense of harmony and calmness that is in direct opposition to the traumatic cultural and historical tensions at the core of the colonial history of the Philippines (i.e., the repeated and traumatic clash of East and West), as explored in this chapter.

Moreover, and as shown here, Manalang Gloria's own version of poetic modernism also constituted a space for shaping a newfound sense of female agency and freedom within the same historical context, which had been previously unavailable as such in the Philippines. Through this three-line poem, Manalang Gloria effectively reconceptualizes the anglophone poetics of imagism in gender and geopolitical terms: she doubly subverts the traditional objectification of mestiza women within the male dominated cultural and historical context of the Philippines, not only as connected to the legacy of the Spanish Empire – as discussed earlier in this chapter in relation to Recto's patriarchal *modernista* poetry – but also as imposed by US colonial and cultural institutions. As Denise Cruz argues, having access to and a connection with a new reading audience in the US allowed a new generation of Filipina writers to counter "dominant representations of Filipinas circulated by the U.S. colonial regime," as well as to contest "racist constructions of women in the Philippines as either savage others or desiring colonial subjects eager for tutelage."[67]

As shown here, Manalang Gloria's engagement with and rearticulation of anglophone modernist poetics effectively changed the trajectory and evolution of Filipinx experimental poetry in English. Her influential work in the late 1920s had a clear impact on the early work of the young Villa himself, extending beyond his own recognition of Manalang Gloria's relevance as the "first of our poets," mentioned above. While Villa's experimentation with language and poetic forms becomes considerably more radical in his later poetry composed in the United States – particularly through his development and widespread use of various experimental techniques, such as his conception of "reverse consonance," described in his author's note included at the end of his 1942 collection *Have Come, Am Here*,[68] and his innovative use of commas in later poems – some of his early poems do show an explicit formal connection with Manalang Gloria's own avant-garde poetic experimentations.

In this regard, a fascinating example of Villa's formal experimentations during this early period is the poem numbered 223 in the "Early Poems" section of Villa's *Selected Poems and New*. This poem is configured by a repeated cinquain that powerfully mirrors Manalang Gloria's own early experimentations with the poetic form invented by Crapsey. Villa's poem is articulated upon the central image of a "withered" "r / ed rose," a poetic image that is strikingly split across the two opening verses of the poem:

> The r
> ed rose withered …[69]

This experimental enjambment-like feature of separating the first consonant from the rest of the first word of the following verse is repeated in four of the five verses of each of the two cinquains in the poem. This same image of the "red rose" central to this poem, as well as Villa's syntactical experimentation, also appears prominently in his piece "Definitions of Poetry," a series of poetic aphorisms defining Villa's own conception of poetry, which was originally published in *Philippine Magazine* in March 1935:

> Poetry is space surging to the heights of music, tossing a red rose that is to be torn into a silver star …
>
> Poetry is music rose-fevered: desire rose-lashed: lighting rose-tamed.[70]

As shown here, Villa's early poetry, and his conception of poetry, not only follows Manalang Gloria's formal innovations through his use of a cinquain as a poetic form, with his added experimental enjambments, but also follows the strong imagistic impulse of Manalang Gloria's own rearticulation of Lowell's "sensuous sense of seeing" through the poetics of imagism – as highlighted by the various poetic transfigurations of the image of the "red rose" ("torn," "withered," "rose-fevered") in Villa's poetry during this period. This particular model of experimental poetics shared by Manalang Gloria's and Villa's early poetry provided a clear foundation for Villa's later experimental poetics as a writer in the US, as well as his own conceptualization and description of his work as a "literary experimenter."[71]

A particularly useful notion for understanding the complex process of translation and recreation of imagist poetics carried out by Manalang Gloria in her early poetry, as well as the clear impact of her late 1920s experimental poetry on the early poetry of Villa, is provided by Brazilian poet, translator, and critic Haroldo de Campos through his influential concept of "transcreation." For de Campos, a "transcreation" constitutes a form of "re-creation," which he defines as "a parallel and autonomous, although reciprocal, translation."[72] De Campos precisely refers to translation here as a creative practice in the work of the originator of imagism, Ezra Pound.[73] As argued by the poet and critic Jerome Rothenberg, de Campos's notion of "transcreation" is connected to the notion of "othering" that Rothenberg considers to be at the heart not just of translation, but ultimately of poetry as a creative practice:

> What Haroldo de Campos called "transcreation" & I called "othering" – as one of the defining characteristics of poetry as a whole … As with other variations – other translations for that matter – the procedure, if it works, doesn't so much annihilate the original version as bring it into a new dimension, where both versions can lead an independent if interlinked existence.[74]

In their early experimental poetry in English, Manalang Gloria and Villa both manage to transcreate – to adopt Rothenberg's conceptualization of Haroldo de Campos's notion here – the anglophone poetics of imagism, in a poetic transfer or "othering" able to effectively "bring to a new dimension" the poetics of anglophone modernism that they both encountered as young college students at the University of the Philippines in the late 1920s. As examined here, the early poetry of both Manalang Gloria and Villa – originally published in various English-language periodicals in the Philippines during the

1920s and 1930s, such as the *Philippines Herald Magazine* and the *Philippine Magazine* – collectively constitutes, like the earlier work of Claro Recto, a priceless historical record not only of the transnational circulation of various forms of modernist and avant-garde poetics in the Philippines, but also of the cultural tension between two imperial and hegemonic forces affecting modern Philippine history and literature.

Comparing the Spectre of Translation in Filipinx Modernism

Despite their divergent political commitments and literary responses, an analysis of the modernist poetry of Recto, Manalang Gloria, and Villa demonstrates how these three poets engaged in a deeply personal and complex process of comparison and translation through which they rearticulated their own positions as Filipinx writers in a rapidly changing world determined by Western colonization. From this perspective, their respective poetics constitute different (post)colonial responses aiming to both critically understand a complex colonial past, and creatively imagine a new future for Filipinx culture, parallel to what Rizal originally described as "el demonio de las comparaciones." In this sense, Recto, Manalang Gloria, and Villa – each through modernist poetry – propose various manifestations of the kind of comparative act originally carried out by Rizal's postcolonial comparison in his foundational novel *Noli me tángere*, transforming this original act of comparison, as Anderson does, into a new version of itself able to enter new cultural registers and historical contexts within the Philippines. As shown in this chapter, their divergent attempts to negotiate and "transcreate" through the language of poetry the deep historical tension between overlapping forms of imperialism in the Philippines – and related understandings of temporality and identity – highlight the different versions of planetary engagement shaping the historical avant-garde in various parts of the world during this period.

While Recto's work represents a political effort to conserve a Spanish-language cultural tradition in the Philippines as a way of resisting US imperialism – by combining through the poetics of *modernismo* the expression of a lyric subjectivity with an explicit rejection of the new imperial paradigm – Manalang Gloria and Villa's early poetry in English attempts to move away from that same Spanish-language tradition, by embracing literary and cultural aspects of the rapidly changing and suddenly shifting logic and material conditions driving US imperialism. In the case of Villa, in his initial embrace and swift rejection of the poetics of Manalang Gloria, we can see how the imperial logic of the

United States quickly altered the way in which anglophone writers in the Philippines tried to acquire a new hegemonic status within the US's literary and historical paradigm. In contrast with these two different male positions represented by the compositions of Recto and Villa, the work of Manalang Gloria shows an alternative commitment to the local sources of Filipinx culture, while embracing the English language as an empowering and transformational medium for her poetry as a woman writer in the Philippines.

Yet the cultural rupture within Filipinx literature that resulted from the US occupation further complicates the kind of comparative reading that allowed both Rizal and Anderson to recognize the exchange value of critical comparison as a way to overcome an original failure of one's own language. In this context, the main complexity at the core of the work of Recto, Manalang Gloria, and Villa, and consequently the main difference from Rizal's original "double vision" in *Noli me tángere*, is rooted in the historical conditions connected to the overlap of the legacy of Spanish colonialism with a new form of imperial domination. In this respect, it is important to highlight that Recto's questioning of the experience of "peace" after the traumatic aftermath of the US occupation in *Bajo los cocoteros* (1911), examined earlier in the chapter, is later mirrored by Villa, from a radically different perspective and ideological position, in his short story "Young Writer in the New Country." At the end of this short story, Villa's first-person narrator, a young writer who has recently immigrated to the United States, poses the following rhetorical question about his complex relation to both his native land and the "new country": "Will the native land forgive? Between your peace and the peace of a strange faraway desert – Between your two peaces – O tell softly, softly. Forgive softly."[75]

As we have seen in this chapter, the particular historical conditions at the core of modernist Philippine literature entail a double erasure of local forms of language and knowledge through the imposition of the norms of the colonizer that complicates the ontological and epistemological status of one's own language – here referring to language at an individual, collective, and national level – as the case of early twentieth-century Filipinx poetry shows. Ultimately, this complex tension and experience of "double vision" at the heart of modernist Filipinx literature in this period not only complicates the kind of comparative reading grounded in the relative stability of one's own language, such as Rizal's and Anderson's, as described above, but also, as Adam Lifshey argues, ultimately "challenges the structures of academic disciplines" traditionally used to understand and produce knowledge on those very cultural and literary forms:

> What literature in Spanish is and can be, what American literature is and can be, suddenly comes up for redefinition when Filipino literature in Spanish is interrogated … If Filipino literature in Spanish after Rizal is quarried and dusted off as an archeological effort aimed at filling in a gap in a national literary history, that would seem to be a justifiable project. But surely a move to fill in a blank space on a map would provoke broader considerations if that move upturned the map altogether.[76]

In filling the "gap" that Lifshey identifies here by carefully tracing the divergent networks and poetic forms of modernist Filipinx literature emerging after Rizal as they take shape in overlapping Spanish and English linguistic forms, this chapter has provided a critical examination of some of the key implications of this "upturned map." As shown here, these are complex experimental literary networks that expand across the world and are determined by and embedded in two imperial ideologies and histories. Overall, what is ultimately emphasized in the three central cases of Recto, Manalang Gloria, and Villa in modernist Filipinx literature is precisely a form of planetary engagement during the historical avant-garde: a committed affirmation through the language of experimental poetry of a deep sense of a postcolonial alterity, of a kind of irreducible otherness within the self that is determined by conflicting historical forces dramatically shaping the local, and which Spivak locates at the core of her original conception of planetarity.

Coda

Ludwig Mies van der Rohe, Lilly Reich, and the Barcelona World's Fair of 1929: Experimental Form as Network and the Traditionalist Politics of Empire

The previous chapters in this book have undertaken a critical re-evaluation of experimental form during the historical avant-garde as it articulates various transnational links between writers, artists, and literary traditions in different parts of the world as specific responses to Iberian colonialism. It is precisely due to the experimental nature of avant-garde poetics – as a radical challenge to and rupture from traditional forms, one that traverses diverse literary, linguistic, and media boundaries – that the particular avant-garde networks studied in this book were able to be established and circulate across various national and continental boundaries. Within this geopolitical context, experimental form can assert a sense of political alterity and critically question received hegemonic histories and traditions, which in my reading emerges as central to the historical avant-garde from a transnational and transcontinental perspective. In other words, and as I have argued here, key works belonging to the historical avant-garde from a formal and temporal perspective – such as Vicente Huidobro's experimental *oeuvre*, Tarsila do Amaral's modernist paintings, or Manalang Gloria's imagist poems, to mention three of the cases studied in this book – while excluded from Eurocentric and Anglo-American scholarly approaches to the period, constitute an intrinsic and crucial part of key larger networks of experimental poetics that were emerging at this time across the world. Part of the objective of this book, albeit limited by its specific scope and archive, has been to fill in some of the geographical gaps pertaining to the historical avant-garde, particularly outside a purely European-centred or centre-periphery model of literary and art history.

The methodological and critical approach to the various avant-garde networks studied in this book has been inspired by Bruno Latour's model for sociohistorical analysis, in particular his examination of social networks developed primarily in *Reassembling the Social*, where

Latour provides a systematic description of actor-network theory as a method of network analysis. Latour highlights the social as a dynamic process of assembling different social properties and actors, and thus presents an approach to social theory through which different social assemblages and associations can be traced back (thus "reassembled") and understood in relation to each other, "following the actors themselves," as Latour puts it succinctly.[1] Within the context of *A Planetary Avant-Garde*, Latour's theory provides a generative methodological foundation for reassembling the social and political dimensions of avant-garde networks. The implications of this method of analysis are considerable for a new understanding of key networks of experimental literature during the historical avant-garde: this is a reassembling through which we can retrace and reconsider previously acknowledged associations (such as the avant-garde network connecting the work of Cendrars and Tarsila explored in chapter 3, and the complex relation between the work of José Garcia Villa and Angela Manalang Gloria in relation to Anglo-American modernism studied in chapter 4); at the same time, by following the actors themselves, we can recreate their circulation and collective existence – the sociohistorical dimensions and "lived relations" of these networks – from a new critical perspective (as in the case of Portuguese Futurism and of Vicente Huidobro's *creacionismo* respectively analysed in chapters 1 and 2).

Parallel to this methodological "reassembling" process, Latour's theory of social analysis also emphasizes the dimension of the network as a complex process that opens up and calls for a series of multiple interpretations – as opposed to emphasizing a specific outcome of or result from a network leading to a single particular interpretation. As studied in this book, the social life of the historical avant-garde from a planetary perspective does not operate in a given, predetermined space, or in a vacuum, for that matter, but rather operates – "acts," in Latour's sense of the verb – through its various forms and assemblages, particularly as these various assemblages form, circulate, and move across various linguistic, national, continental, and aesthetic boundaries in different parts of the world. This experience of form in general and, within the context of the avant-garde, of experimental form more specifically, can be seen as a mode of translation when understood as an integral component of the complex series of sociohistorical relations articulated transnationally by specific experimental literature networks. From this perspective, forms themselves and their circulation as part of a larger process of exchange become key translational actors that facilitate the spatio-temporal development of particular networks, as well as their interrelation with other networks at a local and transnational level.

This conception of form as a mode of translation is highlighted by Latour in the following passage:

> As soon as we concentrate on what circulates from site to site, the first type of entities to snap into focus are *forms*. Few words are more ambiguous, and yet this is just the sort of topic that the shift in social theory allows us to see in a new light. Usually, form is taken not in material but in a formal sense … But as soon as you notice that each site has to pay the connection with another site through some displacement, then the notion of form takes a very concrete and practical sense: a form is simply something which allows something else to be transported from one site to another. Form then becomes one of the most important types of translations.[2]

The particular conception of form as a type of translation in the sense highlighted by Latour, also related to what I have elsewhere called the (un)translatability of form, is central to the examination of the historical avant-garde presented in this book.[3] It is in terms of this understanding of experimental form as capable of translating and thus connecting the (assembled) existence of various avant-garde artworks and actors that my interpretation of the avant-garde in this book opens a new sense of its historicity and geopolitical dimensions that differs considerably from Peter Bürger's sense of the historicity of the avant-garde examined in the introduction.

Seen in relation to each other, the various networks of experimental poetics analysed in the four chapters of this book highlight how the "scattered hegemonies" of Spanish and Portuguese colonialism were actively present in the first three decades of the twentieth century as historical and political forces affecting cultural production across various parts of the world. This was a colonial logic and conception of history that in key instances was precisely identified, challenged, and questioned both outside and within its Iberian metropoles through the experimental artwork itself, as the cases studied in this book demonstrate. Moreover, it is evident that these specific networks were partly determined and defined by the legacies of early modern Iberian colonialism – as well as by renewed colonial efforts by Spain and Portugal during the early twentieth century – including through its inter-imperial overlap with other forms of colonialism, particularly as embodied in the imperial regimes developed from the late nineteenth century by the British Empire, as well as from the early twentieth century by the United States.

By the year 1929, the circulation of experimental poetics across various avant-garde networks had already suffered a gradual process of institutionalization and commodification in the very metropoles of the former Iberian colonial empires. While Futurism had played an important, albeit brief, role in the cultural life of Portugal between 1915 and 1918, as examined in chapter 1, various avant-garde currents, including Futurism, gradually came to occupy an institutional place as well within public life in Spain during the 1920s. In my reading, this co-option of avant-garde and experimental form by Spanish and Portuguese cultural and governmental institutions functioned in a parallel way, in very general terms, to the capitalistic commodification of avant-garde poetics that Greg Dawes traces in Anglo-American modernism, which he describes as a "fenómeno cultural globalizante" (globalizing cultural phenomenon), but which was inflected here by a radically different series of historical, cultural, and political implications.[4] In particular, as I will discuss in the rest of this coda, this gradual commodification of the avant-garde during this period, most of it state-driven, served the purpose of reinforcing a "temporal understanding of modernity," previously mentioned by Puchner in the introduction, in which Europe in general, and Spain and Portugal in particular – or rather, specific understandings of Spain and Portugal as states and political institutions – appear to have been positioning themselves, or at least trying to, as the geographical centre of this sense of modernity, while at the same time defining related ethnocentric and ideologically driven notions of history and historiography.

This institutionalization of avant-garde form, both as a marker of industrial progress and as a "temporal understanding" of modernity, to adopt Puchner's concept, was in fact a process that began earlier, after World War I, and which intensified in the 1920s – parallel to the development of fascism as a political ideology in Spain and Portugal, as well as in Italy. While the institutional co-opting of the avant-garde was perhaps not as wide-ranging in Spain as it was in Italy by the early 1920s – due to Mussolini's incorporation of mainstream Futurism into the fascist ideological project, as well as the proto-fascist dimension of Italian Futurism – the gradual impact of parallel processes in Spain during the 1920s was highly significant. As shown in recent studies of this period in Spain, such as Leslie Harkema's *Spanish Modernism and the Poetics of Youth* and Juli Highfill's *Modernism and Its Merchandise*, this institutional commodification of the avant-garde during the Primo de Rivera regime in the 1920s constitutes one of the key points of inflection within historiographic studies of Iberian avant-garde poetics that still deserves further critical enquiry, particularly concerning the politics of the various avant-garde artists of the period included in groups such as "la joven literatura" movement and the so-called *Generación del 27*.

This process of commodification of the avant-garde in Spain is especially important in terms of the study of the militarization of politics, forms of political repression, and various forms of censorship implemented by the Primo de Rivera dictatorship (1923–30). Highfill's *Modernism and Its Merchandise* provides a crucial account in this context of what she describes as the "new society of spectacle" developed in Spain under Primo de Rivera's military government – namely, the relation between, on the one hand, the material and economic conditions stemming from the Spanish state's "regenerationist" investments in infrastructure and technological development at this time and, on the other, the contemporaneous avant-garde artistic and intellectual production.[5] The impact of Primo de Rivera's policies during the reign of King Alfonso XIII on the cultural and artistic scene of the time, as well as various responses by artists and intellectuals to these sociopolitical conditions, was considerable, particularly around the influential figure of Miguel de Unamuno, who was in fact expelled from the Iberian Peninsula in 1924 by military order and remained in voluntary exile for about six years until 1930.[6]

The gradual commodification and political use of experimental form during the last decade of Alfonso XIII's reign, prior to its collapse and the proclamation of the Spanish Second Republic in 1931, can be traced back at least as far as Primo de Rivera's "Barcelona Manifesto" of 1923. This manifesto constitutes Primo de Rivera's key political pronouncement in which the general, mirroring Mussolini's fascist uprising of 1922 in Italy, publicly presented to the people of Spain what essentially became the *coup d'état* through which the Spanish military deposed the government of then prime minister Manuel García Prieto. Originally published in the newspaper *La vanguardia* on 13 September 1923, the "Barcelona Manifesto" displays the political use of the manifesto form, with evident Futurist tones in terms of both its projected sense of futurity and its performative dimension. The use of the manifesto form in this instance – which is parallel to the use of the manifesto in some of the contemporaneous avant-garde movements developing in Spain and Portugal during this period, as shown in my examination of Futurist manifestos in chapter 1 – is central to the totalitarian politics that Primo de Rivera is trying to declare, establish, and proclaim through this pronouncement. As Primo de Rivera declares in the document, "A manifesto does not admit of further details. Our work will be very soon known, and the nation and history will judge it, for our conscience is at rest as regards our purpose and intent."[7] The performative dimension of the manifesto not only justifies itself as a performative act, but also claims a new political authority and presents it to the Spanish people on behalf of Primo de Rivera, who by this point had effectively taken over the institutions of the Spanish state and government through military force: "Although we may come into being through an act of technical indiscipline, we do represent that true discipline which is due our principles and love of country, and so we shall conceive, practice, and require discipline, not forgetting that, since we are not moved by ambition but … by the spirit of sacrifice, ours is the highest authority."[8]

It is important to emphasize here that this particular totalitarian use both of the rhetoric of the avant-garde and of specific cultural and political institutions in Spain, which appears to have been central to the "new" politics of the Primo de Rivera dictatorship, did not go unnoticed by critics of the regime. In fact, it was repeatedly decried by intellectual figures of the time, including Unamuno. As Harkema has shown, Unamuno tried repeatedly to warn a younger generation of artists and writers in Spain that the apparent modernity, technological progress, and avant-gardism that characterized the rhetoric of the new regime was not only a cover for a totalitarian ideology, but was, in fact, a new version of the old, "defunct" system:

> While Primo worked to frame his government as the antithesis to and solution for the old ways of the past (in this like other European dictators who seized power in the wake of the first World War), Unamuno encouraged Spanish students to see themselves – not the new regime – as the only true source of rejuvenation for their country. In the spring of 1925 he addressed "los estudiantes de España" in an open letter that was published in the anti-regime periodical *España con honra* (*Spain with Honor*). There he warned them that while Primo claimed to have put an end to the *ancien régime* of the Restoration, in reality his dictatorship was the culmination of that defunct order … Unamuno encouraged his young addressees not to be taken in by Primo's rhetoric, and not to act as young recruits to what was in reality an old and abhorrent cause.[9]

Unfortunately, Unamuno's warnings in 1925 went largely unheard by a younger generation of artists, intellectuals, and politicians, as Harkema argues. Hence, there is no doubt that the conscious embrace of a poetics of "youth" and an avant-garde sense of modernity and performativity by Primo de Rivera's dictatorship had an impact on the eventual support provided, implicitly or explicitly, by members of key artistic circles and intellectual elites of the period in Spain.

This gradual commodification of avant-garde rhetoric and experimental form as part of a larger state-apparatus of propaganda and control under the Primo de Rivera military dictatorship can perhaps best be seen in the two international exhibitions or world's fairs that took place in the cities of Barcelona and Seville in 1929.[10] Similar to Primo de Rivera's appropriation of the manifesto form to declare the *coup d'état*, as well as all the resources and institutions of the Spanish state, his government appropriated in this instance two social and political events that had been in the works prior to his ascent to power. Both projects – originally designed by various local institutions in each city aiming to articulate a new sense of modernity for very different regions of Spain – were co-opted by the new regime in order to showcase in 1929 a "new" image of economic and technological progress that the regime had been trying to project both locally and to the world since 1923. As historian Amparo Graciani García has shown, while the Ibero-American Exposition in Seville had been developed locally since 1909, Primo de Rivera soon incorporated it as part of his political and military project for a new Spain:

> Primo de Rivera asimila la idea de la Exposición como parte de su proyecto politico … Más que una exhibición industrial, deseaba propugnar un fraternal americanismo, que por encima de vínculos nacionales, uniera a los países americanos entre sí, y estos con España.)
>
> (Primo de Rivera assimilates the idea of the Exposition as part of his own political project … As opposed to an industrial exhibition, he wanted to project a brotherly Americanism that, above national ties, would unite the American countries among themselves, with Spain.)[11]

While the main political priority of the Seville Exposition was to highlight a sense of neocolonial enterprise between Spain, Portugal, and a number of Latin American nations, the Barcelona World's Fair had a different but complementary focus on technology, industry, and innovation as part of the government's efforts to showcase to the world a "new" and "modern" Spain able to influence world affairs after World War I. The Barcelona Exposition was originally planned as an electrical industry exhibition officially constituted in 1914 by a group of local Barcelona businessmen and politicians. The final plans for the Barcelona Exposition were completed in 1917 and were based on a previous project created by the influential Catalan architect, politician, and urban planner Josep Puig i Cadafalch (1867–1956), and developed in parallel with an urban planning process around the Montjuïc area, which was also approved by the Barcelona municipal authorities in 1914. A series of delays followed, and it was only after Primo de Rivera's coup of 1922 and his subsequent dissolution of the local Mancomunitat de Catalunya

(Commonwealth of Catalonia) as a political entity in 1925 – as part of the totalitarian centralization of power across the country under Primo de Rivera's rule – along with Puig i Cadafalch's resignation from the project, that the original plans were revised and placed in the service of the state and the political ideology of the new regime alongside the Seville Exposition.[12]

This complex political and urban process related to the development and planning of the Barcelona Exposition was fraught with innumerable tensions and complexities at a local economic and political level, which also included the displacement of the local population in the area of the city around the Montjuïc mountain.[13] Finally completed and inaugurated on 20 May 1929, the Barcelona Exposition was presented to the world as an "unsurpassable" achievement of the Spanish nation state under Primo de Rivera, as this passage from the official program of the Exposition ("Plan General del Certamen") asserts:

> In the course of a few years the city of Barcelona has transformed a part of this historical hill on Montjuich into a leafy park of 200 hectares, overlooking the city and the sea and forming a frame of unsurpassable beauty for the Exhibition. This, for its sitting, its splendor, its profusion of lighting effects and fountains, may well be classed as one of the finest Exhibitions ever held in any part of the world.[14]

As the official program of the Exposition also highlights, the city of Barcelona was very important for the Primo de Rivera government in 1929, owing to its growing economic relevance as one of the largest modern cities across the Mediterranean region in Southern Europe, growth that had obviously been the gradual result of considerable financial and urban planning efforts by local Catalan businesses and political institutions over the previous three decades.

As Robert Davidson has shown in *Jazz Age Barcelona*, the Catalan capital had seen a post–World War I economic and urban boom, which was connected to a considerable increase in its cultural relevance across Western Europe as a "spectacle" capital, in terms of what Davidson refers to as the "Europeanization of the spectacle – and the spaces of spectacle" across the city during the Jazz Age.[15] The Barcelona Exposition of 1929 thus represents the culmination of the city's cultural and commercial boom as a European city of "spectacle" during the 1920s on a larger, more official, scale, particularly in relation to the important international ramifications that were, in this case, institutionally driven by the Spanish state under Primo de Rivera, and in coordination with the Ibero-American Exposition in Seville. From this

Figure C.1. Panoramic view of the Barcelona Exposition (1929).
Source: National Archives and Records Administration, Records of the Bureau of Foreign and Domestic Commerce (151-FC-106–67).

perspective, therefore, the main purpose of the Barcelona Exposition was the regime's political need to showcase the sense of "renovating impulse" embodied by the Catalan capital, a commodification of an avant-garde sense of spectacle and "modernity" – referred to by Highfill as the "new society of spectacle"[16] – that was thus projected by the Primo de Rivera dictatorship in order to display and exhibit to the world the economic and political life of a new and modern Spain, as announced in its official program:

> La necesidad de exhibir ante los demás países el estado de adelanto que ha alcanzado Barcelona en los diferentes órdenes de la vida y el convencimiento de que un impulso renovador debe guiar su actividad a fin de asimilarse los diversos y constantes progresos de los tiempos modernos, dieron origen al proyecto de organizar una Exposición internacional, que ha de ser la primera manifestación de esta índole en el mundo después de la gran Guerra.
>
> (The need to expose to other countries the state of progress that Barcelona has achieved in various orders of life and the conviction that a drive of renewal must guide its activity in order to assimilate the range of new advancements of modern times, led to the origins of this project to organize an international Exposition, which is to be the first such demonstration in the world after the Great War.)[17]

"Progress," "new advancements," and "modern times" were thus some of the catchphrases used to promote the Spanish state's self-projected image of modernity and post-war progress through the 1929 Barcelona Exposition and its commodification of the city's own "spectacular" dimension in Davidson's sense, as explored in his *Jazz Age Barcelona*.

As part of this larger process of institutionalization and commodification of "modern times" by the Primo de Rivera regime, and thus of avant-garde form within this context, it is important to highlight the inclusion as part of the Barcelona Exposition of a key modernist work by perhaps the most influential avant-garde architect of the 1920s, Ludwig Mies van der Rohe, as well as by Lilly Reich, artistic director of the German Pavilion at the Exposition. Mies and Reich's Barcelona Pavilion, as it is now generally known, constitutes a paradigmatic and incredibly influential instance of modernist architecture that through its very site of production is intrinsically connected to both a totalitarian politics and a traditionalist understanding of history and progress that is deeply invested in a neocolonial logic of empire. The Barcelona Pavilion itself is generally regarded by art and architecture critics as one of the most important examples of modernist architecture in the world, though these same critics rarely acknowledge the authorial role of Reich, who collaborated with Mies in the design process and was essentially co-author of the project. As has been shown in extensive detail by Christiane Lange, both Mies van der Rohe and Reich collaborated for more than a decade, working together "closely from 1926 to 1939, and … exchanged ideas constantly,"[18] which, in fact, makes the ascription of some of their collaborative work to either one of them an extremely difficult task, as Lange argues: "Even if it were possible to ascribe an individual design to either Mies or to Reich, the examples here shown that we can only do justice to the work of Mies van der Rohe and Lilly Reich if we regard it as the result of a congenial partnership."[19]

From this perspective, the problematic omission of Reich's name in reference to Mies and Reich's Barcelona Pavilion has become commonplace among modern art and architecture critics. For example, Richard Weston highlights the synthesis of materials and approaches that characterize the building, without making any reference to Reich: "Mies was inspired by De Stijl and Suprematism, but the synthesis was uniquely his; it was proclaimed by many who had only seen photographs and drawings as the century's most beautiful building."[20] A similar, and more recent, critical assessment, which also completely ignores Reich's role in the design and creation of the Barcelona Pavilion, is provided by Matt Gibberd and Albert Hill in their recent *Ornament Is Crime: Modernist Architecture* (2017), where they highlight the Pavilion as an essential work in Mies's groundbreaking oeuvre within the field of modernist architecture, and an extremely influential model for modern residential architecture: "His Barcelona Pavilion of 1929, although only intended as a temporary structure, was as influential as Le Corbusier's Villa Savoye. Its clean lines, horizontal emphasis, concrete walls and copious glazing still provide the blueprint for a large proportion of contemporary residential architecture."[21]

One of the defining features highlighted by critics of both Mies and Reich's Barcelona Pavilion over the decades is how the overall sense of form – for example, the "clean lines, horizontal emphasis, concrete walls and copious glazing" described by Gibberd and Hill above – configures a uniquely modern experience that seems to characterize critical assessments of the building. This critical consideration of the form of Mies and Reich's Pavilion as a groundbreaking experience in itself dates back to the building's inauguration as part of the Barcelona Exposition in 1929. As analysed in 1929 by the Catalan writers Àngel Marsà and Luis Marsillach in their essay on the Exposition, *La montaña iluminada* (The Illuminated Mountain), it was precisely the radically experimental rearticulation of forms in the building that provided what they described as a shocking sense of an "architecture of reflections" able to mirror other forms and configurations as intrinsic to the Pavilion's own form:

> The German Pavilion – the Palace of Reflections – is the most authentic expression of Cubism, the chief manifestation of that dead, quartered aesthetic which Picasso invented one gloomy day. The black marble walls drink up the sunlight insatiably, eagerly; and this very sunlight, in its turn, has deigned to kiss the burnished floor and the glass roofs, only to splitter into a thousand flecks of scattered reflections … To have tamed light from above is a great achievement. If a people should adopt this architecture, they will be a people of clear horizons. Such is the German Pavilion: the architecture of reflections. Walls, paving stones and roofs form a prodigious blending of rays and lights which criss-cross freely. And, this precisely, is the soul of the new Germany.[22]

As these descriptions show, there is an attempt to highlight the way in which the avant-garde form of Mies and Reich's Pavilion itself is able not only to incorporate and blend a series of natural elements but also to rearticulate those forms into a new experience and configuration. Marsà and Marsillach, for instance, not only connect the Barcelona Pavilion with the Cubist work of Picasso as a key avant-garde reference relevant to both the local culture of Barcelona and the global culture of the avant-garde, but also emphasize how its experimental and innovative form is related to the way the building works as a reflection of its various materials, in fact as a modernist assemblage of sorts that aims as an artwork at constituting a network of connections within its own space.

As explored throughout *A Planetary Avant-Garde*, the network as process exceeds any of its specific actors and outcomes, a feature also demonstrated here in the case of Mies and Reich's avant-garde Barcelona Pavilion: as highlighted by Marsà and Marsillach, the formal reflection of this artwork also indicates the nationalistic value of the building itself, not only in relation to Germany as the nation represented ("the soul of the new Germany"), but also because this very sense of modernity is inherently connected to the Barcelona Exposition as a national and nationalistic project on behalf of the Spanish state under Primo de Rivera. As the architect and scholar Josep Quetglas has observed in his groundbreaking study of the Barcelona Pavilion, the Pavilion itself as originally conceived was intended as a welcoming space for the reception of King Alfonso XIII at the inauguration of the larger halls that housed the main exhibits of the German section at the Exposition:

> Mies received a complex commission, referring first to one thing, then to another, until the last one comes to renew the cycle of references. Germany's participation in the 1929 Barcelona World's Fair comprised a series of displays on industrial machinery and products in various halls, and a pavilion celebrating electricity, in accord with the fair's original theme. A new space was called for to safeguard protocol. King Alfonso XIII of Spain would inaugurate each participating country's representation at the fair. Germany needed, then, a place where the king could sign the book of ceremony, drink a toast, and have a seat, perhaps in the company of his wife. It would have to provide a setting for the inauguration, a setting that would represent Germany, and to communicate Germany's self-image to the world.[23]

In my reading of both the historical avant-garde and this particular event within it, as developed throughout this book, the connection between nationalism, localized forms of totalitarian politics, and the experience of experimental form embodied in Mies and Reich's building in Barcelona cannot be ignored. In other words, if the original social purpose of the Barcelona Pavilion, one of the key and most influential instances of avant-garde architecture in the world, as briefly outlined here, was in fact to provide a space for the king of Spain to be welcomed to the German section of the 1929 Barcelona Exposition, and thus to provide a protocol location for the inaugural book signing, that geopolitical dimension of the avant-garde artwork as network, and its commodification within this very local context, needs to be accounted for as part of its social life – particularly within the larger examination conducted in this book of both planetary engagement and the "scattered hegemonies" of Iberian colonialism.

Overall, and while they were eventually eclipsed by a series of internal political and economic tensions; the rise of fascism and communism worldwide; and the global economic collapse precipitated by the Wall Street Crash later that year, followed by the Great Depression, the two 1929 exhibitions hold considerable political importance and historical significance, particularly in the context of this book. As examined here, the two government-funded exhibitions were explicit propaganda and promotional efforts by the regime of Alfonso XIII under Primo de Rivera's dictatorship to rearticulate a new imperial impulse after the gradual colonial collapse of Spain in the nineteenth century.[24]

This neocolonial dimension of these two parallel 1929 exhibitions in Spain can be seen explicitly in a speech by Alfonso XIII given in Seville on 7 July 1926 to mark the official provision of land by local organizers of the Ibero-American Exposition in Seville for the construction of the Argentine and Portuguese pavilions. This event in Seville, which, according to historian Alfonso Braojos Garrido, was attended by over 150 guests, including consular representatives of the United States, Portugal, Argentina, and more than ten other Latin American nations,[25] was marked by a royal speech in which Alfonso framed the political relevance of the joint project of these two international exhibitions scheduled for 1929 in the following terms:

> Nuestra raza es hoy fuerte y valerosa. Si España antaño fue pobre y no pudo desarrollarse científica y materialmente en la medida de lo deseable; si no pudo poblar sus territorios, tuvo en cambio corazón y energía. Gracias al esfuerzo de su voluntad ha sabido resurgir y engrandecerse y buscar en la unión con sus hijas de América, esa fuerza que da la unión para que todos unidos laboremos por el engradecimiento de la raza. Madres e hijas, unidas, son las que han de dar al mundo, en lo futuro, la patria de los sentimientos de amor y unión que deben reinar entre los pueblos, como la base del progreso. Y nosotros queremos progreso y paz, porque ellos engrandecen a las naciones … Es preciso que la Exposición sea el modelo de lo que debe ser la España del siglo XX y que no haya solamente en Barcelona Exposición, sino que la haya aquí también para que ambas unidas den la medida del esfuerzo nacional.
>
> (Our race is strong and courageous today. If Spain was once poor and could not develop scientifically and materially as desired; if she could not populate its territories, she had instead heart and energy. Thanks to the effort of her will, she has known how to rise and grow and to seek in union with her daughters in America, that strength that gives unity so that all of us together can work for the appreciation of the race. Mothers and

daughters, united, are those who are to give the world, in the future, the homeland of the feelings of love and union that must reign among peoples, as the basis of progress. And we want progress and peace, because they make the nations great … It is necessary that the Exposition is the model of what should be the Spain of the twentieth century, and that there is not only an Exposition in Barcelona, but that there is also one so that both together give the measure of our national effort.)[26]

This speech by Alfonso highlights, among other key political questions, a series of notions of Spanish history, ideas of progress, and a particular conception of an Ibero-American "race" grounded in a neo-imperial ideology that aims to recuperate the legacy of early modern Iberian colonialism in the historicist and traditionalist terms examined in this book. By fashioning a female motherland able to regenerate "her mothers and daughters," Alfonso is not only recuperating an idealized and patriarchal colonial understanding of the past as part of his political vision for a "modern" Spain in 1926, but also projecting that vision as a potential political future, and thus as the foundation of a "new" Iberian sense of progress and modernity that could be commercialized and exported across the Atlantic, and potentially worldwide. However, this traditionalist understanding of politics and history as a form of "national propaganda" made a clear impression on observers of the Barcelona Exposition outside Spain in 1929, as the following review of the event by the US art historian and critic Helen Appleton Read in the New York–based journal *The Arts* suggests:

A World's Fair, as national propaganda, may be an outworn formula, yet the nations using it broadcast a fairly accurate picture of their industrial and cultural status. The ostensible purpose of the Barcelona World's Fair, only now reaching completion despite its official opening in May, was to proclaim Spain's entry into world's affairs and to establish a reputation as a financial, industrial power. Perhaps the energy and enormous expense of this stupendous undertaking, the lavish electrical displays lighting piled-up masses of bastard baroque and Renaissance exhibition palaces, the elaborate system of tramways, escalators and funiculars conveying visitors up to the Versailles terraces of the exposition grounds, are convincing evidence of a rebirth of the spirit which produced the *Conquistadores*. Culturally the results show that Spain has not roused herself from three hundred years' sleep.[27]

As Appleton Read sharply argues, both the Exposition and the propaganda effort by the Primo de Rivera government led to an image of a

Spain that "had not roused herself from three hundred years' sleep." Ultimately, therefore, despite the financial, architectural, urban, and technological efforts on display at the Exposition, the overall result failed to persuade foreign critics of the sense of modern "rebirth" that the Primo de Rivera and Alfonso XIII regime was so desperately trying to project to the world.

Within the Portuguese context, and as shown in chapter 3, this traditionalist understanding of a colonial past was also central to the political project of the military dictatorship of the *Ditadura Nacional* (National Dictatorship) after the *coup d'état* of 1926 that would eventually lead to Salazar's *Estado Novo*, as well as related political circles in Portugal in the early 1920s. As analysed by António Costa Pinto, these political groups in Portugal had also been greatly influenced by the Primo de Rivera regime, as well as by Mussolini's Italy since 1922, and they "adopted the symbolism of Italian fascism, and in 1923 of the Dictatorship of Primo de Rivera": "The most important factor [u]nifying the new extreme right in the twenties was the 'postponement' of the republic/monarchy cleavage. In this external influences such as Italian fascism, and the Primo de Rivera's Dictatorship, as well as a new generation of young Sorelian integralists played an important role."[28] At the same time, it is important to emphasize that this neocolonial view of the past developing in parallel ways in both Spain and Portugal during this period replicates and is strictly in line with the conception of the nation state at the core of the totalitarian ideology developed by Primo de Rivera. A more developed formulation of this neocolonial and imperial dimension that characterizes Primo de Rivera's "Barcelona Manifesto," mentioned above, is offered in his "Platform of the Patriotic Union," a piece that again uses the manifesto form to present a series of political and ideological tenets, and which elaborates some of the foundations of his dictatorial regime at this historical moment. Of the various precepts, the following three are particularly important as a contextualization of Alfonso XIII's 1926 speech in Seville, analysed above, as well as the role of the two 1929 exhibitions as part of the larger political project.

> 11. Vigilant attention and spiritual, civic, and economic aid to the organization of colonies of Spaniards abroad.
>
> 12. Ever closer spiritual, intellectual, and mercantile relations with the countries of Iberian origin, so that, while the nations preserve the characteristics of their independence, they consider themselves included, especially during difficult moments in worlds affairs, in a great league which is to be sort of comprehensive expression of the genius and the

> duties of the [Hispanic] race and is to tend primarily to the maintenance of peace and justice.
>
> 13. Intervention in national production and in the sale of its products, in order to avoid usury or ruinous competition, undertaking to guarantee the quality of the articles and product exported, in order that the reputation of Spanish business for integrity may not decline and that the national prestige may not suffer.[29]

This section of Primo de Rivera's "Platform of the Patriotic Union" highlights the Iberian origins of his political project as a way of legitimizing a national model of production in which the "products" of Spain are related to a new sense of national reputation and "race." A parallel mythification of history and of the Iberian "race" was developed in Portugal just three years later, centred on the notion of "génio civilizador" (civilizing genius), which Salazar himself defines in his "Princípios fundamentais da revolução política," published in 1930, as a notion rooted in its Iberian "origins" and "que tem de ser a alma da conservação, renascimiento e progreso de Portugal" (which needs to be the soul of the conservation, renaissance, and progress of Portugal):

> Formou-se o País quase de um jacto, desde que se fez a reconquista deste canto da Península, e as nossa fronteiras, inalteráveis desde séculos, não foram fixadas a expensas de qualquer outra nação europeia. Subtraí-nos este facto às competições históricas das conquistas e desforras, permitindo se afirme mais pura a força moral da nossa independência e também da nossa expansão, desde que, firmada a base peninsular, passámos os mares para o alargamento do nosso domínio e manifestação do nosso génio civilizador.
>
> (Our Country was formed almost immediately, once the reconquest of this end of the Peninsula had been carried out, and our borders, unaltered for centuries, were never drawn at the expense of any other European nation. This fact removes us from the historical disputes of conquests and revenges, allowing the moral strength of our own independence to be affirmed more purely, as well as that of our expansion, from the moment that, once our peninsular base was secured, we crossed the seas for the expansion of our dominions and the worldwide manifestation of our civilizing genius.)[30]

Reaching back to a mythic past, Salazar conceives of an Iberian "civilizing genius" as the "natural" nationalist essence that can serve as the new "soul of progress" for Portugal in the late 1920s, and as one of the ideological foundations of his "Princípios fundamentais da revolução política." Hence, as an intrinsic part of this larger totalizing and totalitarian logic that was developed during this period in both Spain and Portugal, the Barcelona and Seville Expositions of 1929 – both of which were direct institutional models for the Exposição do Mundo Português, which took place in Lisbon a decade later in 1940 – were integral to the attempt both to rearticulate the past and to project a "modern" sense of Iberian technological and socio-economic progress within a broader understanding of history and the world economy in the late 1920s.[31]

Overall, while both the Barcelona and Seville Expositions of 1929 tried to present a new institutional image of the state to reflect its contemporary moment, the fact is that the political ideology and conception of history that sustained these social and political projects were pervaded by a traditionalist understanding of politics and history seeking to sustain an old regime in a rapidly changing political and technological landscape. Thus, both projects were ultimately rooted in an idealization and mythification of Spanish history that aimed both to control and to suppress a radically new sense of progress and revolution – embodied in communist and socialist political movements that the dictatorship of Primo de Rivera explicitly tried to repress at the time (in fact, one of the directives of "The Barcelona Manifesto" is the occupation of "communist and revolutionary centers"[32]) – while promoting a traditionalist understanding of Spanish culture and history that was pervaded by a neocolonial and imperial logic, exemplified in the speech by Alfonso XIII and the sections of the "Platform of the Patriotic Union" quoted above.

This traditionalist conceptualization of the past at the core of Primo de Rivera's ideological project for a "new" Spain happens to be on full display in the former Poble Espanyol (Spanish Town) section of the Barcelona Exposition.[33] Designed by a group of architects and artists that included Ramon Reventós, Francesc Folguera, Xavier Nogués, and Miquel Utrillo, and still standing in its original Montjuïc location, this section of the Barcelona Exposition provided a transhistorical representation of some of the traditional urban spaces from various Spanish towns, as well as 117 different homes from various regions of Catalonia and Spain, all condensed into an area of about 49,000 square metres. Poble Espanyol includes replicas of homes and buildings from fifteen different regions in Spain, from Andalucía to Galicia, Extremadura to Catalonia, with a particular focus on "traditional" forms of architecture and life, such as the Romanesque door of San Vicente from Ávila, a street from the city of Arcos de la Frontera in Cádiz, and a traditional Basque *caserío*, Casa Arteche, from the town of Erandio in Biscay.

Figure C.2. Xavier Nogués, "Exposición Internacional Barcelona 1929, 'Pueblo Español'" (1929). Colour lithograph.

Notes: A promotional poster for the 1929 Barcelona Exhibition, the image of Nogués's lithograph includes a representation of the reproduction of the Utebo Bell Tower in the Poble Espanyol (Pueblo Español) section of the Barcelona Exhibition. As documented by Jordana Mendelson in *Documenting Spain* (pp. 23–7), the original tower (part of the Iglesia de Nuestra Señora de la Asunción, in the town of Utebo, province of Zaragoza, Aragón), was photographed by Francesc Folguera (c. 1927–8) as part of the documenting process that led to the design and construction of Poble Espanyol for the Barcelona Exhibition.

Source: Wellcome Collection, provided under Creative Commons licence CC BY 4.0.

By building an idealized "Spanish town" in 1929, the organizers of the Barcelona Exposition created in Poble Espanyol a space that not only collapses different actual spaces and buildings into a new virtual "Spanish" whole, but also condenses different historical events and locations into a new "absolute" spatio-temporal realm that can be relived and experienced outside history. Therefore, the constructed space articulated by Poble Espanyol provides a vision of the "Spanish town" that presents an almost "eternal" version of Spanish history and culture deeply rooted in the past for the contemporary viewer and visitor, as Jordana Mendelson has importantly argued:

> The Poble Espanyol is represented as outside the political dimension of historical time; it is a vision of an idealized Spain that both ignores recent events and replaces them with the spectacle of the distant past or the immediate present … Through the intervention of the architects' plan and the photographers' postcards, the visitor/viewer was encouraged to manufacture and relive a dreamlike, phantasmatic childhood far away from political conflict. The Poble was constructed and perceived by many writers as a site of collective memory for the Spanish people.[34]

As a "constructed" "vision of an idealized Spain" that "ignores recent events and replaces them with the spectacle of the distant past," Poble Espanyol in particular, and the Barcelona Exposition more broadly, provide an instance, and arguably a prototypical model, of what Nil Santiáñez has described in his *Topographies of Fascism* as the fascist "production of space."[35] From this perspective, Poble Espanyol constitutes an example of a fascist production of space in which the "building" – in this case, the "Poble" as constructed space in its totality – represents an absolute "Spanish" space (abstracting "Spain" as a represented culture or nation within the material and spatial bounds of the Poble Espanyol itself). In Santiáñez's terms, this "constructed" or "built" space of fascism – total and totalitarian – is articulated through a complex combination of rhetorical, performative, and material strategies, a "wide array of disciplines, technologies, materials and tools [that] were involved in the fascist politics and production of space":

> We may conclude, thus, that in fascist political discourse the images "edifice" and "to build" condense the grammar and pragmatics of absolute space (the state, the nation, the party), function as instances of relational spacetime (the movement, in this context, is considered as both a "builder" and a "building"), and constitute places and actions located in relative space-time.[36]

The Barcelona Exposition displays a tension between different understandings of temporality and history – that is, the modern as the "new" experimental and experiential sense of form, as in the case of Mies and Reich's Barcelona Pavilion, versus the traditional or the absolute space of an already known past represented by Poble Espanyol. Thus, as a "constructed" space, in Santiáñez's conceptualization, the project of the 1929 Barcelona Exposition itself is dominated by a traditionalist and historicist perspective that collapses the fluidity of historical time into an idealized space-time that reinforces an idea of "origins" and a mythification of the past. Therefore, despite the avant-garde rhetoric and interactions with groundbreaking experimental forms at the core of the Barcelona Exposition, in particular Mies and Reich's Pavilion, as discussed here, the two Expositions organized by the Spanish state in 1929 ultimately constitute the construction of an absolute space. This is part of a larger traditionalist understanding of history and national identity that collapses progress, cultural diversity, and linguistic and ideological difference – both internally and externally, in terms of the multicultural and multi-ethnic past of the Iberian Peninsula, on the one hand, and of the wide diversity of cultures and languages colonized by the Spanish and Portuguese empires, on the other.

Through an understanding of the "temporality of modernity" as originating from a reification of Iberian "spirit" stemming from the early modern period – and the related idealization and mythification of a colonial past that led to an imperial regime of domination and subjection of other cultures and people across the world for more than four hundred years – the commodification of the avant-garde as part of a larger process of state-driven "construction" in Spain and Portugal ends up collapsing its revolutionary potential into a traditionalist understanding of both experimental form and history. All that remained in the wake of the 1929 Expositions in Spain, for instance, were the remnants of a traditional past that was long gone and a constructed image of history that, with the passing of time, also revealed itself to be a mechanism of political control and subjugation. As historian Rodríguez Bernal concludes in relation to the Ibero-American Exposition in Seville, the project itself "looked more towards the past than to the future," thus "constituting a grandiose homage to the imperial past of Spain at a difficult contemporary moment unable to offer a solid foundation to put forward towards a more promising future."[37]

By critically tracing the series of assemblages related to key networks of experimental poetics emerging during the historical avant-garde, this book has explored their specific connection to the legacy and history of Iberian colonialism. As shown here, this colonial and inter-imperial legacy is closely connected to the traditionalist ideology and understanding of the past that was reinscribed politically in Spain and Portugal in the late 1920s – and specifically manifested in the 1929 Expositions – which also emerged in totalitarian form in the subsequent fascist dictatorships of Francisco Franco in Spain and Salazar in Portugal until the 1970s, as earlier Republican efforts were militarily thwarted and repressed in both countries. At the same time, this book has recovered some of the manifestations and social lives of these experimental literature networks, while also highlighting the ways in which the various authors studied here challenged normative, Eurocentric, and historicist understandings of this period, while positing new understandings of the world. At a moment in which contemporary ecological and political movements are radically reshaping our collective understanding of the planet and the difficult legacies and hegemonies of colonialism and imperialism that are still in place – and which are being powerfully confronted, debated, and contested – the recuperation of the forms of planetary engagement explored in this book seems of the utmost critical and scholarly importance today, particularly in light of what Gregory Betts has described as the "historical avant-garde's endeavour to … unleash a new, possible, social reality."[38] There is no doubt that the centrifugal and utopian transnational impulse connected to the notion of planetary engagement in this book partly collapsed by the 1930s due to the various historical forces delineated in this coda. Among other factors, this gradual collapse took place as a result of the impending global economic crisis, increasing labour unrest across the world, and the eventual rise of totalitarian politics that would characterize the 1930s, and which would tragically lead to the military coup against the Second Spanish Republic in 1936 and the ensuing atrocities of the Spanish Civil War and World War II. However, as the commitment to experimental form across the world explored throughout *A Planetary Avant-Garde* showcases, the radical senses of alterity and geopolitical otherness that emerged around a hundred years ago are still traceable and immensely valuable today, not only for a new critical understanding of the historical avant garde, but also for the reimagining of contemporary social and political conditions towards a new, more diverse, and more hopeful future.

Notes

Introduction: Planetary Engagement, the Historical Avant-Garde, and Iberian Colonialism (1909–1929)

1 Perloff, "The Great War and the European Avant-Garde," 142.
2 Levine, *Forms*, 5.
3 Levine, 5.
4 Bürger, *Theory of the Avant-Garde*, 83, 89.
5 Bürger, 89.
6 Bürger, 90.
7 Appadurai's complete definition is as follows: "Globalization is inextricably linked to the current workings of capital on a global basis; in this regard it extends the earlier logics of empire, trade, and political dominion in many parts of the world. Its most striking feature is the runaway quality of global finance, which appears remarkably independent of traditional constraints of information transfer, national regulation, industrial productivity, or 'real' wealth in any particular society, country, or region" ("Grassroots Globalization," 4).
8 Spivak, "'Planetarity,'" 291.
9 Bürger's approach mainly considers German and French avant-garde artists and theoreticians, including Kant, Schiller, Marx, Duchamp, Breton, Magritte, Benjamin, Adorno, and Brecht. While Bürger's approach emphasizes the historicity of the avant-garde, the corpus of his theorization is not representative of this period when considered outside of a purely European centre in general, and Franco-German avant-garde archive in particular.
10 Bürger, *Theory of the Avant-Garde*, 24.
11 In the section of chapter 2 of *Theory of the Avant-Garde* titled "Historicity of Aesthetics Categories," especially pages 15–20, Bürger emphasizes how his attempt to historicize a theory of the avant-garde relates to both

a historicist and historiographic analysis of the present in relation to the past: "In the present context, historicizing a theory will have a different meaning, that is, the insight into the nexus between the unfolding of an object and the categories of a discipline or science. Understood in this fashion, the historicity of a theory is not grounded in its being the expression of a *Zeitgeist* (the historicist view) nor in the circumstance that it incorporates earlier theories (history as a prehistory of the present), but in the fact that the unfolding of object and the elaboration of categories are connected. Historicizing a theory means grasping this connection" (*Theory of the Avant-Garde*, 16).

12 Puchner, *Poetry of the Revolution*, 48. See also Adorno's *Aesthetic Theory*, particularly the sections "Art Beauty," "Coherence and Meaning," and "Draft Introduction," which explicitly engage Adorno's response to Hegel's philosophy as part of his own understanding of the aesthetic and history; see also Ortega y Gasset's *La deshumanización del arte* (The Dehumanization of Art). Ortega y Gasset published a series of studies of Hegel's work, among them *Hegel: Notas de trabajo* and *Kant, Hegel, Dilthey*. For an analysis of the impact and influence of Hegel in Ortega's thought, see Hernández Sánchez, *Estética de la limitación*. For a fascinating examination of Ortega's aesthetic theory of the avant-garde in relation to material culture in 1920s Spain, see Juli Highfill's *Modernism and Its Merchandise*, especially chapter 1, "Ortega's Apples, Ramón's Bottles."

13 Throughout this book I engage key foundational approaches to the historical avant-garde (particularly the work of Peter Bürger, Greg Dawes, Marjorie Perloff, Renato Poggioli, Vicky Unruh, and Gloria Videla, among others), as well as more recent scholarship that approaches the modernist and avant-garde poetics from a wider transnational perspective (such as Carrie Noland, Fernando Rosenberg, and Martin Puchner), as well as studies of the avant-garde with a more national focus (such as recent works by Michelle Clayton, Gregory Betts, Leslie Harkema, and Juli Highfill).

14 Latour, *Inquiry*, 31.

15 Latour, 32 (emphasis in original).

16 Elias and Moraru, "Preface and Acknowledgments," in *Planetary Turn*, vii.

17 These include, among others, art history (such as Terry Smith's research project "Defining Contemporaneity, Imagining Planetarity"), English studies (such as Susan Stanford Friedman in *Planetary Modernisms*; the aforementioned Elias and Moraru in their edited collection *The Planetary Turn*; and, more recently, Cóilín Parsons in "Planetary Parallax"), American studies (such as Wai Chee Dimock and Lawrence Buell in their influential *Shades of the Planet*), urban theory (such as Neil Brenner and Christian Schmid in "Planetary Urbanization"), religious studies (such as Stephen

Moore and Mayra Rivera's edited collection *Planetary Loves*), and history (such as Julie Livingston's *Self-Devouring Growth*). For a more detailed and extensive list of recent uses and applications of the "planetary" in contemporary scholarship in the humanities and social sciences, see Christian Moraru's *Reading for the Planet*, esp. 45–6.

18 In this sense, it is important to emphasize that Friedman's own self-expressed "commitment to planetary modernist studies" is specifically and provocatively conceptualized in terms of "the imperative to develop a framework for the field that encompasses the world across time, in the *longue dureé* of human history" (*Planetary Modernisms*, 12).

19 Friedman, *Planetary Modernisms*, 14. From this perspective, I submit that Friedman's invocation of the notion of the planetary as a longue dureé of modernism at a global scale appears as an avant-garde gesture itself, intendedly shocking and polemical, as acutely argued by Christopher Bush in his review of Friedman's book: "The assertion of a thirteenth- to fourteenth-century Mongol modernity vividly captures the shock if not awe of *Planetary Modernisms*'s agenda to liberate the world and its pasts for 'modernism' and 'modernity'" (Bush, review of *Planetary Modernisms*, 686).

20 Walkowitz, "Planetary Modernisms," 749. It is important to highlight here – based on the evident centrality of Gayatri Spivak's work both for postcolonial studies today and in terms of her original formulation of "planetarity" as described here – that Friedman's approach does not substantially engage with the work of Spivak in her own formulation of the "planetary" as a critical concept in *Planetary Modernisms*, even though, as Friedman confirms in her response to Walkowitz's and Bruce Robbins's reviews of *Planetary Modernisms*, her book constitutes an "adaptation" of postcolonial studies to modernist studies: "*Planetary Modernisms* is unthinkable without postcolonial studies" (Friedman, "Response," 751).

21 Walkowitz, "Planetary Modernisms," 751.

22 Boehmer and Matthews, "Modernism and Colonialism," 285.

23 See Doyle, "Thinking Back through Empires." Doyle defines inter-imperiality as a method in the following terms: "The underlying principle of an inter-imperial method is that polities form relationally – like persons. That is, persons, communities, and states all emerge within a volatile, uneven, and fundamental condition of relationality in which each survives by necessary relations of alliance that are interwoven with relations of coercion and domination – on both microphysical and macropolitical scales. This relationality is always already structured by political histories embedded in material habitats, bodies, and institutions."

24 Shohat and Stam, "Imperial Family." Invoking the notion of "scattered hegemonies" originally developed by Inderpal Grewal and Caren Kaplan, Shohat and Stam argue that colonial hegemonies, despite their "scattered"

status, they continue to shape as relatively fractured and diminished various social and cultural development across the world: "The old imperial hegemonies, many argue, are now more 'dispersed' and 'scattered.' But even within the current situation of dispersed hegemonies, the historical thread or inertia of Western domination remains a powerful presence" (146). Grewal and Kaplan themselves define the very concept in the title of their edited collection of essays using Grewal's own definition of the concept, as "the effects of mobile capital as well as the multiple subjectivities that replace the European unitary subject" (*Scattered Hegemonies*, 7).

25 These scholars include Mabel Moraña's foundational contributions to the field across her oeuvre (particularly Moraña's *Coloniality at Large*, co-edited with Enrique Dussel and Carlos Jáuregui), as well as Alejandro Mejías López (in his influential *Inverted Conquest*), Akiko Tsuchiya and William Acree (in their important edited volume *Empire's End*), and the more recent monographs *Imperial Emotions* by Javier Krauel and *Incomparable Empires* by Gayle Rogers.

26 Begam and Valdez-Moses, introduction to *Modernism and Colonialism*, 1.

27 See Booth and Rigby, *Modernism and Empire*.

28 Esty, *Unseasonable Youth*, 7.

29 Esty, 20. See also Hobsbawm, *Age of Empire*.

30 Another attempt at tracing the relation between empire and modernism is Marjorie Perloff's recent *Edge of Irony*, with a focus on male European figures such as Joseph Roth, Robert Musil, Elias Canetti, and Paul Celan.

31 Resina, *Iberian Modalities*, 11.

32 Resina, vi.

33 Within contemporary Iberian studies, my approach remains particularly indebted to Susan Martin-Márquez's *Disorientations* and Eric Calderwood's *Colonial al-Andalus*. Martin-Márquez's *Disorientations* provides a much-needed reassessment of the extreme importance of a critical analysis of Spanish colonialism in Africa since the nineteenth century – and its related orientalist discourses – for a wide-ranging understanding of the racial, cultural, and socio-economic tensions at the heart of Spain's modernity, as well as the various national identities that it comprises. Calderwood's *Colonial al-Andalus*, on the other hand, provides an outstanding transcultural comparative model for exploring the different forms of relationality that ground Iberian studies today. Calderwood analyzes Spain's complex colonial relation to Morocco and Moroccan culture and literature in the nineteenth and twentieth centuries, and the role played in particular by Andalusian culture within a larger cultural imagining, and across its specific historical manifestations. I share in this book Calderwood's interest in measuring the impact of various manifestations of modern Iberian

colonial ideologies as they reach beyond the confines and limits of the Iberian Peninsula in the twentieth century.

34 Herzog, *Frontiers of Possession*, 11.
35 Herzog, 248.
36 Adelman, *Sovereignty and Revolution*, 6.
37 Adelman, 11.
38 Adelman, 6.
39 Saint-Amour, *Tense Future*, 35.
40 In his published works, José Garcia Villa did not use the diacritical accent ("tilde o acento ortográfico") in his first surname, which is linguistically standard in Spanish. I have maintained this spelling throughout the book.
41 Perloff, "The Great War and the European Avant-Garde," 142.
42 Betts, *Avant-Garde Canadian Literature*, 259.

1. The Geographies and Temporalities of Futurism: Almada Negreiros, Portuguese *Modernismo*, and European Colonialism in Africa

1 Perloff, "Audacity of Hope," 9.
2 Perloff, 10.
3 Perloff, 12.
4 For a comprehensive analysis of the social and political dimension of early Futurism as a radical critique of bourgeois culture, see Günter Berghaus's *Futurism and Politics*.
5 Ram, "Futurist Geographies," 314.
6 For example, Perloff explicitly conceives the Futurist movement as a moment that in her approach terminates in Italy during World War I and the subsequent incorporation of some of its key members into Mussolini's fascist movement: "The heady time of manifestos … was all but over by 1915. Marinetti's call for the 'destruction of syntax,' for 'words in freedom' and for a new sound and visual poetry, … and his exaltation of 'the beauty of speed' met its ironic fate, not in the Piazza San Marco … nor in the Futurist theatre, or the pages of *Lacerba*, but on the battlefield. By 1916, the Futurists had lost what were probably their two most talented visual artists – Sant'Elia and Boccioni. The cénacle dissolved, Carlo Carrà becoming increasingly a 'mystical' salon painter, whereas Balla followed Marinetti into the ranks of Mussolini's Fascists" (Perloff, *Futurist Moment*, xxvi).
7 This key aspect of Futurism, and the wide-ranging ramifications of its circulation across the world and various forms of media during the historical avant-garde are succinctly defined by Salaris ("Programmatic Avant-Garde," 24) as follows:

> The birth of Futurism was felt beyond Western Europe, prompting discussions from Japan and Russia to the Americas. It was met with rather tepid

reception of France, the place Marinetti had most hoped to receive approval. He published a second manifesto to respond to criticism, "Let's Murder the Moonlight!" ("Tuons le clair de lune!"), an allegorical tale describing a war that the Futurists, allies of madmen and ferocious beasts, waged against the inhabitants of Paralysis and Gout. Soon the movement spread to multiple artistic disciplines, resulting in increasingly technical proclamations that were not without the charge of fantasy that had characterized its theoretical approach from the start.

8 Four of the main anthologies and histories of the Futurist movement – Folejswki's *Futurism and Its Place in the Development of Modern Poetry*; Perloff's foundational *Futurist Moment*; Rainey, Poggi, and Whitman's comprehensive anthology of the movement in Italy, *Futurism*; and Buelens, Hendrix, and Jansen's *History of Futurism* – make only nominal reference to Portuguese Futurism, and for that matter to any other manifestation of Iberian Futurism in general. For a study of the transnational circulation of Futurist poetics across the Atlantic, and in particular within the postrevolutionary Mexican avant-garde scene during this period, see Klich, *Noisemakers*.

9 Some of Almada's most influential and best-known works include his famous portraits of Fernando Pessoa, as well as the frescoes of the Alcântara and Rocha do Conde de Óbidos maritime stations.

10 Almada Negreiros lived in Madrid, Spain, from 1927 to 1932. For an extensive analysis of this period of his life, various collaborations established, and his work during this period in Madrid, see Sáez Delgado and Valido-Viegas de Paula-Soares, *Almada Negreiros en Madrid*.

11 Poggioli, *Theory of the Avant-Garde*, 52, 228 (emphasis in the original).

12 Marinetti, "Founding and Manifesto of Futurism," 52.

13 Puchner, *Poetry of the Revolution*, 3.

14 Puchner, 3. In similar terms, Richard Weston considers this historical event itself as essential in the "invention" of the avant-garde: "Fine as some of the paintings and sculptures are, the historical importance of Futurism lies less on the quality of particular works than on the range of the movement's ideas and influence: it defined so much of what we know think of as 'Modern Art.' Marinetti effectively invented the avant-garde movement" (Weston, *Modernism*, 84).

15 Marinetti, "Proclama futurista a los españoles." Unless otherwise noted, all translations from Portuguese and Spanish included in this book are my own.

16 Ram, "Scale of Global Modernisms," 1372.

17 Ram, "Futurist Geographies," 332.

18 Ram, 332.

19 Even though Alves das Neves does not aim to provide a comprehensive study of the period, and presents his project rather as a preliminary study,

O movimento futurista em Portugal does offer an essential anthology that provides a key mapping for the understanding of the origins and key manifestations of the Portuguese Futurist movement. In this work, Alves Das Neves describes some of the key aesthetic and political notions at the core of Marinetti's manifestos, traces the genealogy of the pre-Futurist movement as it starts to appear in the three issues of *Orpheu*, while providing a selection of Futurist pieces by Almada Negreiros, Sá-Carneiro, Pessoa (under his heteronym Álvaro de Campos), António Ferro, and Guilherme de Santa Rita.

20 Alves das Neves, *O movimento futurista em Portugal*, 31.

21 More recently, Sara Afonso Ferreira and Sílvia Laureano Costa have described a similar Futurist genealogy to the standard interpretation provided by Alves das Neves: "Futurism spreads in Portugal thanks to the national press reporting about Marinetti's activities, to the poet Mário de Sá-Carneiro, and the painters Guilherme de Santa Rita and Amadeo de Souza Cardoso (both living in Paris until 1914), and Sonia and Robert Delaunay (who sought to escape the horrors of WWI in Portugal)" (Afonso Ferreira and Laureano Costa, "Almada Negreiros," 23).

22 For a detailed analysis of Pessoa's upbringing and education in South Africa, as well as his early interaction with English poetry and the impact of British Colonialism in his work, see my chapter "Heteronymies of Lusophone Englishness: Colonial Empire, Fetishism, and Simulacrum in Fernando Pessoa *English Poems I–III*," in *After Translation*, 22–50.

23 Aliete Dores Galhoz, "O momento poético do Orpheu," xviii.

24 Ramalho Santos, *Atlantic Poets*, 121.

25 Jackson, *Adverse Genres*, 77.

26 Pessoa, "Opiário," 91.

27 Pessoa, 95.

28 Pessoa, "Ode triunfal," 99.

29 Almada Negreiros, "Ruínas," in *Poesia*, 47.

30 Quoted in Alves das Neves, *O movimento futurista em Portugal*, 50.

31 Marinetti, "Technical Manifesto," 79.

32 Marinetti, 79.

33 Perloff, *Futurist Moment*, 77.

34 Costa Pinto, *Salazar's Dictatorship*, 88.

35 Almada Negreiros, *A cena do ódio*, in *Poesia*, 21.

36 Almada Negreiros, 23.

37 Almada Negreiros, 23.

38 Almada Negreiros, *Manifesto anti-Dantas*, 1.

39 Almada Negreiros, 16.

40 The islands of São Tomé and Príncipe were colonized by the Portuguese around 1470, and eventually became colonial outposts for controlling

maritime trade routes along the Gulf of Guinea for the Portuguese Empire during a long period spanning from the sixteenth to the early twentieth century.

41 Hodges and Newitt, *São Tomé and Príncipe,* 35.

42 António de Almada Negreiros was also the author of a series of important ethnographic studies of the various Portuguese colonies in Africa, including São Tomé e Príncipe (*Colonies portugaises,* published in Lisbon in 1895 and Paris in 1901), Angola (*Angola,* published in Paris in 1901), Mozambique (*Le Mozambique,* published in Paris in 1904), as well as a history of Portuguese colonialism and various studies ranging from agriculture to the judicial organization of the Portuguese colonies (published between 1905 and 1909).

43 Almada Negreiros, *Colonies portugaises,* 51.

44 Quoted in Alves das Neves, *O movimento futurista em Portugal,* 88.

45 For a more detailed examination of the Salazar regime in general, as well as in terms of Almada Negreiros's political and artistic responses to the regime during the 1930s and 1940s, see Sapega, *Consensus and Debate.*

46 Sartini-Blum, "Incorporating the Exotic," 140.

47 Sartini-Blum, 141.

48 *Portugal Futurista* was edited by Carlos Filipe Porfirio, and its only issue included the pieces performed at the Conferência Futurista, as well as other work by Almada Negreiros; visual artwork by José Pacheko and Santa Rita Pintor; a review on Futurism by José Rebelo de Bettencourt; translations of the "Manifeste des peintres futuristes" by Boccioni, Carrà, Russolo, Balla, Giacomo, and Severini; "L'abstractionisme futuriste" by Raúl Leal; "Saltimbancos" by Almada Negreiros; the poem "Arbre" by Apollinaire; "Episódios" and "Ultimatum" by Pessoa; "Tres Poemas" by Mário de Sá-Carneiro; and "Tour Eiffel" by Blaise Cendrars.

49 Halpern Pereira, *First Portuguese Republic,* 19–20.

50 During this particular moment in Portugal, the most famous political "ultimatum" related to Portugal's colonial empire and its own national history, in ways that connect to Almada Negreiros's Futurist project, was the 1890 British Ultimatum issued on behalf of Queen Victoria by prime minister Lord Salisbury to Portugal, through which Portugal withdrew its troops from modern-day Zimbabwe and Malawi. As João Leal has shown, this "Ultimatum" became one of a "series of events, perceived as 'traumatic' for Portuguese national pride. Among them was the British *Ultimatum* (1890). As is well known, the *Ultimatum,* which drastically limited Portuguese colonial claims on Africa, allowed for the British takeover of areas, roughly corresponding to the territories of contemporary Zimbabwe and Malawi, which were also claimed by the Portuguese crown. This directly affected the country's imperial status" (Leal, "Hidden Empire,"

39–40). For a further examination of the impact of the 1890 Ultimatum in Portugal, see Birmingham, *Portugal and Africa.*

51 Poggioli, *Theory of the Avant-Garde*, 69.
52 Puchner, *Poetry of the Revolution*, 89.
53 Almada Negreiros, *Ultimatum Futurista*, 7.
54 Almada Negreiros, 9.
55 Almada Negreiros, 10.
56 Adamson, "Futurism and Italian Intervention," 176.
57 Almada Negreiros, *Ultimatum Futurista*, 19.
58 Perloff, *Futurist Moment*, 35.
59 Perloff, 35.

2. Placing Vicente Huidobro within the Historical Avant-Garde: Experimental Poetics and the Planetary Critique of European Historicism

1 Puchner, *Poetry of the Revolution*, 173.
2 For a more detailed discussion of the translational and intermedial dimension of Huidobro's use of French and Spanish, see my analysis of *Temblor de cielo / Tremblement de ciel* included in chap. 2 of *After Translation* (esp. 58–70).
3 See Wood, "Adán as the Key to Creacionismo" and "Development of 'Creacionismo'"; Tovar, "El adán poético de Vicente Huidobro"; and Pizarro, "El creacionismo de Vicente Huidobro."
4 For example, there is no reference to Huidobro's work in literary histories of the period, such as Dérieux's *La poésie française contemporaine*, or Clancier's *De Rimbaud au surréalisme.*
5 Dawes, *Poetas ante la modernidad*, 82.
6 Huidobro, *Epistolario*, 3.
7 Bürger, *Theory of the Avant-Garde*, 26.
8 Chakrabarty, *Provincializing Europe*, 7 (emphasis in original).
9 Chakrabarty, 7.
10 Huidobro, *Pasando y pasando*, 30.
11 For a further analysis of Huidobro's conceptualization of *poiesis* as a new understanding of poetic creation through his avant garde project of *creacionismo*, see Infante, *After Translation*, chap. 2, esp. 68–76.
12 Huidobro, *Altazor*, in *Obra poética*, 776.
13 Huidobro, 772.
14 Weintraub and Correa-Díaz, "Huidobro's Absolute Modernity/Futurity," 9, 11.
15 In this sense, and going back to *Altazor*, it is important to highlight how the poetic voice of the avant-garde masterpiece presents a material decomposition of language that somehow points towards a location beyond

the realm of particular languages and national cultures, an aspect of Huidobro's poem that is emphasized by Justin Read: "*Altazor* attempts to create a 'new origin' for language and culture by *returning* to the linguistic matter upon which national cultural ideologies have been (and will be) constructed" (Read, *Modern Poetics*, 126).

16 As expressed in the autobiographical essay "Yo," Huidobro was very familiar with Spanish religious history (its key figures such as St. Teresa and St. Ignacio de Loyola, the Spanish Inquisition, the Society of Jesus), as well as some of the key literary figures from the Spanish early modern period (Fray Luis de León, Calderón, and Lope de Vega). *Pasando y Pasando* also contains a laudatory obituary on Marcelino Menéndez Pelayo, in which Huidobro emphasizes the richness and vastness of the Spanish historian's intellectual accomplishments, as well as an essay on the drama of Jacinto Benavente, of whom he states that "no tiene hoy en día quien lo supere en el teatro" (there is no one above him in theatre today; *Pasando y pasando*, 133) and whom he describes as an "artista excelso de la España moderna" (paramount artist in contemporary Spain; 136).

17 De Costa, *Salle XIV*, 98; and *Vicente Huidobro y el creacionismo*, 13. De Costa's interpretation of Huidobro's *creacionismo* is mainly based on the fact that Huidobro developed some of the key manifestos and poetry collections connected to *creacionismo* as a member of the avant-garde scene in Paris from 1916 until the late 1920s. In his canonical interpretation, de Costa also focusses on how Huidobro's work during the period between 1917 and 1925 was produced under the conceptual influence of Cubism as an avant-garde aesthetic.

18 Soria Olmedo, *Vanguardismo*, 97.

19 Unruh, *Latin American Vanguards*, 13.

20 Videla, *Direcciones*, 35. While for Soria Olmedo, this close link between Cubism and *creacionismo* seems to denote a lack of originality and relegates the Chilean poet to a minor role within the Spanish avant-garde, for Videla it explains the relevance of Huidobro's *creacionismo* within her own approach to the literary history of the period in Latin America. According to Videla, Huidobro's poetry not only is endowed with the two key paradigmatic vectors that ground the Latin American avant-garde – "poesía autónoma y cosmopolitismo" (autonomous or absolute poetry and cosmopolitanism; *Direcciones*, 33) – but also constitutes a key element in the circulation of what she refers to as "cubismo-creacionismo," as it "proyecta en otros ámbitos hispanoamericanos" (projects into other Spanish American realms; 51). In this sense, and in line with Videla's argument, Fernando Rosenberg, in his study of the Latin American Avant-Garde, also values Huidobro's cosmopolitanism ("the epitome of the cosmopolitan

writer") and his embrace of European modernity that is "exhibited as cultural capital" (Rosenberg, *Avant-Garde and Geopolitics*, 147).

21 Videla, *Direcciones*, 34.

22 Huidobro, *Epistolario*, 18.

23 Huidobro's fascinating personal and literary relationship with de Torre, Diego, and Larrea can be traced in detail in their extensive correspondence, which has been edited by Gabrielle Morelli and Carlos García (Huidobro, *Epistolario*). In fact, it was due to de Torre's encouragement that Diego first established epistolary contact with Huidobro in April 1920, roughly at the same time that de Torre and the Chilean writer were at odds with one another following their first encounter in Madrid in 1918.

24 Huidobro essentially claimed that some Madrid-based writers had damaged the integrity ("purity") of his own conception of poetry and had attributed his ideas to other key French and European figures. De Torre quickly tried to persuade Huidobro in a subsequent letter that the Chilean poet should in fact be grateful for the "acogida cordialísma que ha tenido en España, y la irradiación de su obra" (extremely cordial reception given in Spain, and the dissemination of his work; Huidobro, *Epistolario*, 21). At that point, however, based on the already evident impact of his work on both sides of the Atlantic, Huidobro was unwilling to assume a secondary role within the contemporary avant-garde scene, as appears to have been suggested by de Torre. Huidobro firmly believed in the originality and truth of his own avant-garde poetics: "Hay una sola verdad en cada época, todo lo demás a su alrededor es farsa. La cosa es saber o mejor sentir cuál es esta verdad" (There is only one truth in each age; everything else around it is false. The thing is to know or, even better, to feel what this truth is; *Epistolario*, 35).

25 See Juli Highfill's *Modernism and Its Merchandise*, esp. chap. 4, "The Technological Prosthetic," for an analysis of de Torre's role within avant-garde circles during this period and, in particular, of de Torre's collection *Hélices* (1923).

26 Torre, *Literaturas europeas*, 87.

27 Torre, 106.

28 Chakrabarty, *Provincializing Europe*, 239.

29 Bary, *Larrea*, 42. By April 1920, when Diego first wrote to Huidobro to express his "verdadera necesidad de comunicarse con usted" (true need to communicate with you; Huidobro, *Epistolario*, 43), Diego and Larrea were committed *creacionistas*: Diego had already given a few talks on *creacionismo* in Bilbao and Santander, and both Diego and Larrea had started writing their own strand of *creacionista* poetry. For a detailed analysis of Diego's *creacionista* work, see del Villar, "Gerardo Diego, poeta creacionista."

30 Latour, *Reassembling the Social*, 46.
31 Torre, *Literaturas europeas*, 100.
32 Huidobro, *Ecuatorial*, in *Obra poética*, 491.
33 Huidobro, 492.
34 Huidobro, 502.
35 Huidobro, "La poésia," in *Obra poética*, 1296.
36 Published in Madrid in 1929 by Compañia Iberoamericana de Publicaciones, *Mío Cid Campeador* is a very loose adaptation of the anonymous medieval Castilian poem *Cantar/Poema de mio Cid* (generally translated into English as *The Cid* or *Song of My Cid*). Huidobro's twentieth-century adaptation of the Castilian epic poem was soon translated into English by Warre B. Wells as *Portrait of a Paladin* and released in New York by the publisher Horace Liveright in 1932.
37 An actor, screenwriter, director, and producer in silent films such as *The Thief of Bagdad*, *Robin Hood*, and *The Mark of Zorro*, and later a founder of United Artists, Fairbanks is arguably one of the most important figures in 1920s American cinema.
38 See Casetti, "Adaptation and Mis-adaptations."
39 Menéndez Pidal, *Poema de Mio Cid*, 7. For a more detailed examination of Menéndez Pidal's philological and historical recuperation of *El Cid* within the wider context of Spanish medieval literature, see Hess's *Ramón Menéndez Pidal*, esp. chap. 3, "Menéndez Pidal and Medieval Spanish Literature."
40 Quoted in Menéndez Pidal, *Poema de Mio Cid*, 56.
41 Menéndez Pidal, 96 (emphasis in original).
42 As Hess describes, Menéndez Pidal spent about fifteen years researching and studying the text and the linguistic features of the medieval poem, which lead to the publication in 1911 of his critical edition of the epic poem, *Cantar de Mio Cid: Texto, gramática y vocabulario* (see Hess, *Ramón Menéndez Pidal*, 133–44).
43 As explained in the preface to *Mío Cid Campeador*, Huidobro cites a Chilean genealogical branch that originates around the figure of King Alfonso X of Castile, asserting that Alfonso X was the great-great-grandson of the Cid via a family line that led directly to Huidobro's own maternal grandfather: "If I speak here of my ancestors, it is because I cannot hide the pride I take in my Spanish blood. Through my ancestors I am Castilian and Galician, Andalusian and Breton. I am Celt and Spaniard, Spaniard and Celt: an aboriginal Celto-Iberian, impervious and hard-headed [that perhaps is softened by Jewishness]" (Huidobro, *Portrait of a Paladin*, vii). The heterogeneous multiplicity of Iberian ethnicities that Huidobro assumes in this genealogical definition of "Spanish blood" from his Chilean perspective is certainly striking here, all the more so because it differs radically from the homogenous notion at work in Menéndez Pidal's imperial

and colonial conception of Spanishness in the Middle Ages, where it represents a form of imperial rule over the different Iberian regions and ethnicities.

44 Huidobro, *Portrait of a Paladin*, viii.
45 Huidobro, *Mío Cid Campeador*, 110.
46 Huidobro, *Portrait of a Paladin*, 98.
47 Huidobro, *Mío Cid Campeador*, 110; and *Portrait of a Paladin*, 98.
48 Huidobro, *Mío Cid Campeador*, 369.
49 Huidobro, *Portrait of a Paladin*, 313.
50 Latour, *Reassembling the Social*, 12.
51 Schulte-Sasse, "Foreword," xiv.
52 Spivak, *Death of a Discipline*, 102.

3. Away from Montmartre: Blaise Cendrars, Tarsila do Amaral, and the Travel Notes of the Historical Avant-Garde

1 In this chapter, I will mostly refer to and analyze the first edition of this poetry collection, originally titled *Le Formose* and published in 1924 by the Paris publisher Au Sans Pareil. This edition also includes the series of original illustrations by Tarsila de Amaral, which will also be the focus of this chapter. Later editions of this collection, published as *Feuilles de route*, include two other parts, as I examine in more detail later in this chapter. This later version of *Feuilles de route*, including all three parts, was first published in English as "Ocean Letters" in Cendrars, *Complete Postcards from the Americas*, and later as "Travel Notes" in Cendrars, *Complete Poems*.
2 For an extensive analysis of this painting by Tarsila, as well as of its history and critical reception, see Kenneth David Jackson's recent *Cannibal Angels*, esp. 62–8.
3 For example, the edition of *Feuilles de route* included in vol. 1 of Cendrars's *Œuvres complètes*, published by Club français du livre in 1968, following the Édition Denöel edition of 1947, does not include any of Tarsila's illustrations within the collection, although a reprint of the cover of *Le Formose* by Tarsila and one of the illustrations are included in the "Iconographie" (Illustrations) section of the volume.
4 The work of both Oswald de Andrade (1890–1954) and Mário de Andrade (1893–1945), two of the key figures of the modernist movement in Brazil and Latin America, will be explored in more detail in the second and third sections of this chapter.
5 Exhibition *Tarsila do Amaral: Inventing Modern Art in Brazil*, 6 October 2017–7 January 2018 at the Art Institute of Chicago, and 11 February–3 June 2018, at MoMA, New York. See D'Alessandro and Pérez-Oramas, *Tarsila do Amaral*.

6 "Le paquebot Formose" (operated by the Compagnie des Chargeurs Réunis Sud Atlantique).
7 Sieburth, "Blaise Cendrars in the Sky."
8 Wall-Romana locates Cendrars's "cinepoetic" style primarily within his earlier work "New York in Flashlight" (originally titled in English and composed in 1912), noting that "'New York in Flashlight' might serve as a form of advertisement for a new cinepoetic project that would include poetic reportages in the form of both telegraphic texts and actual footage" (*Cinepoetry*, 179). Another manifestation of the cinepoetic dimension in Cendrars's work for Wall-Romana is his articulation of an "aesthetics of proximity," which for Wall-Romana constitutes one of Jean Epstein's "two-way homologies between cinema and poetry": "[It] places in correspondence the Griffthian close-up with a new form of condensed phrasing in poetry, both summarizing or virtualizing a longer sequence or development" (123).
9 Cendrars, "Claire de lune," in *Le Formose*, 15.
10 Cendrars, 15.
11 Noland, *Poetry at Stake*, 9. See also Noland's chapter "Blaise Cendrars and the Heterogeneous Discourses of the Lyric Subject," in *Poetry at Stake*.
12 Healey, *Modernist Traveler*, 56.
13 Cendrars, "Claire de lune," in *Le Formose*, 15.
14 *Oxford English Dictionary*, s.v. "roadmap," accessed 25 October 2022, https://www.oed.com/view/Entry/274812; s.v. "waybill," accessed 25 October 2022, https://www.oed.com/view/Entry/226477.
15 Cendrars, "En route pour Dakar," in *Le Formose*, 21.
16 Cendrars, 21.
17 Cendrars, 21.
18 Cendrars, 21.
19 Cendrars, "Profound Today," 267.
20 Cendrars, "Sur les côtes du Portugal," in *Le Formose*, 20.
21 Cendrars, "Pedro Álvarez Cabral," in *Le Formose*, 21.
22 Cortesão, *A expedição de Pedro Alvares Cabral*, 201.
23 Burbank and Cooper, *Empires in World History*, 157.
24 Cortesão, *A expedição de Pedro Alvares Cabral*, 210.
25 First printed in 1572, and generally considered one of the most influential works of Portuguese literature, *Os Lusíadas* by Luís Vaz de Camões (1524–80) is an epic poem that describes the sea journey to India undertaken by Vasco da Gama. Within the context of *A Planetary Avant-Garde*, Cortesão's historiographic recuperation of the figure of Álvares Cabral contrasts with the rupture with the past proposed in Futurist terms just five years earlier by Almada Negreiros, as examined in chap. 1.
26 As shown by historian Miriam Halpern Pereira, this imperial and neo-colonial political ideology gradually developed in Portugal during

the First Portuguese Republic (1910–26), gaining widespread institutional and political support during the 1920s: "The idea that Portugal's mission in the world was connected to its civilizing function and that its national survival depended on the Empire was unanimously accepted by the Portuguese elite of the mid 1920s, as can be seen in the 'Movement for the defence of the colonies,' in response to the appeal of the Geographical Society, whose members came from all walks of political life" (Halpern Pereira, *First Portuguese Republic*, 155). Both the colonial ethos of Portuguese society during the 1920s mentioned by Pereira and the aggrandizing and mythification of Portugal's colonial history displayed by Cortesão in his historiographic study of Álvares Cabral would eventually prove pivotal to the development of the *Estado Novo* in Portugal as one of the "principles" of the "political revolution" proposed by Salazar.

27 Salazar, *Discursos*, 1:42.

28 In Salazar's colonial and totalitarian political logic, Portugal's colonial possessions can only exist as proof and evidence of this very same categorical imperative of Portugal's political existence as a nation state. By assuming that Portugal's political reality is determined by its territorial rights to its colonial possessions (and their potential expansion through the *Estado Novo*), Salazar is embracing Portuguese colonialism as a universal condition of Portugal as a modern nation, and thus as a dimension intrinsic to its own political sovereignty.

29 Cendrars, "Ignorance," in *Le Formose*, 70.

30 Cendrars, "Sào-Paulo," in *Le Formose*, 70.

31 Cendrars, "Sào-Paulo," in *Le Formose*, 70.

32 Cendrars, "Sào-Paulo," in *Le Formose*, 70.

33 See Amaral, *Blaise Cendrars no Brasil*; Eulalio, "L'aventure brésilienne"; Roig, "Blaise Cendrars et le Bresil"; and Roig, *Blaise Cendrars*.

34 For a more detailed examination of the 1922 *Semana de Arte Moderna*, see, among others, Camargos, *Semana de 22*; Gonçalves, *1922*; Boaventura, *22 por 22*; and Schwartz, *Vanguarda e cosmopolitismo*; and *Las vanguardias latinoamericanas*.

35 As Andrade argues in his preface to *Paulicea Desvairada*, the Brazilian foundation and expression of his modernist project is also central to its influential geopolitical dimension: "Pronomes? Escrevo brasilero. Si uso ortografia portuguesa é porquê, não alterando o resultado, dá-me uma ortografia" (Andrade, *Paulicea Desvairada*, 33 ["Pronouns? I write in Brazilian. If I use a Portuguese orthography, it is because, without changing the outcome, it provides me with an orthography"; Andrade, *Hallucinated City*, 16]).

36 Read, *Modern Poetics*, 91.

37 Amaral, "Tarsila: La magia y lo racional," 43. According to Amaral, it was Cendrars who gave "a helping hand" to Oswald de Andrade and Tarsila by providing the couple with access to a key group of avant-garde artists in Paris: "A través de *main amie* del poeta suizo-francés Blaise Cendrars, visitado en Paris por la pareja Tarsila y Oswald en mayo 1923 y durante toda la década (hasta 1929), gran amigo de la pareja, al abrirles las puertas en Paris a la amistad y contactos con los Supervielle, Gleizes y Juliette Roche, Léonce Rosenberg, Léger, Cocteau, Delaunay, Brancusi, Satie, entre otros" (Through the *main amie* of the Swiss-French poet Blaise Cendrars, visited in Paris by the couple Tarsila and Oswald in May 1923 and throughout the decade – until 1929 – a great friend of the couple, by opening the doors in Paris to friendship and contacts with a group that included Supervielle, Gleizes and Juliette Roche, Léonce Rosenberg, Léger, Cocteau, Delaunay, Brancusi, Satie, among others; Amaral, 43).

38 *Tarsila do Amaral (Fundación Juan March).*

39 Bonet, "'Quest' for Tarsila," 78.

40 It is important to mention here, particularly in order to highlight the extensive reach and interconnections of the various avant-garde networks from this period explored in this book, that Delaunay also produced an illustration of the Eiffel Tower for Vicente Huidobro's visual poem "Tour Eiffel," published in Madrid by Imprenta Pueyo in 1918.

41 The exhibition of Delaunay's *Champs de Mars: The Red Tower* at the Conservatório Dramático e Musical of São Paulo on 12 June 1924 is listed in the Art Institute of Chicago record for the painting. Cendrars's lecture "The Eiffel Tower" was also given on the same date, thus coinciding with the exhibition of the painting. This is stated at the end of Cendrars's "Eiffel Tower" essay, with a brief note that reads, "Extract from Lecture Delivered June 12, 1924 at São Paulo, Brazil" (Cendrars, "Eiffel Tower," 240).

42 For an examination of Cendrars's collaboration with Sonia Delaunay during this period, as well as in relation to the avant-garde poetics of simultaneity also central to Robert Delaunay's work during this time, see Carrie Noland's chapter "High Decoration: Sonia Delaunay, Blaise Cendrars and the Poem as Fashion Design," in *Poetry at Stake*.

43 Cendrars, "Eiffel Tower," 234.

44 Cendrars, 237–8.

45 As also shown in other European-centred critical interpretations of this moment, as in the case of Bonet explored above, this is a European neo-colonial categorical imperative that reappears in later interpretations of the avant-garde, as well as in its "historical" and historicist interpretation presented by Peter Bürger in his foundational *Theory of the Avant-Garde*, as mentioned in previous sections of this book.

46 Art curator Matthew Drutt locates the production of *Champs de Mars: The Red Tower* right after the autumn of 1911, and between the production of two other pieces in the series (*The Eiffel Tower* [1911], and *Red Eiffel Tower*), emphasizing a radical new sense of "simultaneity" as central to this specific Delaunay painting: "Thus we not only see the tower from simultaneous angles frontally, but the view from the air brings new spatial and temporal elements into the work. As if to celebrate this new development, Delaunay gave the painting to his friend Apollinaire, with an inscription referring to simultaneity. It is the first time Delaunay associated the concept of simultaneity with his art" (Drutt, "Simultaneous Expressions," 33).

47 Amaral, "Delaunay y la Torre Eiffel," 211.

48 Amaral, 211–12.

49 Roland Wetzel provides a brief summary of the relevance of the series within Delaunay's work during this time, as well as some of its key formal and critical features: "The Eiffel Tower, despite being twenty years old at the time, symbolized modernity. Not just here but in many other paintings, Delaunay made the tower his 'iron muse,' also referring it as his 'fruit bowl'. Unlike the Cubist painters, he does not formally analyse still life painting to overcome the central perspective paradigm that has dominated the previous 400 years of painting. The dynamism of the city space, the new dimensions of the view from the air and the acceleration of appearance of the theme of this series. During the three years that he worked on them, the individual Tour Eiffel paintings vary significantly. They illustrate the fruitfulness of working of different motif cycles simultaneously" (Wetzel, *Robert Delaunay*, 61–4).

50 Amaral, "Delaunay y la Torre Eiffel," 211.

51 Amaral, "Confissão geral, 1950," 728.

52 See Jáuregui's *Canibalia*, particularly the section on *Pau Brasil* on pp. 401–7. For other similarly important approaches to the anthropophagic impulse within Latin American culture, within a transhistorical framework, see Jens Andermann's "Antropofagia," as well as Kenneth David Jackson's *Cannibal Angels*, particularly chap. 3, "The Cannibal Magazine and the Cannibal Manifesto." In his book, Jackson examines the *antropofagia* movement within the larger history of the Brazilian avant-garde, with a transatlantic approach to modernism and a particular focus on the notions of travel, portraiture, improvisation, primitivism, and utopia.

53 The nine different sections of the *Pau Brasil* collection are as follows: "Historia do Brazil," "Poemas da Colonização," São Martinho," "RP I," "Carnaval," "Secretario dos Amantes," "Poste da Light," "Roteiro das Minas," and "Loyde Brasiliero."

54 Andrade, *Poesias reunidas*, 3.

55 For a closer and more detailed analysis of the formal connections between Cendrars's *Feuilles de route* and Andrade's *Pau Brasil*, see Tessa Sermet's "Blaise Cendrars e o modernismo brasileiro." Sermet focuses on the formal dimensions of both works in relation to each other, based primarily on what Sermet defines as a "poetry of facts":

> Uma poesia dos fatos ('poésie des faits'), para utilizar uma expressão de Cendrars – o tom dos poemas pertence à conversa cotidiana, a forma e a linguagem se simplificam, e, além disso, ambos os autores usam a técnica da colagem dadaísta e integram números, títulos de jornais, e nomes de prédios nos poemas, com o intuito de enriquecer o ponto de vista visual e sonoro.
>
> (A poetry of facts ["poésie des faits"], to use an expression of Cendrars's – the tone of poetry is related to everyday speech, forms and language are simplified, and, moreover, both authors use Dadaist collage as a technique, including in the poems' numbers, newspaper titles, and names of buildings, in order to enrich their visual and sonic dimensions; 136).

56 Andrade, "Pau Brasil" in *Poesias reunidas*, 68.

57 Andrade, "Pau Brasil," trans. Cisneros, 135.

58 Cendrars, "Ignorance," in *Le Formose*, 70.

59 D'Alessandro, "A Negra, Abaporou, and Tarsila's Anthropophagy," 47. This symbolic and cultural recuperation in Brazil of a local natural product as the symbol of a new experimental rearticualtion of local national culture as part of Latin American avant-garde movements also appeared in Peruvian cultural circles during this period. As Michelle Clayton has shown in the case of the Peruvian avant-garde, it is the groundmass material of guano that acquires a parallel dimension, particularly in the avant-garde poetry of César Vallejo and in his masterpiece *Trilce* (1922): "The appearance of guano in *Trilce* condenses a particular kind of investment in history and reveals a commitment to the question of representation, to the reinstallation of materialism and the recovery of repressed origins. Guano can be read here as both completely material and completely metaphorical, as something that is both resolutely itself and potentially other, encouraging the production of other elements, sprouting from the soil in which it is invested" (Clayton, *Poetry in Pieces*, 125–6).

60 Cendrars's name is included in the epigraph to the first edition of *Pau Brasil*, but is absent from later editions. According to Saulo Gouveia, the first edition was originally planned to be dedicated to Paulo Prado, but this changed when the collection was first published in 1925 by Cendrars's publisher, Au Sans Pareil, in Paris: "It was not by coincidence that Paulo Prado wrote a preface in praise of *Pau-Brasil* at the time of its first publication in 1925. In fact, the preface is more than just an endorsement. It was also a gesture of gratitude toward Oswald. Originally, *Pau-Brasil* was

dedicated to Paulo Prado" (Gouveia, *Triumph of Brazilian Modernism*, 227). Cendrars's name is removed from the epigraph to the collection from the version of *Pau Brasil* included in Andrade's *Poesias reunidas*, published by Difusão Européia do Livro in 1966.

61 Latour, *Inquiry*, 32.

62 Cendrars, "Départ," in *Œuvres complètes*, 1:199.

63 A similar incorporation – or, to use Carrie Noland's term, "modernist appropriation" ("The Metaphysics of Coffee," 402) – of Brazil within Cendrars's avant-garde project to the one analyzed here in relation to *Feuilles de route* is also represented – perhaps with a more complex economic and philosophical perspective than in the 1924 poetry collection – in Cendrars's later essay "La métaphysique du café" (1927). In a critical effort to highlight the emergence of an understanding of hybridity from Cendrars's perspective in relation to both the economic specificity of Brazil and Kantian aesthetics, Noland argues how this essay by Cendrars displays "the irreducible strangeness and singularity of Cendrars's own role in the modern cross-fertilization of cultures" (403).

64 The importance of this kind of historicizing of particular poetry networks, and the critical and historical retracing of the actual forms and structures at the core of these instances of modernist and avant-garde poetry, is also a particular point stressed by Justin Read, as a way to critique previously normative understandings of modernist poetry as somehow unrelated to specific historical processes and social contexts. Read thus highlights the importance of reading poetic forms and structures "with respect to the locations in which they appear and operate" (Read, *Modern Poetics*, 28): "Such historicization, finally, allows us to correct several critical and theoretical problems, especially reading modernist poetry … Translated into literary and cultural studies, formalism and structuralism have by and large fallen into disrepute as ahistorical, and therefore as blinded to social conflicts of race, gender and sexuality. This has been particular detrimental to the image of modernist poetry – of poetic movements defined by their emphasis on poetic form and structure … One must pay attention to the historical contexts in which poetic forms appear as well as the forms themselves" (28–9).

65 Andrade, "França / Feuilles de route."

66 Andrade, "Pau-Brasil e Antropofagia," 684.

67 For a detailed analysis of the impact of travel in the avant-garde poetics of Mário de Andrade and its relation to the *antropofagia* movement in Brazil and the Latin American avant-garde, see Rosenberg, *Avant-Garde and Geopolitics*, esp. chap. 4, "*Macunaíma* in the Mouth of the Cannibal," and chap. 5, "Leaving Home: Cosmopolitanism and Travel."

68 Among the series of figures represented in this sixth illustration, Tarsila juxtaposes a series of sketches of plants and natural objects, together with

a few local buildings (which appear to be small homes, a church, and a school), a few agricultural instruments (a cart, a pulley), and architectural components (windows, roofs, fences), in a complex amalgamation of images, which is centred overall around the sketch of a Black male figure.

69 Gabara, *Errant Modernism*, 40 (emphasis in original).

70 Gabara, 41–2.

71 Cendrars, "Christophe Colomb," in *Œuvres complètes*, 1:213.

72 Millet, "Tarsila do Amaral," 230.

73 Andrade, "Pau Brasil," in *Poesias reunidas*, 68; translation in Andrade, "Pau Brasil," trans. Cisneros, 135.

74 Roffino, "Towering Brazilian Modernist."

4. The Spectre of Translation: Angela Manalang Gloria, José Garcia Villa, Claro Recto, and the Comparative Poetics of Modernism in the Philippines

1 Anderson, *Spectre of Comparisons*, 2.

2 Apart from the spatial and historical separation inherent in this particular act of double vision as interpreted by Anderson, the original Manila city scene within Rizal's novel is also endowed with a series of rich temporal and sensorial implications that are partly lost in Anderson's critical reading of the same passage, quoted here in the original (followed by my own translation):

> A la bajada del Puente los caballos tomaron el trote, dirigiéndose hacia el Paseo de la Sabana. A la izquierda, la fábrica de Tabacos de Arroceros dejaba oír el estruendo que hacen las cigarreras golpeando las hojas. Ibarra no pudo menos de sonreír, acordándose de aquel fuerte olor que a las cinco de la tarde saturaba el puente de Barcas y le mareaba cuando niño. Las animadas conversaciones, los chistes llevaron maquinalmente su imaginación al barrio de Lavapiés en Madrid con sus motines de cigarreras, tan fatales para los desgraciados guindillas, etc. El jardín botánico ahuyentó sus risueños recuerdos: el demonio de las comparaciones le puso delante de los jardines botánicos de Europa, en los países donde se necesitaba mucha voluntad y mucho oro para que brote una hoja y abra su cáliz una flor; recordó los de las colonias, ricos y bien cuidados y abiertos todos al público.
>
> (As they were going down the Bridge, the horses began to trot, heading towards the Paseo de la Sabana. On the left was the Arroceros Tobacco Factory, with the loud noise made by the cigar-makers hitting the leaves. Ibarra could not help but smile, remembering how that strong smell saturated the Barcas Bridge at five in the afternoon, making him dizzy as a child. The animated conversations and jokes mechanically took his imagination to the Lavapiés neighbourhood in Madrid, with the riots of cigar workers, so perilous for the

unfortunate local policemen, etc. The botanical garden scared away his amusing memories: the demon of comparisons placed him in front of the botanical gardens in Europe, in countries where plenty of will and plenty of gold were needed for a leaf to sprout, and for a flower to open its calyx; he recalled those from the colonies, rich and well maintained and all open to the public; Rizal, Noli me tángere (novela tagala), 82).

3 Rizal first travelled to Europe between 1882 and 1887. He left for Spain in May 1882 to study medicine at the Universidad Central de Madrid. After completing his degree in Madrid, he studied at the University of Paris and the University of Heidelberg.

4 Rizal, *Noli me tángere (novela tagala)*, 82.

5 Anderson, *Spectre of Comparisons*, 2.

6 In fact, in the two available English translations of Rizal's *Noli me tángere*, Charles Derbyshire translates the sentence as "the demon of comparison" (*Social Cancer*, 62), while Harold Augenbraum goes with "the devilry of comparison" (*Noli Me Tangere (Touch Me Not)*, 54), both establishing a closer semantic relation to the original phrase, particularly within the context of Rizal's revolutionary *ilustrado* nationalism in the face of Spanish colonialism in the last decade of the nineteenth century in the Philippines.

7 According to Sevilla Muñoz and Zurdo Ruíz-Ayúcar's *Refranero multilingüe*, the saying or proverbial phrase "Las comparaciones son odiosas" or "Toda comparación es odiosa" has the following meaning in Spanish: "Significado: No conviene comparar personas o cosas entre sí, para evitar que alguna se sienta menospreciada o porque cada una tiene sus propios valores. Observaciones: *Toda comparación es odiosa* (*La Celestina* IX 35). *Las comparaciones son siempre odiosas* (*El Quijote* II, 22). *Toda comparación es odiosa* (*El Quijote* II 23)" (Meaning: It is not convenient to compare people or things with each other, in order to avoid people feeling belittled or because every person has its own values. Observations: *All comparisons are hateful* [*La Celestina*, IX 35]. *Comparisons are always hateful* [*Don Quixote*, II 22]. *Every comparison is hateful* [*Don Quixote*, II 23]). See *Refranero multilingüe*, s.v. "Las comparaciones son odiosas," accessed 26 October 2022, https://cvc.cervantes.es/lengua/refranero/ficha.aspx?Par=58928&Lng=0.

8 Anderson, *Spectre of Comparisons*, 2.

9 Anderson, 3.

10 A relevant instance of the spectral and haunting theoretical implications of Anderson's critique appears in a key passage of *Imagined Communities* in which Anderson describes the tradition in modern nations of creating tombs and cenotaphs to the Unknown Soldier: "This is why so many different nations have such tombs without feeling any need to specify the nationality of their absent occupants. What else could they be *but* Germans, Americans, Argentinians …?" For Anderson, these monuments are

"saturated with ghostly *national* imaginings" (*Imagined Communities*, 10; emphasis in original).

11 Derrida, *Specters of Marx*, 188–9.

12 Derrida, 188.

13 Gémino Abad has succinctly described the key three historical stages of the US occupation of the Philippines as follows: "On April Fools' Day by the American calendar, 1901, Gen. Emilio Aguinaldo, captive president of the First Philippine Republic, took his oath of allegiance to the United States, and two months later, on July 4 ironically, William Hoard Taft became the first civil governor during more than three decades of American rule and government tutelage. The first decade, which set the stage for 'special relations' even to the present time, was characterized by (1) 'pacification' or, as recommended by Gen. Arthur MacArthur, the Philippines's last military governor, 'bayonet treatment for at least a decade'; (2) the suppression of Filipino nationalism or, more precisely, the ilustrados' nonviolent campaign for immediate political independence (from Spanish times through the short-lived Malolos Republic 1899–1901, they were the ruling socioeconomic and political elite;) and (3), for more than three decades of American domination, the subtle de-Filipinization or, if you will, Americanization of the native-Hispanic culture, chiefly through the American public school system and 'free trade'" (Abad, *Our Scene So Fair*, 45–6).

14 Part of the reason for the relevance of this double process of colonization in the Philippines, which determines Filipinx writing of this period, is that, as Adam Lifshey has described, it has generally been unacknowledged in scholarly fields outside of the field of Filipinx history and literature precisely because "it challenges the structures of academic disciplines": "The Philippines remains virtually unacknowledged by Spanish departments despite over three centuries of Spanish colonialism; by English departments despite being, according to some measurements, perhaps the fourth largest anglophone country in the world; and by Asian departments, despite geography, because of all the successive Western presence in the islands. The ceaseless flux of cultures and languages and peoples that constitute the Philippines, however, is precisely what makes its literature in Spanish a leading example of the unsettled and asymmetrical forces of modernity" (Lifshey, *Magellan Fallacy*, 16).

15 Rafael, *White Love*, 168.

16 Rafael, 168.

17 Constantino, *Making of a Filipino*, 7–8.

18 As historians Greg Bankoff and Kathleen Weekley have argued in their analysis of the development of a postcolonial sense of national identity in the Philippines, Christianity played a central role in its development and articulation: "Whatever the nature of the Philippine Revolution, whether

it was shaped mostly by an implanted European liberal ideology or belonged more to an indigenous tradition of millenarian popular uprisings, is was quintessentially a Christian affair. The main events surrounding its inception, the growth and leadership of the Katipunan (the secret society that instigated the revolt in August 1896), most of the soldiers who constituted the revolutionary army, the first president of the Republic, and the delegates who met at Malolos to frame the constitution in 1899 were Christians, largely, in fact, from the Tagalog provinces of Central Luzon" (Bankoff and Weekley, *Post-colonial National Identity*, 3–4).

19 Ponce, *Beyond the Nation*, 17.

20 According to Megan Thomas, it was their unique Dominican ethos, which instilled in them as part of their core mission a drive to provide the native population in the Philippines with the academic basis to acquire a global concept of knowledge, that allowed the *ilustrado* elite to produce wide-ranging scholarly work "about their homeland, entering international scholarly worlds, and pressing against the limits of Spanish national-colonial politics": "For the Dominican University of Santo Tomás was not only the oldest university in Asia; it was also, until 1857 in Calcutta, the only [one] in which 'natives' were taught, and it had no comparable peer anywhere in Southeast Asia during the nineteenth century. The Dominicans of the university, caught between their commitment to Thomistic philosophy and pressures to modernize the curriculum, had to admit subjects and curricula whose teachers were not always Dominican. These young men were armed with scholarly languages (Latin, Greek, and often French), versed in the classics, and living in a world where science and technology progressed by leaps and bounds" (Thomas, *Orientalists, Propagandists, and Ilustrados*, 17).

21 Constantino, *Making of a Filipino*, 4.

22 Constantino, 24.

23 *Bajo los cocoteros* includes a prologue ("introito") by Fernando María Guerrero, a brief laudatory piece ("elogio") by Cecilio Apóstol – both of whom were also graduates of the University of Santo Tomás – and an "epilogue" by Teodoro Kalaw. Due to its inclusion of introductory pieces by key Spanish-language writers on the importance of Guerrero and Apóstol, as well as the epilogue by Kalaw, the publication of Recto's poetry collection was clearly regarded as an important event within contemporary Philippine culture by the key Spanish-language writers at the time in Manila.

24 For a more detailed exploration of the work of José Martí and Filipinx writers at the end of the nineteenth century, particularly the work of Rizal, see Hagimoto, *Between Empires*. Hagimoto focuses his analysis on his notion of an "intercolonial alliance" between Cuba and the Philippines through a comparative reading of the work of Rizal and Martí and their

respective plights against Spanish colonialism and empire. Although he does mention other Filipinx writers as part of his study, Hagimoto does not refer to Recto's work. It is precisely because of his position as a writer responding not only to Spanish colonialism but also to US imperialism that Recto's work constitutes a fascinating counterpoint to that of Martí, in a connection that becomes more relevant when one considers their respective uses of *modernista* poetics.

25 Originating in Latin America and spanning across the Atlantic and beyond, Spanish American *modernismo* emerged around the 1880s and lasted through the 1920s. As an intrinsically Latin American response to modernity, *modernismo* was aimed primarily at the radical renovation of Spanish-language literature and its earlier dependence on Spanish colonial models and literary tradition, and was also intended as a response to a shared colonial past that strove towards a liberating form of aesthetic, cultural, and political autonomy. For a more detailed examination of *modernismo* in its various facets and contexts, see any of the following critical works, listed alphabetically: Aching, *Spanish American Modernismo*; Gullón, *Direcciones del modernismo*; Henríquez Ureña, *Breve historia del modernismo*; Jrade, *Modernismo, Modernity*; Mejías-López, *Inverted Conquest*; Montaldo, *La sensibilidad amenazada*; Rotker, *American Chronicles of José Martí*; Schulman and González, *Martí, Darío y el modernismo*; and Yurkiévich, *Celebración del modernismo*.

26 Guerrero, "Introito," xiv–xv.

27 For a more in-depth reading of Darío's *Azul*, particularly within the larger, and brilliantly presented, geopolitical context of Spanish American *modernismo* and in relation to the Spanish Empire and its colonial legacy, see Mejías-López, *Inverted Conquest*, esp. chap. 3, "The Conquest of the Metropolitan Literary Field."

28 Recto, "Rosas de carne," in *Bajo los cocoteros*, 61.

29 The literary figure of the "cisne" (swan) has a long history within both Spanish American *modernista* poetry and Symbolist poetry. For detailed study of the various implications of this figure as part of Darío's modernist poetics in particular, see Jrade, *Rubén Darío*, as well as Acereda and Guevara, *Modernism*.

30 Recto, "Rosas de carne," in *Bajo los cocoteros*, 61.

31 Darío, "Leda," in *Obras completas*, 1:286.

32 Jrade, *Rubén Darío*, 104.

33 Jrade, 103.

34 Recto, "Rosas de carne," in *Bajo los cocoteros*, 62.

35 Recto, "Rosas de Eros," in *Bajo los cocoteros*, 67.

36 As Cruz also points out in her study, during the first two decades of the twentieth century, "transpacific Filipina elites found themselves caught

between two popular models of Filipina femininity as produced by the United States: the indigenous Filipina, inscrutable and potentially frightening yet ultimately disciplined and controlled; and an elite Filipina who might achieve her true potential through benevolent influence" (*Transpacific Femininities*, 43).

37 Ngai, *Ugly Feelings*, 210.

38 Ngai, 247.

39 Cruz, *Transpacific Femininities*, 79. In this groundbreaking study of femininity in modern Filipinx culture across the Pacific, Cruz shows how this *ilustrado* ideal of femininity in the Philippines is paradigmatically embodied in Rizal's character of Maria Clara in *Noli*: "Despite Rizal's view that women needed access to education and his plea for Filipinas to depart from blindly following Spanish friar rule, he believed women should behave with 'spotless conduct'" (*Transpacific Femininities*, 79).

40 Recto, "En aquellos días," in *Bajo los cocoteros*, 200–2.

41 There is another connection here with the work of Rubén Darío, particularly his "Oda a Roosevelt" of 1904, included in *Cantos de vida y esperanza* (1907), in which the Nicaraguan poet develops a critique of US imperialism, particularly from his Latin American perspective, and of the United States ("Los Estados Unidos son potentes y grandes" (The United States is powerful and big; 38), as a "future invasor" (future invader; 36) of Spanish America.

42 Recto, *Monroismo asiático*, 109.

43 In an essay included in *Monroismo asiático*, "El castellano como factor de nuestra nacionalidad," originally published in November 1927, Recto makes the following statement:

> Cumplió la ley del destino de todos los imperialismos el imperialismo de Carlos V, pero, al ser expulsado de su último reducto en esta parte del globo, nos dejó, en desagravio de pretéritas ofensas, el legado espiritual de su idioma que, purificado de toda escoria materialista en el crisol de la revolución, ha sido desde entonces, como será en lo sucesivo, no ya el paladión de una cultura que, en el curso de los siglos, hizo acopio de las más prodigiosas creaciones del ingenio humano; no ya el símbolo y el recuerdo de aquella cantera espiritual que ha suministrado a las edades el mármol necesario para eternizar lo mas grande y elevado en el pensamiento de la Historia; sino un componente inseparable del conjunto de afirmaciones que forman el sistema básico, sustantivo, de nuestra nacionalidad; una de las fuerzas de moderación y resistencia destinadas a condicionar, según el patrón de un nacionalismo sin tacha, la corriente de influencias invasoras que aspiran a deformar en su incontenido avance la fisionomía peculiar de nuestro pueblo.
>
> (The imperialism of Charles V fulfilled the law of the fate of all imperialisms, but, being expelled from its last stronghold in this part of the world, left us,

in reparation of past offences, the spiritual legacy of their language, which, purged of all materialistic dross in the crucible of the revolution, has since been, as it will be hereinafter, no longer the palladium of a culture that, in the course of the centuries, mustered the most prodigious creations of human ingenuity; no longer the symbol and the memory of that spiritual quarry that has supplied to the ages the marble needed to perpetuate what has been greatest and loftiest in thought throughout History; but an inseparable component of the set of affirmations that form the basic, substantive system of our nationality; one of the forces of moderation and endurance designed to condition, according to the pattern of an unblemished nationalism, the current of invasive influences that aspire to deform in its uncontained advance the peculiar physiognomy of our people; *Monroismo asiático*, 109–10).

44 San Juan, *Reading the West / Writing the East*, 4–5.

45 Jonathan Chua describes this process as follows: "The systematic Americanization of the islands, chiefly through public education, however, soon contained the tide of nationalism and ushered in new structures of thinking, feeling, and valuation. Philippine literature was inevitably and radically implicated in this process of colonial restructuring. In the 1930s, the time that Villa was most active as a critic, the foundations that the nationalist Tagalog critics had established were being shaken … Another symptom of this change was the place that Tagalog literature occupied vis-à-vis Philippine literature in English, then in its emergent phase. Tagalog literature was thought of as sentimental, didactic, formulaic; its writers dismissed as 'literary quacks.'… Philippine literary criticism, it seems, had ceased to operate from a generally mimetic framework to an expressive framework; the critic was resubjectified from being a vanguard of nationalism to an evaluator of taste, which at the time was American-influenced" (Chua, *The Critical Villa*, 10–11).

46 San Juan, *Philippine Temptation*, 173.

47 Ponce, *Beyond the Nation*, 58.

48 For a detailed analysis of the publication of Villa's "Man-Songs" in 1929, as well as a fascinating approach to Villa's queer poetics within the larger historical context of the 1920s in the Philippines, see Ponce, *Beyond the Nation*, esp. chap. 3, "The Queer Erotics of Garcia Villa's Modernism," 58–66.

49 Villa, *Selected Poems and New*, vii.

50 For example, one of the poems published in the *Philippines Herald Magazine* as "Man-Songs" in 1929, "Song IX: Song of Ripeness," appears as the first poem included under "Early Poems" in *Selected Poems and New*, under the title "The Coconut Poem" (poem 211 in the collection).

51 Villa, "One hemisphere the heart," in *Selected Poems and New*, 219.

52 Villa, "One hemisphere the heart," in *Selected Poems and New*, 219.

53 Villa, "Man-Songs," 10.

54 Villa, "The Best Poems of 1931," in *Critical Villa*, 64.

55 During her time at the University of the Philippines, Manalang Gloria studied under the US scholar Cecil V. Wicker, who would later become a professor of English at the University of New Mexico. Wicker himself held a Master of Arts degree from the University of Michigan and, having been previously an instructor of rhetoric at Michigan, joined the University of the Philippines in 1924 for three years, as assistant professor of English. Wicker would then join the faculty of the University of New Mexico in 1927. According to the University of Pittsburgh English department website, he later obtained his doctoral degree in English from the University of Pittsburgh in 1940: "He left New Mexico to complete his PhD at Pitt, then returned to UNM in 1942 and taught there until his retirement in 1960. He wrote on Steinbeck, and he published *The American Technical Writer* with his UNM colleague, William P Albrecht" (University of Pittsburgh, Department of English, "History of the English Department 1940s").

56 Villa, "The Best Poems of 1931," in *Critical Villa*, 64.

57 Zapanta Manlapaz, *Angela Manalang Gloria*, 2. As Manlapaz has extensively documented in her biography of Manalang Gloria, her decision to switch from the field of law to the study of literature took place while she was studying with two American scholars teaching at the University of the Philippines, Cecil V. Wicker and George Pope Shannon, who exposed Manalang Gloria and her fellow students to key anglophone writers of the period. Based on the evidence referred to by Manlapaz, included some of Manalang Gloria's graded college essays, it seems that Wicker had the strongest influence on the young Manalang Gloria. Shannon was acting associate professor of English at Stanford in 1933, and would later teach at the University of New Mexico and the University of Alabama.

58 Zapanta Manlapaz, *Angela Manalang Gloria*, 20.

59 As explained by Linda Wagner-Martin, one of the key features of imagism as a modernist movement was the fact that there were a number of highly influential women writers associated with it, including most of the American poets that, as I have mentioned, were studied at the University of the Philippines in the late 1920s: "Along with Marianne Moore, always a credible member of the Imagist school – though writing in much more complicated stanza forms – there were some excellent women poets who became largely known through Imagism. (Their presence is one of the reasons Amy Lowell took over the editing of what were then called Imagiste Anthologies.) Adelaide Crapsey practiced tanka and haiku to perfection, and created a five-line form called the cinquain; Sarah Teasdale was given numerous accolades for her short poems, as was Elinor Wylie, who later turn to writing novels; Hazel Hall wrote about disability and work; Edna St. Vincent Millay was one of twentieth century's most beloved – and most famous – poets, known specially for her sonnets and sonnets sequences" (Wagner-Martin, *Introduction to American Modernism*, 53).

60 A graduate of Vassar College, Crapsey (1878–1914) spent three years in Europe between 1908 and 1911, with part of this time spent in Rome, Paris, and London, where she studied English prosody at the British Museum, overlapping, while never formally associated with, some of the writers connected to the Imagiste group. As a result of her time in Europe, Crapsey developed the cinquain, a five-verse poem that happened to be inspired by the Japanese haiku. As Susan Sutton Smith argues in her introduction to Crapsey's *Complete Poems and Collected Letters*, perhaps the key connection between Crapsey and the imagists was their interest in Asian literary traditions: "Crapsey shared with the Imagists, of course, an interest in Japanese poetry. She probably made her notes on Michel Revon and Yone Noguchi before Pound began his work on the manuscripts of Ernest Fenollosa in 1912" (Crapsey, *Complete Poems*, 31).
61 Crapsey, "The Warning," in *Verse*, 46.
62 Manalang Gloria, "The Closed Heart," originally published in the *Philippines Herald Magazine*, 30 October 1927. Reprinted in *Complete Poems*, 45.
63 Lowell, "Time," in *Pictures of the Floating World*, 19.
64 Lowell, *Pictures of the Floating World*, vi.
65 Thacker, *Imagist Poets*, 100.
66 Manalang Gloria, "To a Mestiza," originally published in the *Philippines Herald Magazine*, 25 September 1927. Reprinted in *Complete Poems*, 41.
67 Cruz, *Transpacific Femininities*, 25.
68 Villa, *Have Come, Am Here*, 151–2.
69 Villa, *Selected Poems and New*, 219.
70 Villa, "Definitions of Poetry," 140–1.
71 Villa, "About the Author," in *Selected Poems and New*, 236.
72 Campos, "Translation as Creation and Criticism," 315.
73 For a more detailed analysis of the impact and retranslation of Pound's modernist conception of translation by the Campos brothers and the Brazilian concrete movement, see my chapter "Transferring the 'Luminous Detail': Sousândrade, Pound, and the Imagist Origins of Brazilian Concrete Poetry," in *After Translation*, 117–45.
74 Rothenberg, *Seven Hells of Jigoku Zoshi*, n.p.
75 Villa, "Young Writer in the New Country," in *Footnote to Youth*, 303–4.
76 Lifshey, "Introduction to Forum Kritika," 97.

Coda: Ludwig Mies van der Rohe, Lilly Reich, and the Barcelona World's Fair of 1929: Experimental Form as Network and the Traditionalist Politics of Empire

1 Latour, *Reassembling the Social*, 12.
2 Latour, 222–3 (emphasis in original).

3 See Infante, "(Un)translatability."
4 Dawes, *Poetas ante la modernidad*, 164. See also Dawes's epilogue and pp. 163–6 for his full, and immensely important, analysis and critique of the commodification of the avant-garde within Anglo-American modernism.
5 Highfill, *Modernism and Its Merchandise*, 4.
6 On this particular aspect of this period, see Harkema, *Spanish Modernism*, esp. chap. 3, "Un joven auténtico de 366 años." See in particular the introduction and afterword to Highfill's *Modernism and Its Merchandise* for this aspect of Highfill's argument.
7 Primo de Rivera, "Barcelona Manifesto," 128.
8 Primo de Rivera, 128.
9 Harkema, *Spanish Modernism*, 143.
10 Another important example of the commodification of experimental form in this period, among many instances that deserve further critical examination, is provided by the modernist sculptor and artist Gertrude Vanderbilt Whitney's massive sculpture commemorating the figure of Christopher Columbus in Huelva, located in Punta del Sebo. Planned and constructed in the mid 1920s, this monument, officially called the "Monumento a la Fe Descubridora" (Monument to the Discovering Faith) is characterized by a Cubist style and is more than 37 metres in height. While funded by the US, Gertrude Vanderbilt Whitney's then experimental piece was approved by local authorities and officially inaugurated by the Spanish government on 21 April 1929, with Primo de Rivera and the US ambassador to Spain in attendance. For a more detailed analysis of the planning and inauguration of Whitney's "Monumento a la Fe Descubridora," see Márquez Macias, *Huelva y América*.
11 Graciani García, *Participación internacional y colonial*, 22–3. According to the historian Rodríguez Bernal, Primo de Rivera soon realized the potential for establishing political and commercial links with the former colonies through the project of the Seville Exposition, which had been originally conceived in 1909 as an international Spanish American exposition to create a series of cultural, economic, and political connections across the Atlantic and whose first organizing committee was established by the Ayuntamiento de Sevilla (city council) in 1910, and officially approved by the Spanish government in 1911 (30). According to Rodríguez Bernal, it was after 1923 that Primo de Rivera officially incorporated the Seville Exposition into his political project:

> El general mostró su interés por la culminación del Certamen desde los primeros momentos, pues comprendió que sus objetivos políticos de acercamiento a Ibero-América debían ser asumidos por el Estado dentro de la línea de política exterior por él impulsada de potenciar las relaciones con este continente. Por eso su intervencionismo no se hizo esperar. Ya el 14 de noviembre

de 1923 firmó un Real Decreto en cuyo preámbulo el Gobierno se identificaba plenamente con las aspiraciones del Certamen, de tal manera que numerosos textos legales posteriores se refieren a él como el que otorgó un carácter nacional a la Exposición Ibero-Americana. Esta calificación resulta transcendental pues significa la incautación estatal de una empresa que hasta entonces había sido dirigida por el Ayuntamiento.

(The general showed an interest in the culmination of the Exposition early on, since he understood that his political objectives of rapprochement with Ibero-America should be assumed by the State within the line of foreign policy he promoted to strengthen international relations with this continent. Thus, his interventionism was immediate. Already on 14 November 1923, he signed a Royal Decree in whose preamble the government fully identified with the aspirations of the Exposition, a fact shown by the ways in which numerous subsequent official documents refer to that decree as the one that gave a national character to the Ibero-American Exposition. This qualification is crucial since it meant that the state took over the organization of the event that up until then had been controlled by the City Council; *La Exposición Ibero-Americana de Sevilla*, 38–9).

12 This process is described in more detail by Ignasi de Solà-Morales in his work *La exposición internacional de Barcelona, 1914–1929*:

El golpe de Estado del general Primo de Rivera afectó a la dirección de la Exposición y detuvo un programa que, ya en aquel momento, era en extremo errático, pues la Exposición Internacional de Industrias Eléctricas tampoco estaba del todo organizada. La disolución de la *Mancomunitat de Catalunya*, después de la dimisión de Puig i Cadafalch, y la dimisión también de otros cargos políticos de la dirección de la Exposición—como el mismo Cambó—provocaron una nueva detención que duraría, aproximadamente hasta el año 1925. A partir de aquel momento, cierto *entente* entre la burguesía catalana y la dictadura permitió desbloquear la situación creada. Se nombró al marqués de Foronda nuevo comisario para la Exposición y, con la potenciación simultánea de otra exposición en Sevilla—la Hispano-Americana—, volvió a emprenderse la actividad en Montjuïc.

(General Primo de Rivera's *coup d'état* affected the management of the Exposition and stopped a program that, at that time, was rather erratic, since the International Exposition of Electrical Industries was not a fully organized enterprise either. The dissolution of the Mancomunitat de Catalunya, after the resignation of Puig i Cadafalch, as well as the resignation of other political officials involved in the direction of the Exhibition – like Cambó himself – caused a new delay that would last until approximately 1925. At that point, there appears to have been an agreement between the Catalan bourgeoisie and the dictatorship that allowed the situation to be unblocked. The Marquis of Foronda was appointed the new curator for the Exposition and, with the simultaneous support of another exhibition in Seville – the Ibero-American – activity began again in Montjuïc; Solà-Morales, *Exposición internacional de Barcelona*, 68–9).

13 For a detailed examination of the urban growth of the city of Barcelona, see Carrión, *Barcelona*. Carrión refers to the Barcelona Exposition and the related population displacements on pp. 14–15.

14 *Exposición de Barcelona*, n.p.

15 Davidson, *Jazz Age Barcelona*, 9.

16 Highfill, *Modernism and Its Merchandise*, 4.

17 The official program of the Barcelona World's Fair reads as follows:

> PLAN GENERAL DEL CERTAMEN.— Bajo el alto patronato de Su Majestad el Rey de España y con la cooperación del Gobierno español, el Ayuntamiento de Barcelona prepara este gran Certamen internacional, que se inagurará en el año 1929 y cuyo presupuesto se cifra en 130 millones de pesetas. Barcelona es el centro fabril y comercial de mayor importancia de España. Por el número de sus habitantes, que ya alcanza el millón, sobrepuja a todas las ciudades del Mediterraneo. La necesidad de exhibir ante los demas paises el estado de adelanto que ha alcanzado Barcelona en los diferentes órdenes de la vida y el convencimiento de que un impulso renovador debe guiar su actividad a fin de asimilarse los diversos y constantes progresos de los tiempos modernos, dieron origen al proyecto de organizar una Exposición internacional, que ha de ser la primera manifestacion de esta índole en el mundo despues de la gran Guerra.
>
> (GENERAL PLAN OF THE COMPETITION. – Under the high patronage of His Majesty the King of Spain and with the cooperation of the Spanish Government, the Barcelona City Council is preparing this great international Exposition, which will open in 1929 and whose budget is estimated at 130 million pesetas. Barcelona is the most important manufacturing and commercial centre in Spain. Due to its population, which has already reached one million, it surpasses all the cities of the Mediterranean. The need to show other countries the great progress that Barcelona has made in the different orders of life, and the conviction that an innovative drive must guide its activity in order to assimilate the advances and progress of modern times, gave rise to the project to organize an International Exposition, which is to be the first such demonstration in the world after the Great War; *Exposición de Barcelona*, n.p.).

18 Lange, *Ludwig Mies van der Rohe & Lilly Reich*, 10.

19 Lange, 114.

20 Weston, *Modernism*, 170.

21 Gibberd and Hill, *Ornament Is Crime*, 9.

22 Quoted in English translation in Quetglas, *Fear of Glass*, 15. The full title of Marsà and Marsillach's work is *La montaña iluminada. Itinerario espiritual de la Exposición de Barcelona, 1929–1930* (The Illuminated Mountain: Spiritual Itinerary of the Barcelona Exposition, 1929–30).

23 Quetglas, *Fear of Glass*, 27.

24 At the same time, the Iberian dimension of the project was previously acknowledged in a Real Decreto of 9 November 1922, providing the denomination of Ibero-Americana and requesting the budget for the event to Congress, as documented by Rodríguez Bernal:

> El Gobierno de V.M. estima de suma importancia fijar definitivamente el carácter general de dicha Exposición, que deberá responder a los designios que a la hora presente alberga el pueblo español, respondiendo a los dictados de su geografía y su historia. Ambas, de consuno, muestran a las claras cómo por encima de las diferencias nacidas de la separación de los Estados, los pueblos que conviven en el marco geográfico de la Península Ibérica, tienen en muchas direcciones de la actividad social ideales semejantes nacidos de comunes empresas realizadas en las pasadas centurias, que se espiritualizan y se funden en idénticos pensamientos en el crisol de los siglos y en modernas orientaciones que responden sin duda a direcciones aparentemente contrapuestas pero que en el fondo no los son, y en todo caso, será obra provechosa, el estrechar relaciones y coordinar esfuerzos entre los que vivimos en el mismo solar y por multitud de razones debemos confraternizar, aunando nuestras respectivas labores.
>
> (His Majesty's Government considers it of the utmost importance to establish the general character of said Exhibition, which must respond to the will of the Spanish people at the present time, responding to the dictates of their geography and history. Both, jointly, show clearly how over and above the differences arising from the separation of the States, the peoples who coexist within the geographical framework of the Iberian Peninsula have similar ideals across their societies born out of common enterprises carried out over past centuries, which are spiritualized and merged in identical thoughts across the centuries and in modern attitudes that undoubtedly respond to seemingly opposite directions but that, in the end, are not, and in any case, it will be a profitable enterprise in order to strengthen relations and coordinate efforts between those of us who live on the same land, and for many reasons we must establish a fellowship, uniting our respective projects; *Real Decreto* of 9 November 1922, originally published in *Gaceta de Madrid*, 10 November 1922, quoted in Bernal, *Historia*, 90).

25 There is an important conceptual and historical connection between the Barcelona and Seville Expositions of 1929 as a joint national project and the nineteenth-century international exhibitions taking place across the world, as well as the national expositions taking place throughout Latin

America during the same period. These important nineteenth-century universal exhibitions provide different models in particular for the Ibero-American dimension of the Seville Exposition. For further analysis of these nineteenth-century exhibitions and their representations of modernity, particularly in relation to the national projects of Argentina and Brazil, see in particular Jens Andermann's "Tournaments of Value." Andermann focuses in this essay on how, during the "Age of Exhibitions," Latin American nations, in particular Argentina and Brazil, "had to negotiate the material and symbolic value of their commodities and cultural samples with a host of agents" (333). Andermann analyzes the "national pavilion" as the key structure for the articulation of these international Expositions as providing "'contact zones,' performative spaces for the exchange of objects, gazes and words" (333). For a wider study of this phenomenon across the nineteenth and early twentieth centuries, as well as its impact across Latin America, see Beatriz González Stephan and Jens Andermann's edited collection *Galerias del progreso*.

26 Quoted in Braojos Garrido, *Alfonso XIII y la Exposición Iberoamericana*, 90.

27 Appleton Read, "Germany at the Barcelona World's Fair," 112.

28 Costa Pinto, *Salazar's Dictatorship*, 116, 138.

29 Primo de Rivera, "Platform of the Patriotic Union," 130–1.

30 Salazar, *Discursos*, 43.

31 The Exposição do Mundo Português of 1940 provides another example of the Iberian dimension of this tension between the experimental and the traditional that characterized this state-driven institutionalization process as part of a larger traditionalist framing of national "progress." While this 1940 Exposition, inaugurated during World War II, was connected to the development of a series of institutional strategies by the Salazar *Estado Novo* aiming at a reconstruction of national identity and the projection of a sense of progress or modernity, the constructed "newness" of the Portuguese "New State" was ultimately determined by a traditionalist and historicist interpretation of national history and identity, as Costa Pinto argues:

> The cultural combination of the modern and the traditional was openly dominated by the latter. Like other authoritarian regimes, Salazarism's cultural project sought the 'systematic restoration of traditional values.' Particular attention was given to a whole 'ethnographic folkloric' movement which included the revitalization of local folk groups, the restoration of the symbols of the 'Christian reconquest' as well as the social deployment of these images. The title 'most Portuguese' became the object of official competitions such as the 'most Portuguese village in Portugal,' destined to 'increase in the Portuguese the cult of tradition,' developing one of the basic elements of the 'New State': the village as a microcosm of a traditional society … (Costa Pinto, *Salazar's Dictatorship*, 195–6).

32 Primo de Rivera, "Barcelona Manifesto," 128.

33 Another relevant manifestation of this understanding of Spanish cultural identity and history is explicitly portrayed in the official poster of the Barcelona Exposition by Josep Rojas Assens, which presents a medieval Barcelona "macer" over a landscape of the city, an example of medieval iconography also shared by Francesc de Assís Galí's poster for the exhibition's section "El arte en España." For a wider analysis of the Poble Espanyol in relation to the urban development of Barcelona across various historical periods, see Epps, "Modern Spaces: Building Barcelona."
34 Mendelson, *Documenting Spain*, 29.
35 Santiáñez, *Topographies of Fascism*, 31.
36 Santiáñez, 31, 29–30.
37 Bernal, *Historia*, 386–7. Bernal describes the closing of the Seville Exposition as follows:

> La clausura del Certamen sucedió el 21 de junio de 1930 sin la solemnidad dada a la inauguración … Los objetivos de aproximación económica y cultural tantas veces manifestados quedaron sólo en bellas palabras … En conjunto da la impresión que la Ibero-Americana fue sobre todo una Exposición histórica y cultural. Miró mas al pasado que al futuro, en oposición a lo que ocurría en otras exposiciones internacionales de carácter general. La aspiración de enaltecer la Historia de España, los historicimos predominantes de sus edificios, la omisión de una Exposición de Arte Moderno de todos los países participantes y la ausencia de adelantos técnicos, así lo demuestran. Ello tal vez conecte con los ideales primitivos que la hicieron nacer, que no eran en esencia otros que realizar un gran homenaje al pasado colonizador de España en un presente difícil que no ofrecía tampoco bases sólidas para aventurar un futuro mas prometedor.
>
> (The closing of the Exposition happened on 21 June 1930, without the solemnity given to the inauguration … The objectives of economic and cultural approach so often expressed ended up being just beautiful words … As a whole, it seems that the Ibero-American [Exposition] was above all a historical and cultural exhibition. It looked more to the past than to the future, in opposition to what happened in other international exhibitions of a more general nature. This is demonstrated by the aspirations to exalt the history of Spain, the predominant historicisms apparent in its buildings, the omission of an Exhibition of Modern Art from all the participating countries, and the absence of any technical advances. This perhaps connects with the original ideals that gave birth to the Exposition, which were essentially no other than a grandiose homage to the imperial past of Spain at a difficult contemporary moment unable to offer a solid foundation to put forward towards a more promising future; 386–7).

38 Betts, *Avant-Garde Canadian Literature*, 259.

Bibliography

Abad, Gémino H. *Our Scene So Fair: Filipino Poetry in English, 1905 to 1955.* Diliman, Quezon City: University of the Philippines Press, 2008.

Acereda, Alberto, and Rigoberto Guevara. *Modernism, Rubén Darío, and the Poetics of Despair*. Dallas: University Press of America, 2004.

Aching, Gerard. *The Politics* of *Spanish American Modernismo: By Exquisite Design*. Cambridge: Cambridge University Press, 1997.

Adamson, Walter. "Futurism and Italian Intervention in World War I." In *Futurism, 1909–1944: Reconstructing the Universe*, edited by Vivien Greene, 175–83. New York: Guggenheim Museum Publications, 2014.

Adelman, Jeremy. *Sovereignty and Revolution in the Iberian Atlantic*. Princeton, NJ: Princeton University Press, 2006.

Adorno, Theodor W. *Aesthetic Theory*. Edited by Gretel Adorno and Rolf Tiedemann. Translated and with an introduction by Robert Hullot-Kentor. Minneapolis: University of Minnesota Press, 1997.

Afonso Ferreira, Sara, and Sílvia Laureano Costa. "Almada Negreiros: A Futurist Poet, and Much More. International Symposium at the Calouste Gulbenkian Foundation in Lisbon, 13–15 November 2013." In *International Yearbook of Futurism Studies*, vol. 4, edited by Günter Berghaus, 21–6. Berlin: Walter de Gruyter, 2014.

Aliete Dores Galhoz, Maria. "O momento poético do *Orpheu*." In *Orpheu* (reissue of no. 1), xiii–liii. Lisbon: Edições Ática, 1959.

Almada Negreiros, António de. *L'agriculture dans les colonies portugaises. Programme de réformes à appliquer aux colonies d'origine latine. Mémoire présenté à la première "Réunion internationale d'agronomie coloniale" de Paris*. Paris: A. Challamel, 1905.

Almada Negreiros, António de. *Angola*. Paris: Alcan-Lévy, 1901.

Almada Negreiros, António de. *Colonies portugaises. Île de San-Thomé; avec cartes*. Paris: A. Challamel, 1901.

Almada Negreiros, António de. *Le Mozambique*. Paris: A. Challamel, 1904.

Almada Negreiros, José de. *Manifesto anti-Dantas e por extenso*. Porto: Documentos Literários, 1970.

Almada Negreiros, José de. *Obras completas*. Vol. 4, *Poesia*. Lisbon: Editorial Estampa, 1971.

Almada Negreiros, José de. *Ultimatum Futurista às gerações portuguesas do século XX*. Lisbon: Pedro Veiga, 1917.

Alves das Neves, João. *O movimento futurista em Portugal*. Porto: Livraria Divulgação, 1966.

Amaral, Aracy. *Blaise Cendrars no Brasil e os modernistas*. São Paulo: Martins, 1970.

Amaral, Aracy. "Tarsila: La magia y lo racional en el modernismo brasileño." In *Tarsila, Frida, Amelia: Tarsila do Amaral, Frida Kahlo, Amelia Peláez*, edited by Irma Arestizábal, 38–52. Barcelona: Fundación La Caixa, 1997.

Amaral, Tarsila do. "Confissão geral, 1950." In *Crônicas e outros escritos de Tarsila do Amaral*, edited by Laura Taddei Brandini, 727–8. Campinas: Editora Unicamp, 2008.

Amaral, Tarsila do. "Delaunay y la Torre Eiffel." In *Tarsila do Amaral (Fundación Juan March)*, 211–12.

Amaral, Tarsila do. "Pau-Brasil e Antropofagia." In *Crônicas e outros escritos de Tarsila do Amaral*, edited by Laura Taddei Brandini, 684–5. Campinas: Editora Unicamp, 2008.

Andermann, Jens. "Antropofagia: Testimonios y silencios." *Revista Iberoamericana* 68, no. 198 (January–March 2002): 79–89.

Andermann, Jens. "Tournaments of Value: Argentina and Brazil in the Age of Exhibitions." *Journal of Material Culture* 14, no. 3 (September 2009): 333–63. https://doi.org/10.1177/13591835091064.

Anderson, Benedict. *Imagined Communities: Reflections of the Origin and Spread of Nationalism*. New York: Verso, 1983.

Anderson, Benedict. *The Spectre of Comparisons: Nationalism, Southeast Asia, and the World*. New York: Verso, 1998.

Andrade, Mário de. "França / Feuilles de route." *A Revista* 1, no. 1 (July 1925): 54.

Andrade, Mário de. *Hallucinated City (Paulicéia Desvairada)*. Translated by Jack E. Tomlins. Nashville, TN: Vanderbilt University Press, 1968.

Andrade, Mário de. *Paulicea Desvairada*. São Paulo: Casa Mayença, 1922.

Andrade, Oswald de. "Pau Brasil." In *The Oxford Book of Latin American Poetry*, edited by Cecilia Vicuña and Ernesto Livon-Grosman, translated by Odile Cisneros, 135–7. Oxford: Oxford University Press, 2009.

Andrade, Oswald de. *Poesias reunidas*. São Paulo: Difusão Européia do Livro, 1966.

Appadurai, Arjun. "Grassroots Globalization and the Research Imagination." In *Globalization*, edited by Arjun Appadurai, 1–22. Durham, NC: Duke University Press, 2001.

Appleton Read, Helen. "Germany at the Barcelona World's Fair." *The Arts*, no. 16, September 1929–May 1930, 112–13.

Bankoff, Greg, and Kathleen Weekley. *Post-colonial National Identity in the Philippines: Celebrating the Centennial of Independence*. Aldershot: Ashgate, 2002.

Bary, David. *Larrea: Poesía y transfiguración*. Barcelona: Planeta, 1976.

Begam, Richard, and Michael Valdez-Moses, eds. *Modernism and Colonialism: British and Irish Literature, 1899–1939*. Durham, NC: Duke University Press, 2007.

Berghaus, Günter. *Futurism and Politics: Between Anarchist Rebellion and Fascist Reaction, 1909–1944*. Providence, RI: Berghahn Books, 1996.

Betts, Gregory. *Avant-Garde Canadian Literature: The Early Manifestations*. Toronto: University of Toronto Press, 2013.

Birmingham, David. *Portugal and Africa*. Houndmills: Macmillan; New York: St. Martin's Press, 1999.

Boaventura, Maria Eugênia da Gama Alves. *22 por 22: A Semana de Arte Moderna vista pelos seus contemporâneos*. São Paulo: EDUSP, 2000.

Boehmer, Elleke, and Steven Matthews, "Modernism and Colonialism." In *The Cambridge Companion to Modernism*, edited by Michael Levenson, 284–300. Cambridge: Cambridge University Press, 2011.

Bonet, Juan Manuel. "A 'Quest' for Tarsila." In *Tarsila do Amaral (Fundación Juan March)*, 67–92.

Booth, Howard J., and Nigel Rigby, eds. *Modernism and Empire: Writing and British Coloniality, 1890–1940*. Manchester: Manchester University Press, 2000.

Braojos Garrido, Alfonso. *Alfonso XIII y la Exposición Iberoamericana de Sevilla de 1929*. Seville: Secretariado de Publicaciones, Universidad de Sevilla, 1992.

Brenner, Neil, and Christian Schmid. "Planetary Urbanization." In *Urban Constellations*, edited by Matthew Gandy, 10–13. Berlin: Jovis, 2012.

Buelens, Geert, Harald Hendrix, and Monica Jansen, eds. *The History of Futurism: The Precursors, Protagonists, and Legacies*. Lanham, MD: Lexington Books, 2012.

Burbank, Jane, and Frederick Cooper. *Empires in World History: Power and the Politics of Difference*. Princeton, NJ: Princeton University Press, 2010.

Bürger, Peter. *Theory of the Avant-Garde*. Translated by Michael Shaw. Foreword by Jochen Schulte-Sasse. Minneapolis: University of Minnesota Press, 1984.

Bush, Christopher. Review of *Planetary Modernisms: Provocations on Modernity across Time*, by Susan Stanford Friedman. *Modernism/modernity* 23, no. 3 (September 2016): 686–8.

Calderwood, Eric. *Colonial al-Andalus: Spain and the Making of Modern Moroccan Culture*. Cambridge, MA: Belknap Press of Harvard University Press, 2018.

Camargos, Marcia. *Semana de 22: Entre vaias e aplausos*. São Paulo: Boitempo, 2006.

Camões, Luís de. *Os Lusíadas*. Edited by Reis Brasil. Lisbon: Editorial Minerva, 1964.

Campos, Haroldo de. "Translation as Creation and Criticism." In *Novas: Selected Writings*, edited and with an introduction by Antonio Sergio Bessa and Odile Cisneros, foreword by Roland Greene, 312–26. Evanston, IL: Northwestern University Press, 2007.

Carrión, Jorge. *Barcelona. Libro de los pasajes*. Barcelona: Galaxia Gutenberg, 2017.

Casetti, Francesco. "Adaptation and Mis-adaptations: Film, Literature, and Social Discourses." In *A Companion to Literature and Film*, edited by Robert Stam and Alessandra Raengo, 81–91. Malden, MA: Blackwell, 2007.

Cendrars, Blaise. *Complete Poems*. Translated by Ron Padgett. With an introduction by Jay Bochner. Berkeley: University of California Press, 1992.

Cendrars, Blaise. *Complete Postcards from the Americas: Poems of Road and Sea*. Translated and with an introduction by Monique Chefdor. Berkeley: University of California Press, 1976.

Cendrars, Blaise. "The Eiffel Tower." In *Selected Writings of Blaise Cendrars*, edited by Walter Albert, 234–40. New York: New Directions, 1966.

Cendrars, Blaise. *Feuilles de route*. Vol. 1, *Le Formose*. Paris: Au Sans Pareil, 1924.

Cendrars, Blaise. *Œuvres complètes*. Vol. 1, *Introduction à la lecture de Blaise Cendrars, par Raymond Dumay*. With the assistance of Nino Frank. Paris: Club français du livre, 1968.

Cendrars, Blaise. "Profound Today." Translated by Harold A. Loeb. *BROOM (An International Magazine of the Arts)* 1, no. 3 (1922): 265–8.

Césaire, Aimé. *Cahier d'un retour au pays natal*. With a preface by Petar Guberina. Paris: Présence Africaine, 1956.

Chakrabarty, Dipesh. *Provincializing Europe: Postcolonial Thought and Historical Difference*. Princeton, NJ: Princeton University Press, 2000.

Chua, Jonathan, ed. and comp. *The Critical Villa: Essays in Literary Criticism by Jose Garcia Villa*. Quezon City: Ateneo de Manila University Press, 2002.

Chua, Jonathan. "Introduction." In *The Critical Villa: Essays in Literary Criticism by Jose Garcia Villa*, edited and compiled by Jonathan Chua, 1–32. Quezon City: Ateneo de Manila University Press, 2002.

Clancier, George-Emmanuel. *De Rimbaud au surréalisme : Panorama critique*. Paris: Pierre Seghers, 1953.

Clayton, Michelle. *Poetry in Pieces: César Vallejo and Lyric Modernity*. Berkeley: University of California Press, 2011.

Constantino, Renato. *The Making of a Filipino*. Quezon City: Malaya Books, 1969.

Cortesão, Jaime. *A expedição de Pedro Alvares Cabral e o descobrimento do Brazil*. Lisbon: Aillaud e Bertrand, 1922.

Costa, René de. *Salle XIV, Vicente Huidobro y las artes plásticas*. Madrid: Museo Nacional Centro de Arte Reina Sofía, 2001.

Costa, René de, ed. *Vicente Huidobro y el creacionismo*. Madrid: Taurus, 1975.
Costa Pinto, António. *Salazar's Dictatorship and European Fascism: Problems of Interpretation*. Boulder, CO: Social Science Monographs; New York: Distributed by Columbia University Press, 1995.
Crapsey, Adelaide. *The Complete Poems and Collected Letters of Adelaide Crapsey*. Edited with an introduction and notes by Susan Sutton Smith. Albany: State University of New York Press, 1977.
Crapsey, Adelaide. *Verse*. Rochester, NY: Manas Press, 1915.
Cruz, Denise. *Transpacific Femininities: The Making of the Modern Filipina*. Durham, NC: Duke University Press, 2012.
D'Alessandro, Stephanie. "*A Negra*, *Abaporou*, and Tarsila's Anthropophagy." In D'Alessandro and Pérez-Oramas, *Tarsila do Amaral*, 38–56.
D'Alessandro, Stephanie, and Luis Pérez-Oramas. *Tarsila do Amaral: Inventing Modern Art in Brazil*. Chicago: Art Institute of Chicago; New York: Museum of Modern Art, 2017.
Darío, Rubén. *Azul*. With a foreword by Juan Valera. Buenos Aires: La Nación, 1905.
Darío, Rubén. *Cantos de vida y esperanza. Los cisnes, y otros poemas*. Barcelona: F. Granada, 1907.
Darío, Rubén. *Obras completas*. Edited by Julio Ortega, with the collaboration of Nicanor Vélez and José Emilio Pacheco. Barcelona: Galaxia Gutenberg / Círculo de Lectores, 2007.
Davidson, Robert A. *Jazz Age Barcelona*. Toronto: University of Toronto Press, 2009.
Dawes, Greg. *Poetas ante la modernidad: Las ideas estéticas y políticas de Vallejo, Huidobro y Paz*. Madrid: Editorial Fundamentos, 2009.
Dérieux, Henry. *La poésie française contemporaine, 1885–1935*. Paris: Mercure de France, 1935.
Derrida, Jacques. *Specters of Marx*. Translated by Peggy Kamuf. New York: Routledge, 1994.
Diego, Gerardo. "Poesía y creacionismo de Vicente Huidobro," in de Costa, *Vicente Huidobro y el creacionimo*, 209–29.
Dimock, Wai Chee, and Lawrence Buell, eds. *Shades of the Planet: American Literature as World Literature*. Princeton, NJ: Princeton University Press, 2007.
Doyle, Laura. "Thinking Back through Empires." *Modernism/modernity Print Plus* 2, no. 4 (2018). https://doi.org/10.26597/mod.0037.
Drutt, Matthew. "Simultaneous Expressions: Robert Delaunay's Early Series." In *Visions of Paris: Robert Delaunay's Series*, organized by Mark Rosenthal, 15–46. New York: Guggenheim Museum, 1997.
Elias, Amy J., and Christian Moraru, eds. *The Planetary Turn: Relationality and Geoaesthetics in the Twenty-First Century*. Evanston, IL: Northwestern University Press, 2015.

Epps, Bradley. "Modern Spaces: Building Barcelona." In *Iberian Cities*, edited by Joan Ramon Resina, 148–97. New York: Routledge, 2001.
Esty, Jed. *Unseasonable Youth: Modernism, Colonialism, and the Fiction of Development*. New York: Oxford University Press, 2012.
Eulalio, Alexandre. "L'aventure brésilienne de Blaise Cendrars." *Études portugaises et brésiliennes*, no. 5 (1969): 19–55.
Exposición de Barcelona, Plan general del certamen. Barcelona: Exposición Internacional Barcelona, 1929.
Folejewski, Zbigniew. *Futurism and Its Place in the Development of Modern Poetry: A Comparative Study and Anthology*. Ottawa: University of Ottawa Press, 1980.
Friedman, Susan Stanford. "Planetarity: Musing Modernist Studies." *Modernism/modernity* 17, no. 3 (September 2010): 471–99.
Friedman, Susan Stanford. *Planetary Modernisms: Provocations on Modernity across Time*. New York: Columbia University Press, 2015.
Friedman, Susan Stanford. "Response to Robbins and Walkowitz." *Interventions* 18, no. 5 (2016): 750–6. https://doi.org/10.1080/1369801X.2016.1173955.
Gabara, Esther. *Errant Modernism: The Ethos of Photography in Mexico and Brazil*. Durham, NC: Duke University Press, 2008.
Gibberd, Matt, and Albert Hill. *Ornament Is Crime: Modernist Architecture*. London: Phaidon, 2017.
Gonçalves, Marcos Augusto. *1922: A semana que não terminou*. Rio de Janeiro: Companhia das Letras, 2012.
González Stephan, Beatriz, and Jens Andermann, eds. *Galerias del progreso. Museos, exposiciones y cultura visual en América Latina*. Rosario: Beatriz Viterbo Editora, 2006.
Gouveia, Saulo. *The Triumph of Brazilian Modernism: The Metanarrative of Emancipation and Counter-narratives*. Chapel Hill: University of North Carolina Press, 2013.
Graciani García, Amparo. *La participación internacional y colonial en la exposición iberoaméricana de Sevilla de 1929*. Seville: ICAS, Universidad de Sevilla, Departamento de Publicaciones, 2010.
Grewal, Inderpal, and Caren Kaplan, eds. *Scattered Hegemonies: Postmodernity and Transnational Feminist Practices*. Minneapolis: University of Minnesota Press, 1994.
Guerrero, Fernando María. "Introito." In *Bajo los cocoteros (almas y panoramas)*, by Claro M. Recto, ix–xx. Manila: Libreria "Manila Filatélica," 1911.
Gullón, Ricardo. *Direcciones del modernismo*. Madrid: Gredos, 1963.
Hagimoto, Koichi. *Between Empires: Martí, Rizal and the Intercolonial Alliance*. New York: Palgrave Macmillan, 2013.
Halpern Pereira, Miriam. *The First Portuguese Republic: Between Liberalism and Democracy (1910–1926)*. Brighton: Sussex Academic Press, 2019.

Harkema, Leslie J. *Spanish Modernism and the Poetics of Youth: From Miguel de Unamuno to* La Joven Literatura. Toronto: University of Toronto Press, 2017.

Healey, Kimberley J. *The Modernist Traveler: French Detours, 1900–1930.* Lincoln: University of Nebraska Press, 2003.

Henríquez Ureña, Max. *Breve historia del modernismo.* Mexico City: Fondo de Cultura Económica, 1954.

Hernández Sánchez, Domingo. *Estética de la limitación. La recepción de Hegel por Ortega y Gasset.* Salamanca: Ediciones Universidad de Salamanca, 2000.

Herzog, Tamar. *Frontiers of Possession: Spain and Portugal in Europe and the Americas.* Cambridge, MA: Harvard University Press, 2015.

Hess, Steven. *Ramón Menéndez Pidal: The Practice and Politics of Philology in Twentieth-Century Spain.* Newark, DE: Juan de la Cuesta Hispanic Monograhs, 2014.

Highfill, Juli. *Modernism and Its Merchandise: The Spanish Avant-Garde and Material Culture, 1920–1930.* University Park: Pennsylvania State University Press, 2014.

Hobsbawm, Eric J. *The Age of Empire, 1875–1914.* New York: Pantheon Books, 1987.

Hodges, Tony, and Malyn Newitt. *São Tomé and Príncipe: From Plantation Colony to Microstate.* Boulder, CO: Westview Press, 1988.

Huidobro, Vicente. *Epistolario.* Edited by Gabrielle Morelli and Carlos García. Madrid: Residencia de Estudiantes, 2009.

Huidobro, Vicente. *Mío Cid Campeador. Hazaña.* Santiago: Ediciones Ercilla, 1949.

Huidobro, Vicente. *Obra poética. Edición crítica.* Co-ordinated by Cedomil Goic. Madrid: ALLCA XX, 2003.

Huidobro, Vicente. *Pasando y pasando.* Santiago: Imprenta de Chile, 1914.

Huidobro, Vicente. *Portrait of a Paladin.* Translated by Warre B. Wells. New York: H. Liveright, 1932.

Infante, Ignacio. *After Translation: The Transfer and Circulation of Modern Poetics across the Atlantic.* New York: Fordham University Press, 2013.

Infante, Ignacio. "On the (Un)translatability of Literary Form: Framing Contemporary Translational Literature." *Translation Review* 95, no. 1 (2016): 1–7. https://doi.org/10.1080/07374836.2016.1174503.

Jackson, Kenneth David. *Adverse Genres in Fernando Pessoa.* New York: Oxford University Press, 2010.

Jackson, Kenneth David. *Cannibal Angels: Transatlantic Modernism and the Brazilian Avant-Garde.* Bern: Peter Lang, 2021.

Jáuregui, Carlos A. *Canibalia: Canibalismo, calibanismo, antropofagia cultural y consumo en América Latina.* Madrid: Iberoamericana, 2008.

Jiménez, Juan Ramón. *El modernismo.* Madrid: Aguillar, 1962.

Jrade, Cathy L. Modernismo*, Modernity, and the Development of Spanish American Literature.* Austin: University of Texas Press, 1998.

Jrade, Cathy L. *Rubén Darío and the Romantic Search for Unity: The Modernist Recourse to Esoteric Tradition*. Austin: University of Texas Press, 1983.

Klich, Lynda. *The Noisemakers: Estridentismo, Vanguardism, and Social Action in Postrevolutionary Mexico*. Oakland: University of California Press, 2018.

Krauel, Javier. *Imperial Emotions: Cultural Responses to Myths of Empire in* Fin-de-Siècle *Spain*. Liverpool: Liverpool University Press, 2013.

Lange, Christiane. *Ludwig Mies van der Rohe & Lilly Reich: Furniture and Interiors*. Ostfildern: Hatje Cantz, 2006.

Latour, Bruno. *An Inquiry into Modes of Existence: An Anthropology of the Moderns*. Translated by Catherine Porter. Cambridge, MA: Harvard University Press, 2013.

Latour, Bruno. *Reassembling the Social: An Introduction to Actor-Network Theory*. Oxford: Oxford University Press, 2005.

Leal, João. "The Hidden Empire: Peasants, Nation Building, and the Empire in Portuguese Anthropology." In *Recasting Culture and Space in Iberian Contexts*, edited by Sharon R. Roseman and Shawn S. Parkhurst, 35–54. Albany: State University of New York Press, 2008.

Levine, Caroline. *Forms: Whole, Rhythm, Hierarchy, Network*. Princeton, NJ: Princeton University Press, 2015.

Lifshey, Adam. "An Introduction to Forum Kritika: Philippine Literature in Spanish." *Kritika Kultura*, no. 20 (2013): 95–8. https://doi.org/10.13185/KK2013.02005.

Lifshey, Adam. *The Magellan Fallacy: Globalization and the Emergence of Asian and African Literature in Spanish*. Ann Arbor: University of Michigan Press, 2012.

Lifshey, Adam. *Subversions of the American Century: Filipino Literature in Spanish and the Transpacific Transformation of the United States*. Ann Arbor: University of Michigan Press, 2015.

Livingston, Julie. *Self-Devouring Growth: A Planetary Parable as Told from Southern Africa*. Durham, NC: Duke University Press, 2019.

Lowell, Amy. *Pictures of the Floating World*. New York: Macmillan, 1919.

Manalang Gloria, Angela. *The Complete Poems of Angela Manalang Gloria*. Edited and with an introduction by Edna Zapanta Manlapaz. Quezon City: Ateneo de Manila University Press, 1993.

Marinetti, F.T. "The Founding and Manifesto of Futurism." In *Futurism: An Anthology*, edited by Lawrence Rainey, Christine Poggi, and Laura Wittman, 49–53. New Haven, CT: Yale University Press, 2009.

Marinetti, F.T. "Proclama futurista a los españoles." Translated by Ramón Gómez de la Serna. *Prometeo (Revista Social y Literaria)* 3, no. 20 (1910): 517–31.

Marinetti, F.T. "Technical Manifesto of Futurist Literature." In *Selected Poems and Related Prose*, selected by Luce Marinetti, translated by Elizabeth R.

Napier and Barbara R. Studholme, with an essay by Paolo Valesio, 77–80. New Haven, CT: Yale University Press, 2002.

Márquez Macias, Rosario. *Huelva y América: Cien años de Americanismo. Revista "La Rábida" (1911–1933).* Seville: Universidad Internacional de Andalucía, 2012.

Marsà, Àngel, and Luis Marsillach. *La montaña iluminada. Itinerario espiritual de la Exposición de Barcelona, 1929–1930.* Barcelona: Ediciones Horizonte, 1930.

Martí, José. *Selected Writings.* Translated and edited by Esther Allen. New York: Penguin, 2002.

Martin-Márquez, Susan. *Disorientations: Spanish Colonialism in Africa and the Performance of Identity.* New Haven, CT: Yale University Press, 2008.

Mejías López, Alejandro. *The Inverted Conquest: The Myth of Modernity and the Transatlantic Onset of Modernism.* Nashville, TN: Vanderbilt University Press, 2009.

Mendelson, Jordana. *Documenting Spain: Artists, Exhibition Culture, and the Modern Nation, 1929–1939.* University Park: Pennsylvania State University Press, 2005.

Menéndez Pidal, Ramón, ed. *Poema de Mio Cid.* Madrid: Espasa-Calpe, 1911.

Millet, Sergio. "Tarsila do Amaral." In *Tarsila do Amaral (Fundación Juan March),* 227–30.

Montaldo, Graciela. *La sensibilidad amenazada, fin de siglo y modernismo.* Rosario: Beatriz Viterbo Editora, 1994.

Moore, Stephen, and Mayra Rivera, eds. *Planetary Loves: Spivak, Postcoloniality, Theology.* New York: Fordham University Press, 2011.

Moraña, Mabel, Enrique Dussel, and Carlos A. Jáuregui, eds. *Coloniality at Large: Latin America and the Postcolonial Debate.* Durham, NC: Duke University Press, 2008.

Moraru, Christian. *Reading for the Planet: Toward a Geomethodology.* Ann Arbor: University of Michigan Press, 2015.

Ngai, Sianne. *Ugly Feelings.* Cambridge, MA: Harvard University Press, 2007.

Noland, Carrie. "The Metaphysics of Coffee: Blaise Cendrars, Modernist Standardization, and Brazil." *Modernism/modernity* 7, no. 3 (September 2000): 401–22. https://doi.org/10.1353/mod.2000.0068.

Noland, Carrie. *Poetry at Stake: Lyric Aesthetics and the Challenge of Technology.* Princeton, NJ: Princeton University Press, 1999.

Orpheu (reissue of no. 1). Lisbon: Edições Ática, 1959.

Ortega y Gasset, José. *La deshumanización del arte y otros ensayos de estética.* Barcelona: Espasa Libros, 2017.

Ortega y Gasset, José. *Hegel: Notas de trabajo.* Edited by Domingo Hernández Sánchez. Madrid: Abada Editorial, 2007.

Ortega y Gasset, José. *Kant, Hegel, Dilthey.* Madrid: Revista de Occidente, 1961.

Parsons, Cóilín. "Planetary Parallax: *Ulysses*, the Stars, and South Africa." *Modernism/modernity* 24, no. 1 (January 2017): 67–85. https://doi.org/10.1353/mod.2017.0003.

Patke, Rajeev S. *Modernist Literature and Postcolonial Studies*. Edinburgh: Edinburgh University Press, 2013.

Perloff, Marjorie. "The Audacity of Hope: The Foundational Futurist Manifestos." In *The History of Futurism: The Precursors, Protagonists, and Legacies*, edited by Geert Buelens, Harald Hendrix, and Monica Jansen, 9–30. Lanham, MD: Lexington Books, 2012.

Perloff, Marjorie. *Edge of Irony: Modernism in the Shadow of the Habsburg Empire*. Chicago: University of Chicago Press, 2016.

Perloff, Marjorie. *The Futurist Moment: Avant-Garde, Avant Guerre, and the Language of Rupture*. Chicago: University of Chicago Press, 2003.

Perloff, Marjorie. "The Great War and the European Avant-Garde." In *The Cambridge Companion to the Literature of the First World War*, edited by Vincent Sherry, 141–65. Cambridge: Cambridge University Press, 2005.

Pessoa, Fernando [Álvaro de Campos, pseud.]. "'Opiário' e 'Ode triunfal.' Duas composições de Alvaro de Campos, publicadas por Fernando Pessoa." In *Orpheu* (reissue of no. 1), 89–108. Lisbon: Edições Ática, 1959.

Pitcher, M. Anne. *Politics in the Portuguese Empire: The State, Industry, and Cotton, 1926–1974*. Oxford: Clarendon Press, 1993.

Pizarro, Ana. "El creacionismo de Vicente Huidobro y sus orígenes (1969)." In *Vicente Huidobro y el creacionismo*, edited by René de Costa, 229–48. Madrid: Taurus, 1975.

Poggioli, Renato. *The Theory of the Avant-Garde*. Translated by Gerald Fitzgerald. Cambridge, MA: Belknap Press of Harvard University Press, 1968.

Ponce, Martin Joseph. *Beyond the Nation: Diasporic Filipino Literature and Queer Reading*. New York: New York University Press, 2012.

Primo de Rivera, Miguel. "The Barcelona Manifesto." In *Modern Spain (A Documentary History)*, edited by Jon Cowans, 126–8. Philadelphia: University of Pennsylvania Press, 2003.

Primo de Rivera, Miguel. "Platform of the Patriotic Union." In *Modern Spain (A Documentary History)*, edited by Jon Cowans, 129–31. Philadelphia: University of Pennsylvania Press, 2003.

Puchner, Martin. *Poetry of the Revolution: Marx, Manifestos, and the Avant-Gardes*. Princeton, NJ: Princeton University Press, 2006.

Quetglas, Josep. *Fear of Glass: Mies van der Rohe's Pavilion in Barcelona*. With an introduction by Rafael Moneo, and drawings by Ricardo Daza, Margarita González, and Toni Sánchez. Translated by John Stone and Rosa Roig. Basel: Birkhäuser, 2001.

Rafael, Vicente. *White Love*. Durham, NC: Duke University Press, 2000.

Rainey, Lawrence, Christine Poggi, and Laura Wittman, eds. *Futurism: An Anthology*. New Haven, CT: Yale University Press, 2009.

Ram, Harsha. "Futurist Geographies: Centre, Periphery, and the Struggle for Aesthetic Autonomy: Paris, Italy, Russia, 1909–1914." In *The Oxford Handbook of Global Modernisms*, edited by Mark Wollaeger, 313–40. New York: Oxford University Press, 2012.

Ram, Harsha. "The Scale of Global Modernisms: Imperial, National, Regional, Local." *PMLA* 131, no. 5 (2016): 1372–85. https://doi.org/10.1632/pmla.2016.131.5.1372.

Ramalho Santos, Irene. *Atlantic Poets: Fernando Pessoa's Turn in Anglo-American Modernism*. Hanover: University Press of New England, 2003.

Read, Justin. *Modern Poetics and Hemispheric American Cultural Studies*. New York: Palgrave Macmillan, 2009.

Recto, Claro M. *Bajo los cocoteros (almas y panoramas)*. Manila: Libreria "Manila Filatélica," 1911.

Recto, Claro. *Monroismo asiático (artículos de polémica) y otros ensayos*. Manila: Imprenta de Juan Fajardo, 1921.

Resina, Joan Ramon. *Iberian Modalities: A Relational Approach to the Study of Culture in the Iberian Peninsula*. Edited by Joan Ramon Resina. Liverpool: Liverpool University Press, 2013.

Rizal, José. *Noli me tángere (novela tagala)*. Illustrated and with annotations by R. Sempau. Barcelona: Casa Editorial Maucci, 1909.

Rizal, José. *Noli Me Tángere (Touch Me Not)*. Translated by Harold Augenbraum. New York: Penguin, 2006.

Rizal, José. *The Social Cancer: A Complete Version of Noli me tangere from the Spanish of José Rizal*. Translated by Charles Derbyshire. Manila: Philippine Education Company; New York: World Book Company, 1956.

Rodríguez Bernal, Eduardo. *La Exposición Ibero-Americana de Sevilla*. Seville: Instituto de la Cultura y las Artes, 2006.

Rodríguez Bernal, Eduardo. *Historia de la Exposición Ibero-Americana de Sevilla de 1929*. Seville: Servicio de Publicaciones del Ayuntamiento, 1994.

Roffino, Sara. "Why MoMA's Exhibition of Towering Brazilian Modernist Tarsila do Amaral Misses the Mark." *Artnet News*, 1 March 2018. https://news.artnet.com/opinion/moma-tarsila-amaral-review-1231778.

Rogers, Gayle. *Incomparable Empires: Modernism and the Translation of Spanish and American Literature*. New York: Columbia University Press, 2016.

Roig, Adrien. "Blaise Cendrars et le Bresil: Le grand film bresilien, la traduction de *A selva*, le *Morro azul* et la *Tour Eiffel Siderale*." In *Portugal, Brésil, France: Histoire et culture. Actes du colloque, Paris, 25–27 mai 1987*, 273–98. Paris: Foundation Calouste Gulbenkian, Centre Culturel Portugais, 1988.

Roig, Adrien. *Blaise Cendrars, o Aleijadinho e o modernismo brasileiro*. Rio de Janeiro: Edições Tempo Brasileiro, 1984.

Rosenberg, Fernando J. *The Avant-Garde and Geopolitics in Latin America*. Pittsburgh: University of Pittsburgh Press, 2006.

Rothenberg, Jerome. *The Seven Hells of Jigoku Zoshi*. New York: Trobar, 1962.

Rotker, Susana. *The American Chronicles of José Martí: Journalism and Modernity in Spanish America*. Translated by Jennifer French and Katherine Semler. Hanover: University Press of New England, 2000.

Sáez Delgado, Antonio, and Filipa María Valido-Viegas de Paula-Soares, eds. *Almada Negreiros en Madrid*. Madrid: Ediciones Universidad Autónoma de Madrid, 2016.

Saint-Amour, Paul K. *Tense Future: Modernism, Total War, Encyclopedic Form*. New York: Oxford University Press, 2015.

Salaris, Claudia. "The Invention of the Programmatic Avant-Garde." In *Italian Futurism, 1909–1944: Reconstructing the Universe*, edited by Vivien Greene, 22–49. New York: Guggenheim Museum, 2014.

Salazar, António de Oliveira. *Discursos*. Vol. 1, *Salazar: Discursos, notas relatorios, teses, artigos e entrevistas, 1909–1955. Antología*. Lisbon: Vanguarda, 1955.

San Juan, E., Jr. *Reading the West / Writing the East: Studies in Comparative Literature and Culture*. New York: Peter Lang, 1992.

San Juan, E., Jr. *The Philippine Temptation: Dialectics of Philippines–U.S. Literary Relations*. Philadelphia: Temple University Press, 1996.

Santiáñez, Nil. *Topographies of Fascism: Habitus, Space, and Writing in Twentieth-Century Spain*. Toronto: University of Toronto Press, 2013.

Sapega, Ellen W. *Consensus and Debate in Salazar's Portugal: Visual and Literary Negotiations of the National Text, 1933–1948*. University Park: Pennsylvania State University Press, 2008.

Sartini-Blum, Cynthia. "Incorporating the Exotic: From Futurist Excess to Postmodern Impasse." In *A Place in the Sun: Africa in Italian Colonial Culture from Post-Unification to the Present*, edited by Patrizia Palumbo, 138–62. Berkeley: University of California Press, 2003.

Schulman, Iván A., and Manuel Pedro González. *Martí, Darío y el modernismo*. Madrid: Gredos, 1969.

Schulte-Sasse, Jochen. "Foreword." In *Theory of the Avant-Garde*, by Peter Bürger, translated by Michael Shaw, vii–xlvii. Minneapolis: University of Minnesota Press, 1984.

Schwartz, Jorge. *Vanguarda e cosmopolitismo na década de 20: Oliverio Girondo e Oswald de Andrade*. Translated by Mary Amazonas Leite de Barros and Jorge Schwartz. Edited by Jorge Schwartz and Plínio Martins. São Paulo: Editora Perspectiva, 1983.

Schwartz, Jorge. *Las vanguardias latinoamericanas. Textos programáticos y críticos*. Madrid: Cátedra, 1991.

Sermet, Tessa. "Blaise Cendrars e o modernismo brasileiro: A (re)descoberta do Brasil." *Spanish and Portuguese Review*, no. 2 (2016): 135–50.

Shohat, Ella, and Robert Stam. "From the Imperial Family to the Transnational Imaginary: Media Spectatorship in the Age of Globalization." In *Global/ Local: Cultural Production and the Transnational Imaginary*, edited by Wimal Dissanayake and Rob Wilson, 145–72. Durham, NC: Duke University Press, 1996.

Sieburth, Richard. "Blaise Cendrars in the Sky." *Times Literary Supplement*, 24 September 2014, 3–5.

Solà-Morales, Ignasi. *La exposición internacional de Barcelona, 1914–1929: Arquitectura y ciudad*. Barcelona: Feria de Barcelona, 1985.

Soria Olmedo, Andrés. *Vanguardismo y crítica literaria en España (1910–1930)*. Madrid: Istmo, 1988.

Spivak, Gayatri Chakravorty. *Death of a Discipline*. New York: Columbia University Press, 2003.

Spivak, Gayatri Chakravorty. "'Planetarity' (Box 4, WELT)." *Paragraph* 38, no. 2 (July 2015): 290–2.

Tarsila do Amaral (Fundación Juan March, Madrid, del 6 de febrero al 3 de mayo de 2009). Madrid: Fundación Juan March, 2009.

Thacker, Andrew. *The Imagist Poets*. Liverpool: Liverpool University Press, 2011.

Thomas, Megan C. *Orientalists, Propagandists, and Ilustrados: Filipino Scholarship and the End of Spanish Colonialism*. Minneapolis: University of Minnesota Press, 2012.

Tibbetts, John C., and James M. Welsh. *Douglas Fairbanks and the American Century*. Jackson: University Press of Mississippi, 2014.

Torre, Guillermo de. *Historia de las literaturas de vanguardia*. Madrid: Ediciones Guadarrama, 1965.

Torre, Guillermo de. *Literaturas europeas de vanguardia*. Madrid: R. Caro Raggio, 1925.

Tovar, Francisco. "El adán poético de Vicente Huidobro: Pautas de un proceso creacionista." *Quaderni ibero americani: Attualità culturale della Penisola Iberica e dell'America Latina*, no. 92 (2002): 174–85.

Tsuchiya, Akiko, and William G. Acree, eds. *Empire's End: Transnational Connections in the Hispanic World*. Nashville, TN: Vanderbilt University Press, 2016.

University of Pittsburgh, Department of English. "History of the English Department 1940s." Accessed 23 August 2022. https://www.english.pitt .edu/history-english-department-1940s.

Unruh, Vicky. *Latin American Vanguards: The Art of Contentious Encounters*. Berkeley: University of California Press, 1994.

Vicuña, Cecilia, and Ernesto Livon-Grosman, eds. *The Oxford Book of Latin American Poetry: A Bilingual Anthology*. Oxford: Oxford University Press, 2009.

Videla, Gloria. *Direcciones del vanguardismo hispano-americano: Estudios sobre poesía de vanguardia, 1920–1930. Documentos*. Mendoza: Editorial de la Universidad Nacional de Cuyo, 2011.

Vigié-Lecocq, E. *La poésie contemporaine, 1884–1896*. Paris: Société du Mercure de France, 1896.

Villa, José Garcia. "Definitions of Poetry." *Philippine Magazine*, vol. 32, no. 3 (323), March 1935, 140–1, 152–3.

Villa, José Garcia. *Footnote to Youth: Tales of the Philippines and Others*. New York: Charles Scribner's Sons, 1933.

Villa, José Garcia. *Have Come, Am Here: Poems*. New York: Viking Press, 1942.

Villa, José Garcia [O. Sevilla, pseud.]. "Man-Songs." *Philippines Herald Magazine*, 2 June 1929, 7–10.

Villa, José Garcia. *Selected Poems and New*. With an introduction by Edith Sitwell. New York: McDowell, Obolensky, 1958.

Villar, Arturo del. "Gerardo Diego, poeta creacionista." *Cuadernos Hispanoamericanos*, nos. 361–2 (July–August 1980): 152–69.

Wagner-Martin, Linda. *The Routledge Introduction to American Modernism*. Abingdon: Routledge, 2016.

Walkowitz, Rebecca L. "Planetary Modernisms: Provocations on Modernity across Time." *Interventions* 18, no. 5 (2016): 748–50. https://doi.org/10.1080/1369801X.2016.1173961.

Wall-Romana, Christophe. *Cinepoetry: Imaginary Cinemas in French Poetry*. New York: Fordham University Press, 2013.

Weintraub, Scott, and Luis Correa-Díaz. "Huidobro's Absolute Modernity /Futurity: An Introduction." In *Huidobro's Futurity: Twenty-First Century Approaches*, edited by Luis Correa-Díaz and Scott Weintraub, 1–13. Hispanic Issues Online. Minneapolis: University of Minnesota, College of Liberal Arts, 2010. https://cla.umn.edu/hispanic-issues/online/huidobros-futurity-twenty-first-century-approaches.

Weston, Richard. *Modernism*. London: Phaidon, 1996.

Wetzel, Roland. *Robert Delaunay: Hommage à Blériot*. Bielefeld: Kerber Verlag; New York: Distributed Art Publishers, 2008.

Wood, Cecil G. "*Adán* as the Key to *Creacionismo*." *Kentucky Romance Quarterly* 24, no. 1 (1977): 35–45. https://doi.org/10.1080/03648664.1977.9928126.

Wood, Cecil G. "The Development of 'Creacionismo': A Study of Four Early Poems of Vicente Huidobro." *Hispania* 61, no. 1 (1978): 5–13.

Yurkiévich, Saúl. *Celebración del modernismo*. Barcelona: Tusquets, 1976.

Zapanta Manlapaz, Edna. *Angela Manalang Gloria: A Literary Biography*. Quezon City: Ateneo de Manila University Press, 1993.

Index

Toronto Iberic

CO-EDITORS: Robert Davidson (Toronto) and Frederick A. de Armas (Chicago)

EDITORIAL BOARD: Josiah Blackmore (Harvard); Marina Brownlee (Princeton); Anthony J. Cascardi (Berkeley); Justin Crumbaugh (Mt Holyoke); Emily Francomano (Georgetown); Jordana Mendelson (NYU); Joan Ramon Resina (Stanford); Enrique García Santo-Tomás (U Michigan); H. Rosi Song (Durham); Kathleen Vernon (SUNY Stony Brook)

1 Anthony J. Cascardi, *Cervantes, Literature, and the Discourse of Politics*
2 Jessica A. Boon, *The Mystical Science of the Soul: Medieval Cognition in Bernardino de Laredo's Recollection Method*
3 Susan Byrne, *Law and History in Cervantes'* Don Quixote
4 Mary E. Barnard and Frederick A. de Armas (eds.), *Objects of Culture in the Literature of Imperial Spain*
5 Nil Santiáñez, *Topographies of Fascism: Habitus, Space, and Writing in Twentieth-Century Spain*
6 Nelson Orringer, *Lorca in Tune with Falla: Literary and Musical Interludes*
7 Ana M. Gómez-Bravo, *Textual Agency: Writing Culture and Social Networks in Fifteenth-Century Spain*
8 Javier Irigoyen-García, *The Spanish Arcadia: Sheep Herding, Pastoral Discourse, and Ethnicity in Early Modern Spain*
9 Stephanie Sieburth, *Survival Songs: Conchita Piquer's* Coplas *and Franco's Regime of Terror*
10 Christine Arkinstall, *Spanish Female Writers and the Freethinking Press, 1879–1926*

11 Margaret E. Boyle, *Unruly Women: Performance, Penitence, and Punishment in Early Modern Spain*

12 Evelina Gužauskytė, *Christopher Columbus's Naming in the* diarios *of the Four Voyages (1492–1504): A Discourse of Negotiation*

13 Mary E. Barnard, *Garcilaso de la Vega and the Material Culture of Renaissance Europe*

14 William Viestenz, *By the Grace of God: Francoist Spain and the Sacred Roots of Political Imagination*

15 Michael Scham, Lector Ludens*: The Representation of Games and Play in Cervantes*

16 Stephen Rupp, *Heroic Forms: Cervantes and the Literature of War*

17 Enrique Fernandez, *Anxieties of Interiority and Dissection in Early Modern Spain*

18 Susan Byrne, *Ficino in Spain*

19 Patricia M. Keller, *Ghostly Landscapes: Film, Photography, and the Aesthetics of Haunting in Contemporary Spanish Culture*

20 Carolyn A. Nadeau, *Food Matters: Alonso Quijano's Diet and the Discourse of Food in Early Modern Spain*

21 Cristian Berco, *From Body to Community: Venereal Disease and Society in Baroque Spain*

22 Elizabeth R. Wright, *The Epic of Juan Latino: Dilemmas of Race and Religion in Renaissance Spain*

23 Ryan D. Giles, *Inscribed Power: Amulets and Magic in Early Spanish Literature*

24 Jorge Pérez, *Confessional Cinema: Religion, Film, and Modernity in Spain's Development Years, 1960–1975*

25 Joan Ramon Resina, *Josep Pla: Seeing the World in the Form of Articles*

26 Javier Irigoyen-García, *"Moors Dressed as Moors": Clothing, Social Distinction, and Ethnicity in Early Modern Iberia*

27 Jean Dangler, *Edging toward Iberia*

28 Ryan D. Giles and Steven Wagschal (eds.), *Beyond Sight: Engaging the Senses in Iberian Literatures and Cultures, 1200–1750*

29 Silvia Bermúdez, *Rocking the Boat: Migration and Race in Contemporary Spanish Music*

30 Hilaire Kallendorf, *Ambiguous Antidotes: Virtue as Vaccine for Vice in Early Modern Spain*

31 Leslie Harkema, *Spanish Modernism and the Poetics of Youth: From Miguel de Unamuno to* La Joven Literatura

32 Benjamin Fraser, *Cognitive Disability Aesthetics: Visual Culture, Disability Representations, and the (In)Visibility of Cognitive Difference*

33 Robert Patrick Newcomb, *Iberianism and Crisis: Spain and Portugal at the Turn of the Twentieth Century*

34 Sara J. Brenneis, *Spaniards in Mauthausen: Representations of a Nazi Concentration Camp, 1940-2015*
35 Silvia Bermúdez and Roberta Johnson (eds.), *A New History of Iberian Feminisms*
36 Steven Wagschal, *Minding Animals in the Old and New Worlds: A Cognitive Historical Analysis*
37 Heather Bamford, *Cultures of the Fragment: Uses of the Iberian Manuscript, 1100–1600*
38 Enrique García Santo-Tomás (ed.), *Science on Stage in Early Modern Spain*
39 Marina Brownlee (ed.), *Cervantes'* Persiles *and the Travails of Romance*
40 Sarah Thomas, *Inhabiting the In-Between: Childhood and Cinema in Spain's Long Transition*
41 David A. Wacks, *Medieval Iberian Crusade Fiction and the Mediterranean World*
42 Rosilie Hernández, *Immaculate Conceptions: The Power of the Religious Imagination in Early Modern Spain*
43 Mary Coffey and Margot Versteeg (eds.), *Imagined Truths: Realism in Modern Spanish Literature and Culture*
44 Diana Aramburu, *Resisting Invisibility: Detecting the Female Body in Spanish Crime Fiction*
45 Samuel Amago and Matthew J. Marr (eds.), *Consequential Art: Comics Culture in Contemporary Spain*
46 Richard P. Kinkade, *Dawn of a Dynasty: The Life and Times of Infante Manuel of Castile*
47 Jill Robbins, *Poetry and Crisis: Cultural Politics and Citizenship in the Wake of the Madrid Bombings*
48 Ana María Laguna and John Beusterien (eds.), *Goodbye Eros: Recasting Forms and Norms of Love in the Age of Cervantes*
49 Sara J. Brenneis and Gina Herrmann (eds.), *Spain, World War II, and the Holocaust: History and Representation*
50 Francisco Fernández de Alba, *Sex, Drugs, and Fashion in 1970s Madrid*
51 Daniel Aguirre-Oteiza, *This Ghostly Poetry: Reading Spanish Republican Exiles between Literary History and Poetic Memory*
52 Lara Anderson, *Control and Resistance: Food Discourse in Franco Spain*
53 Faith Harden, *Arms and Letters: Military Life Writing in Early Modern Spain*
54 Erin Alice Cowling, Tania de Miguel Magro, Mina García Jordán, and Glenda Y. Nieto-Cuebas (eds.), *Social Justice in Spanish Golden Age Theatre*

55 Paul Michael Johnson, *Affective Geographies: Cervantes, Emotion, and the Literary Mediterranean*
56 Justin Crumbaugh and Nil Santiáñez (eds.), *Spanish Fascist Writing: An Anthology*
57 Margaret E. Boyle and Sarah E. Owens (eds.), *Health and Healing in the Early Modern Iberian World: A Gendered Perspective*
58 Leticia Álvarez-Recio (ed.), *Iberian Chivalric Romance: Translations and Cultural Transmission in Early Modern England*
59 Henry Berlin, *Alone Together: Poetics of the Passions in Late Medieval Iberia*
60 Adrian Shubert, *The Sword of Luchana: Baldomero Espartero and the Making of Modern Spain, 1793–1879*
61 Jorge Pérez, *Fashioning Spanish Cinema: Costume, Identity, and Stardom*
62 Enriqueta Zafra, *Lazarillo de Tormes: A Graphic Novel*
63 Erin Alice Cowling, *Chocolate: How a New World Commodity Conquered Spanish Literature*
64 Mary E. Barnard, *A Poetry of Things: The Material Lyric in Habsburg Spain*
65 Frederick A. de Armas and James Mandrell (eds.), *The Gastronomical Arts in Spain: Food and Etiquette*
66 Catherine Infante, *The Arts of Encounter: Christians, Muslims, and the Power of Images in Early Modern Spain*
67 Robert Richmond Ellis, *Bibliophiles, Murderous Bookmen, and Mad Librarians: The Story of Books in Modern Spain*
68 Beatriz de Alba-Koch (ed.), *The Ibero-American Baroque*
69 Deborah R. Forteza, *The English Reformation in the Spanish Imagination: Rewriting Nero, Jezebel, and the Dragon*
70 Olga Sendra Ferrer, *Barcelona, City of Margins*
71 Dale Shuger, *God Made Word: An Archaeology of Mystic Discourse in Early Modern Spain*
72 Xosé M. Núñez Seixas, *The Spanish Blue Division on the Eastern Front, 1941-45: War Experience, Occupation, Memory*
73 Julia Domínguez, *Quixotic Memories: Cervantes and Memory in Early Modern Spain*
74 Anna Casas Aguilar, *Bilingual Legacies: Father Figures in Self-Writing from Barcelona, 1975-2005*
75 Julia H. Chang, *Blood Novels: Gender, Caste, and Race in Spanish Realism*
76 Frederick A. de Armas, *Cervantes' Architectures: The Dangers Outside*
77 Michael Iarocci, *The Art of Witnessing: Francisco de Goya's* Disasters of War

78 Esther Fernández and Adrienne L. Martín (eds.), *Drawing the Curtain: Cervantes's Theatrical Revelations*

79 Emiro Martinez-Osorio and Mercedes Blanco (eds.), *The War Trumpet: Iberian Epic Poetry, 1543–1639*

80 Christine Arkinstall, *Women on War in Spain's Long Nineteenth Century: Virtue, Patriotism, Citizenship*

81 Ignacio Infante, *A Planetary Avant-Garde: Experimental Literature Networks and the Legacy of Iberian Colonialism*